FRED BASSET YEARBOOK 2010–2011

Summersdale Publishers Ltd
46 West Street
Chichester
West Sussex
PO19 1RP
UK

www.summersdale.com

Printed and bound in Malta

Drawings by Alex Graham and Michael Martin

ISBN: 978-1-84953-083-5

FRED BASSET

2010–2011

Ok, Fred—You can't put it off any longer. It's got to be done!
Deep breath— Brave face— Your public awaits
'Morning folks!

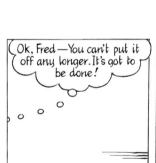

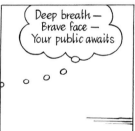

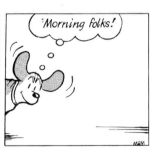

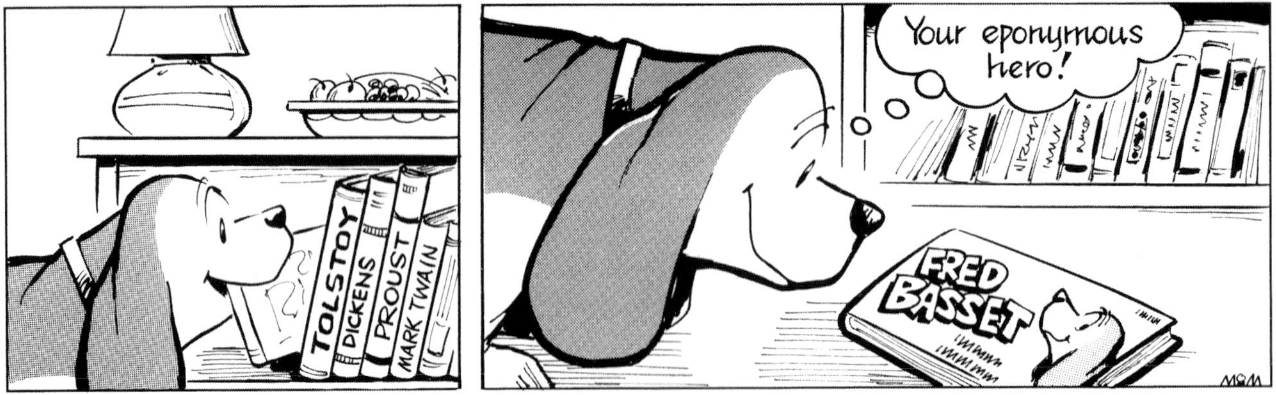
TOLSTOY
DICKENS
PROUST
MARK TWAIN
Your eponymous hero!
FRED BASSET

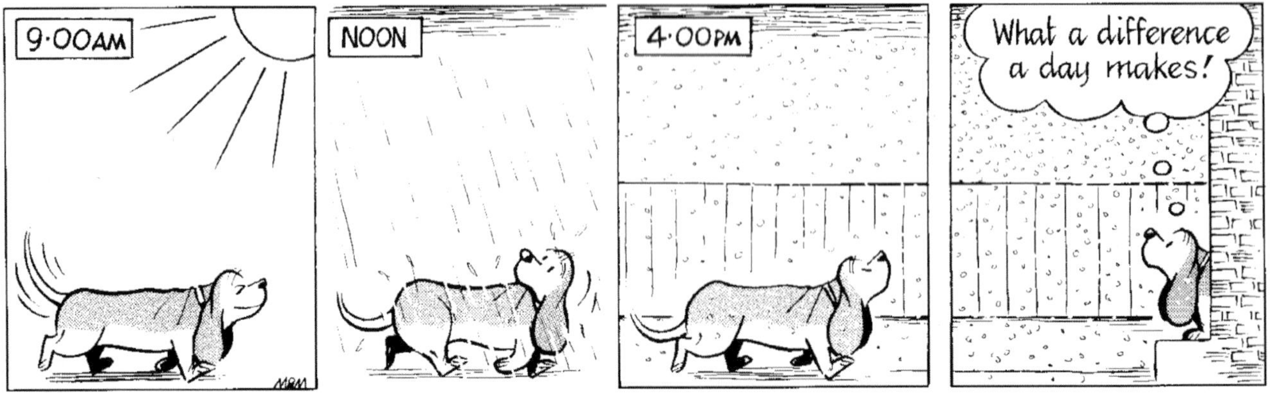
9·00AM
NOON
4·00PM
What a difference a day makes!

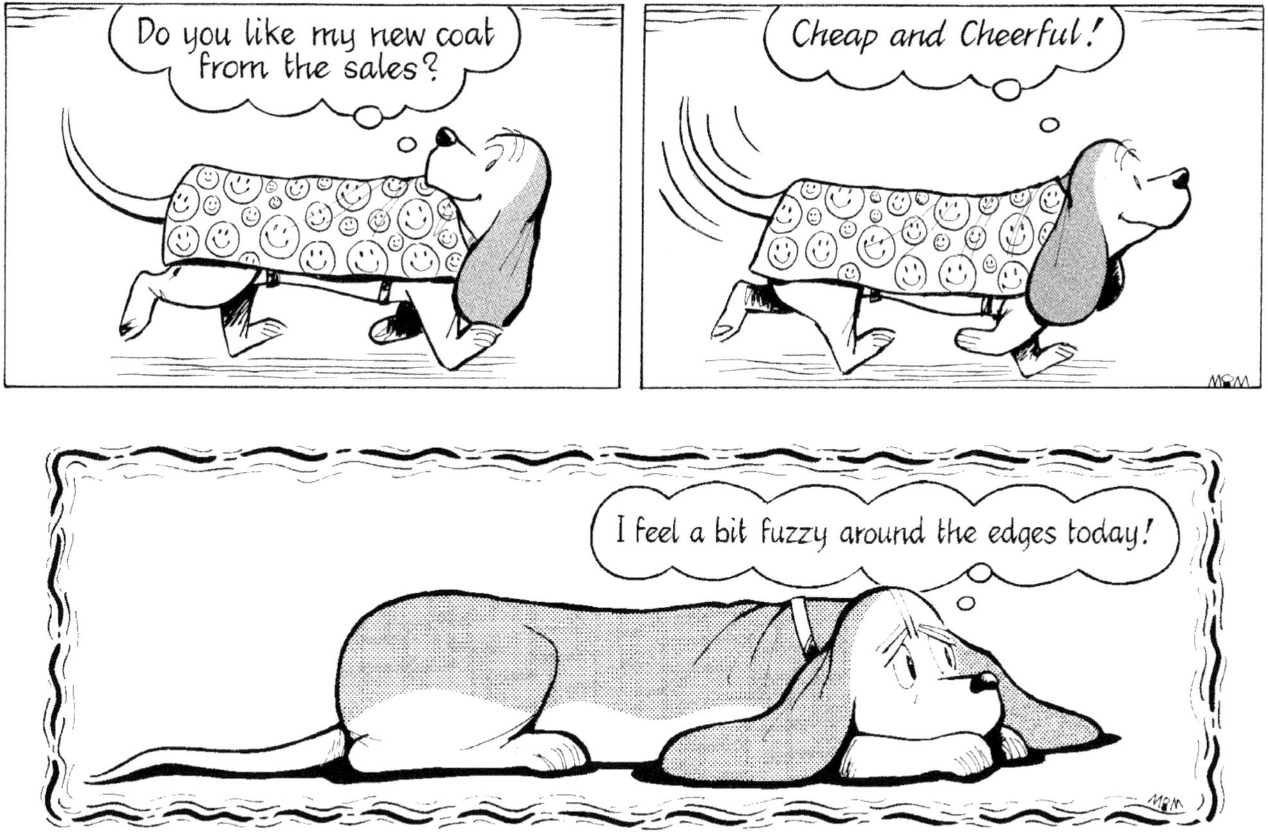
Do you like my new coat from the sales?
Cheap and Cheerful!
I feel a bit fuzzy around the edges today!

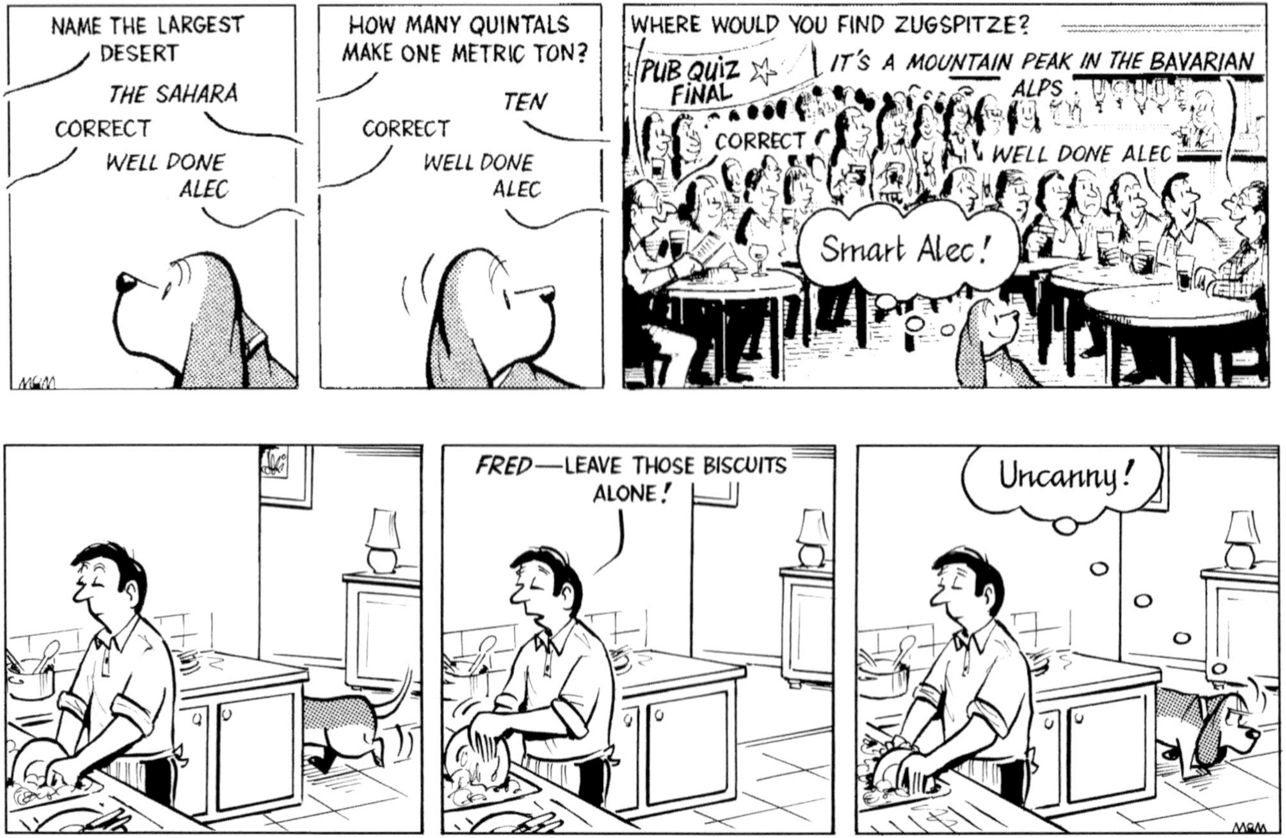
NAME THE LARGEST DESERT
THE SAHARA
CORRECT
WELL DONE ALEC
HOW MANY QUINTALS MAKE ONE METRIC TON?
TEN
CORRECT
WELL DONE ALEC
WHERE WOULD YOU FIND ZUGSPITZE?
PUB QUIZ FINAL
IT'S A MOUNTAIN PEAK IN THE BAVARIAN ALPS
CORRECT
WELL DONE ALEC
Smart Alec!
FRED—LEAVE THOSE BISCUITS ALONE!
Uncanny!

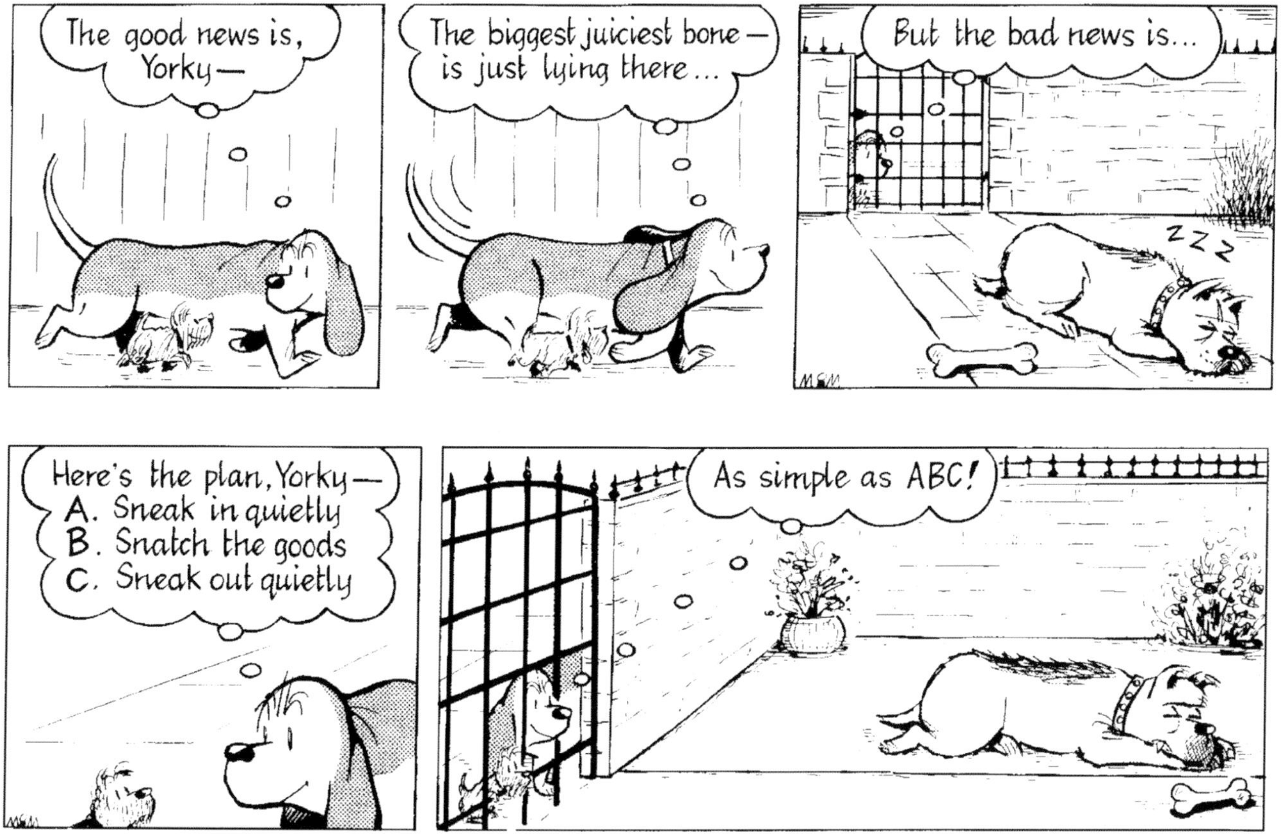
The good news is, Yorky—
The biggest juiciest bone— is just lying there...
But the bad news is...
ZZZ
Here's the plan, Yorky— A. Sneak in quietly B. Snatch the goods C. Sneak out quietly
As simple as ABC!

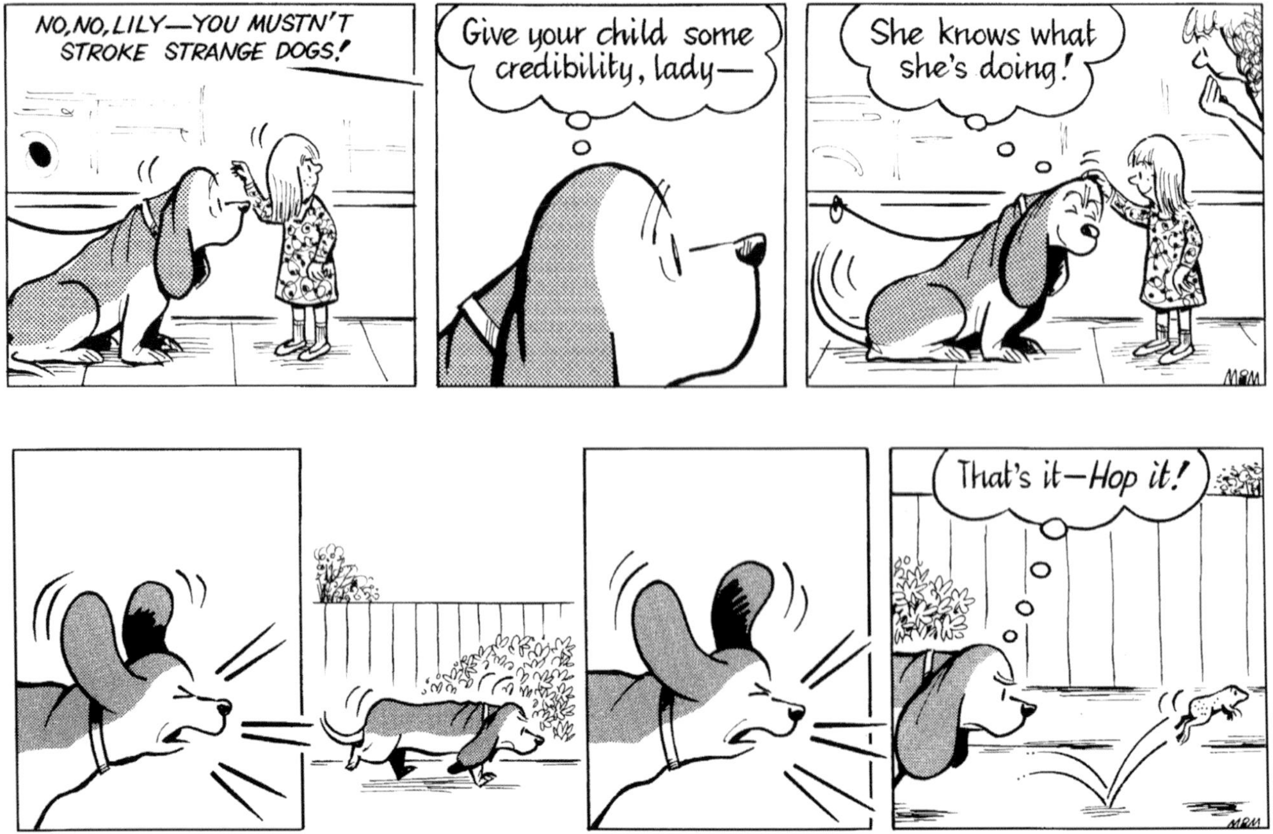
NO, NO, LILY—YOU MUSTN'T STROKE STRANGE DOGS!
Give your child some credibility, lady—
She knows what she's doing!
MBM
That's it—Hop it!
MBM

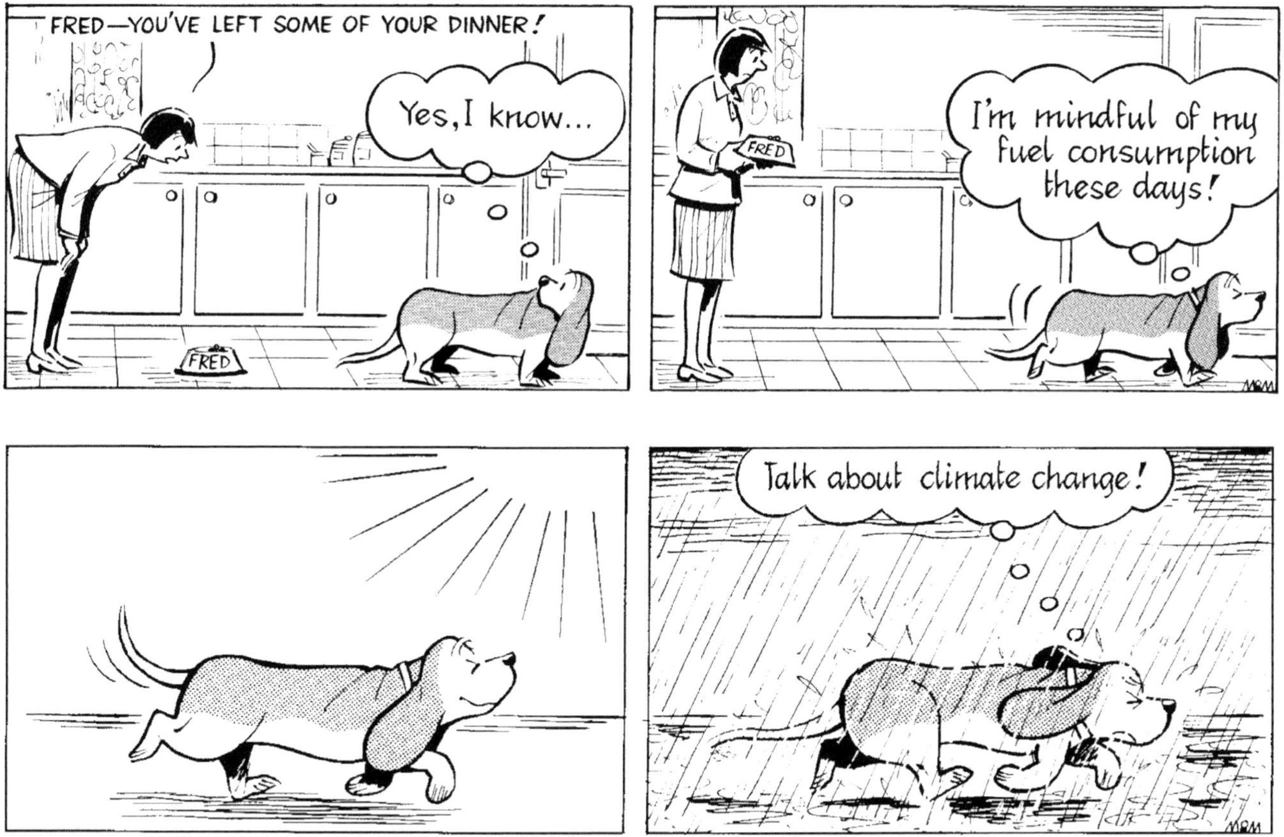
FRED—YOU'VE LEFT SOME OF YOUR DINNER!
Yes, I know...
FRED
FRED
I'm mindful of my fuel consumption these days!
Talk about climate change!

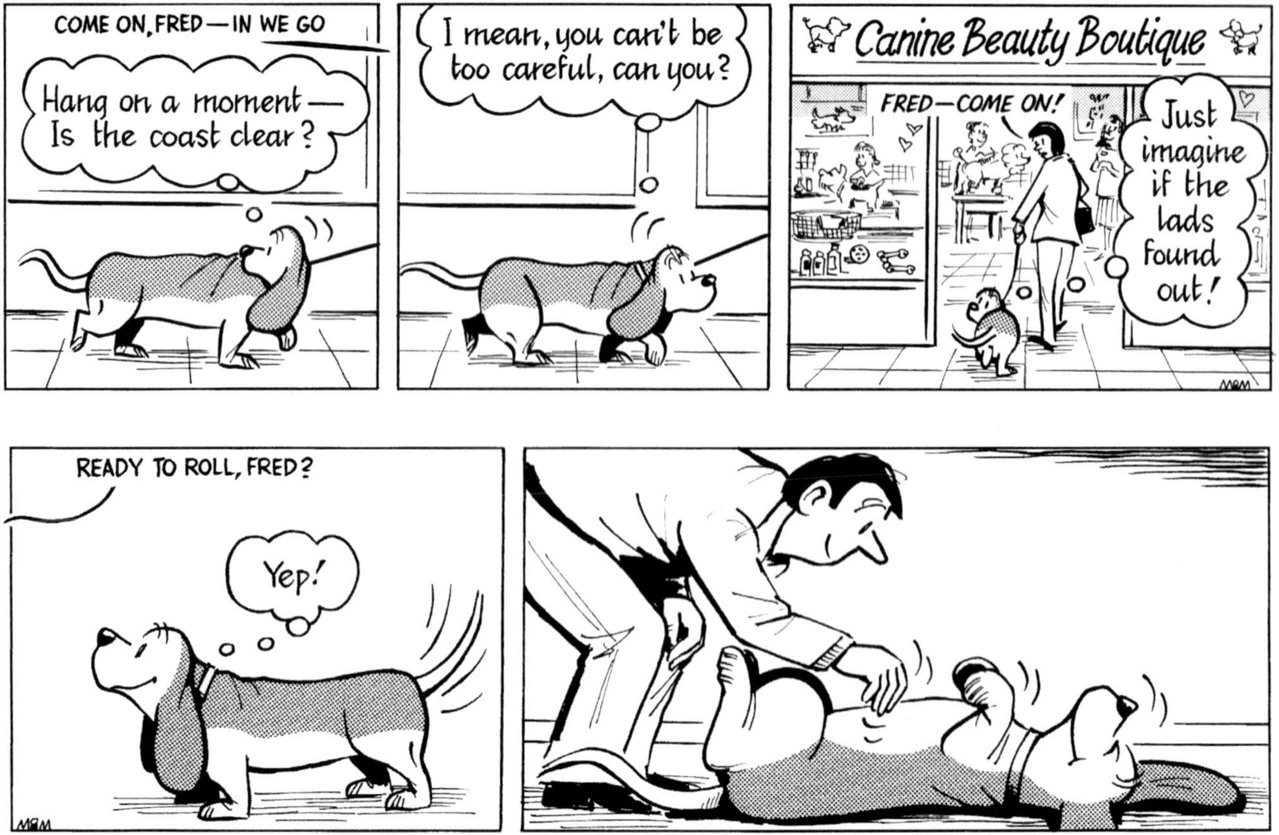
COME ON, FRED — IN WE GO
Hang on a moment — Is the coast clear?
I mean, you can't be too careful, can you?
Canine Beauty Boutique
FRED — COME ON!
Just imagine if the lads found out!
READY TO ROLL, FRED?
Yep!

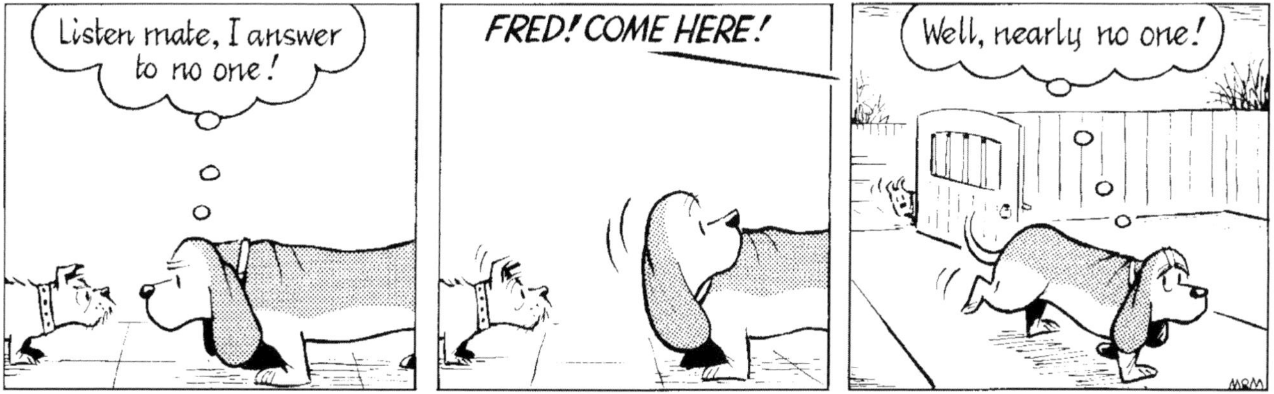
Listen mate, I answer to no one!
FRED! COME HERE!
Well, nearly no one!

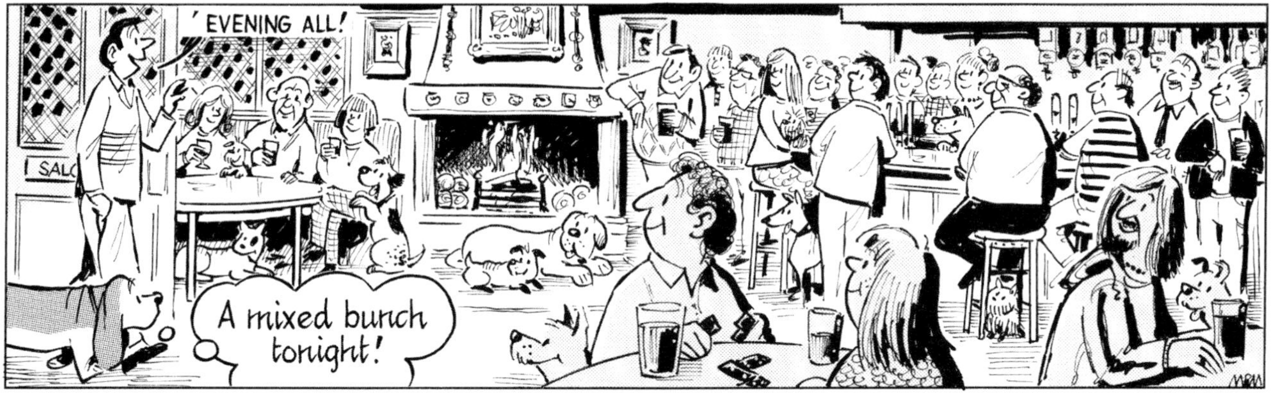
'EVENING ALL!
A mixed bunch tonight!

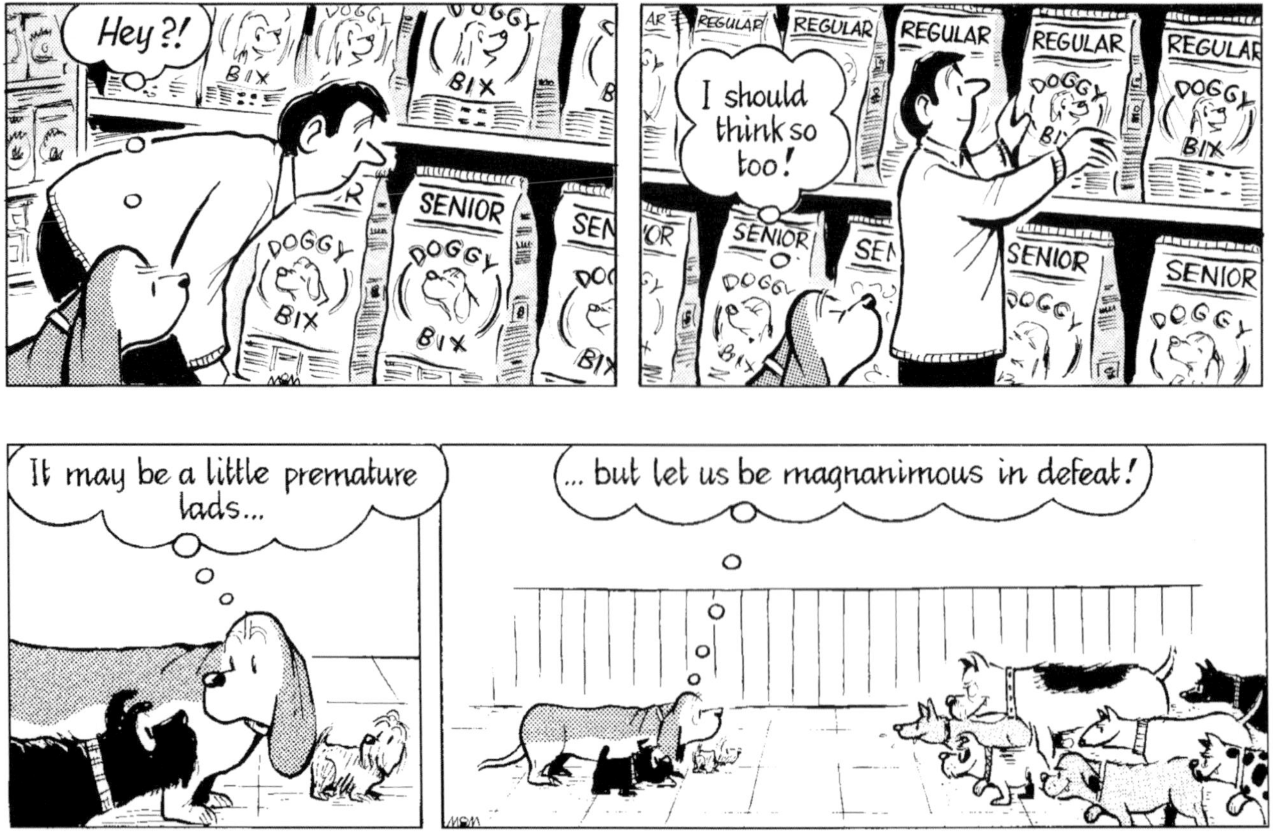
Hey?!
I should think so too!
It may be a little premature lads...
... but let us be magnanimous in defeat!

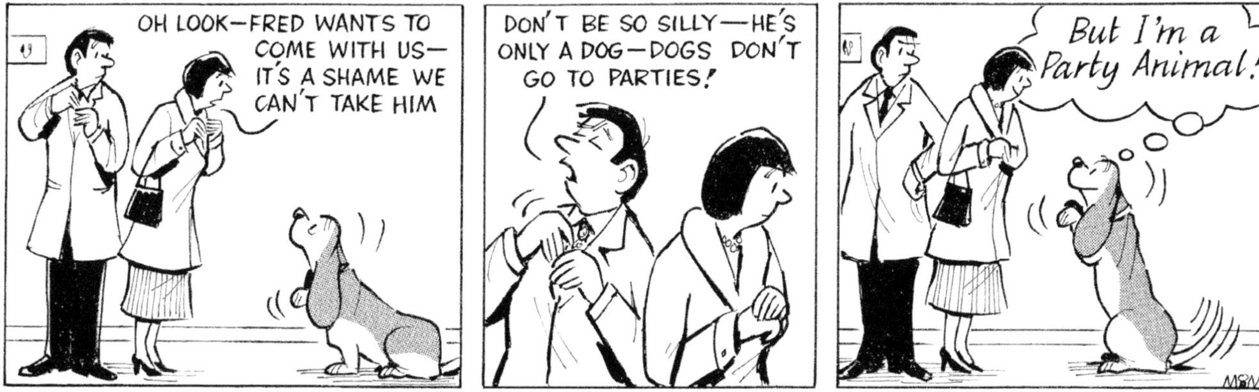

OH LOOK—FRED WANTS TO COME WITH US—IT'S A SHAME WE CAN'T TAKE HIM
DON'T BE SO SILLY—HE'S ONLY A DOG—DOGS DON'T GO TO PARTIES!
But I'm a Party Animal!
M&M

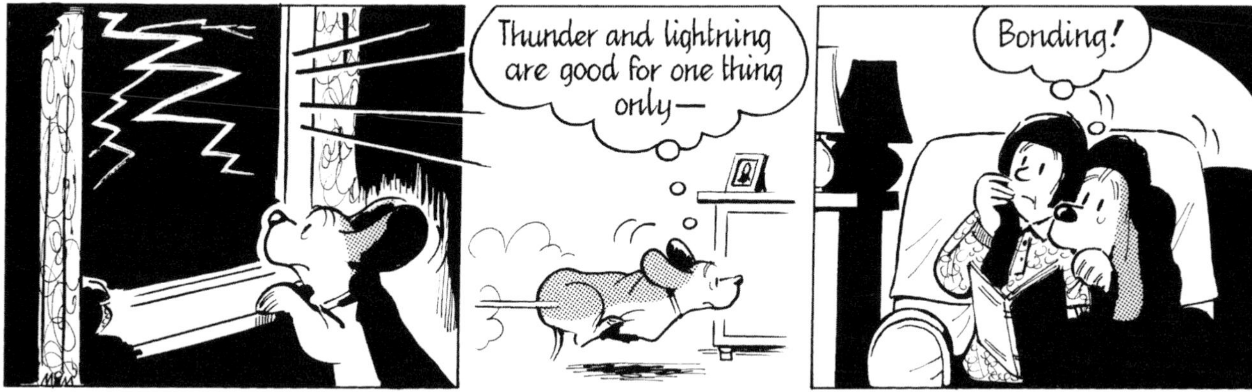

Thunder and lightning are good for one thing only—
Bonding!

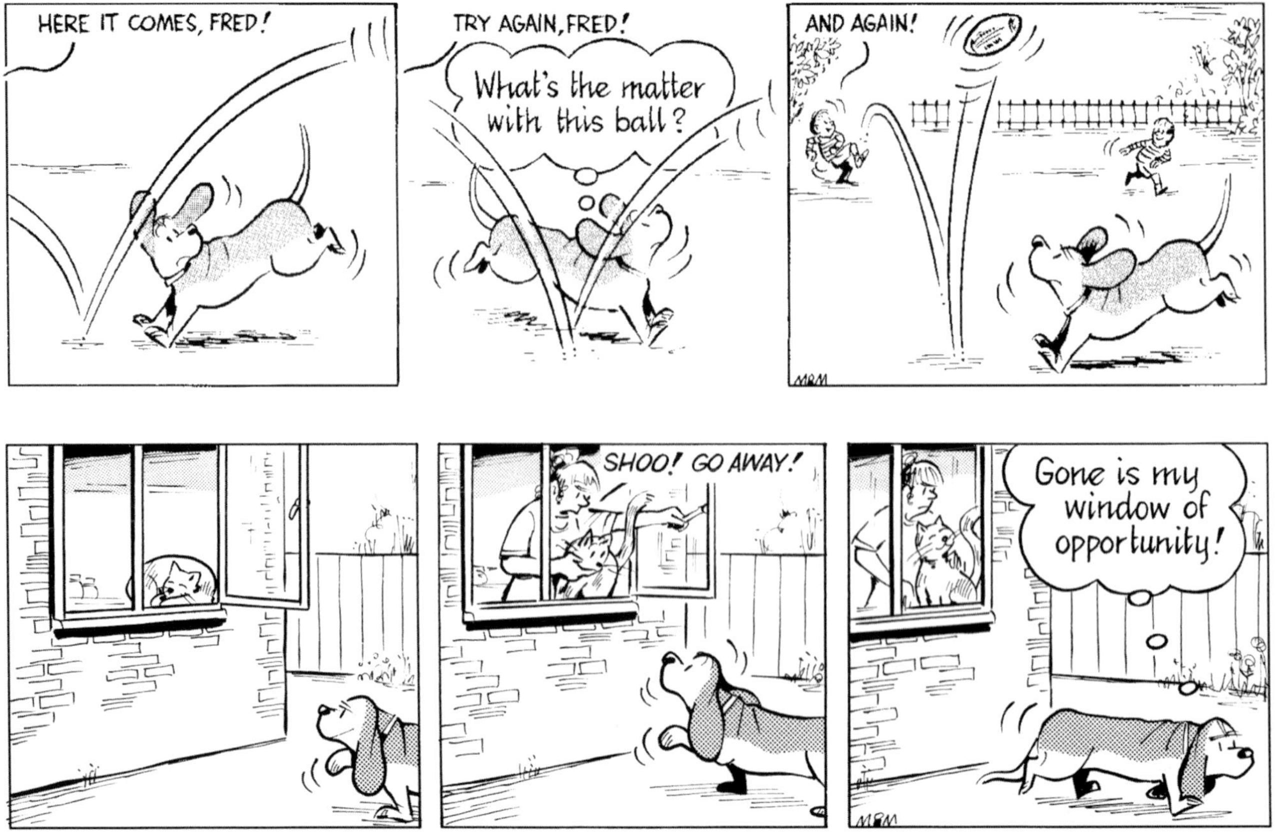
HERE IT COMES, FRED!
TRY AGAIN, FRED!
What's the matter with this ball?
AND AGAIN!
MRM
SHOO! GO AWAY!
Gone is my window of opportunity!
MRM

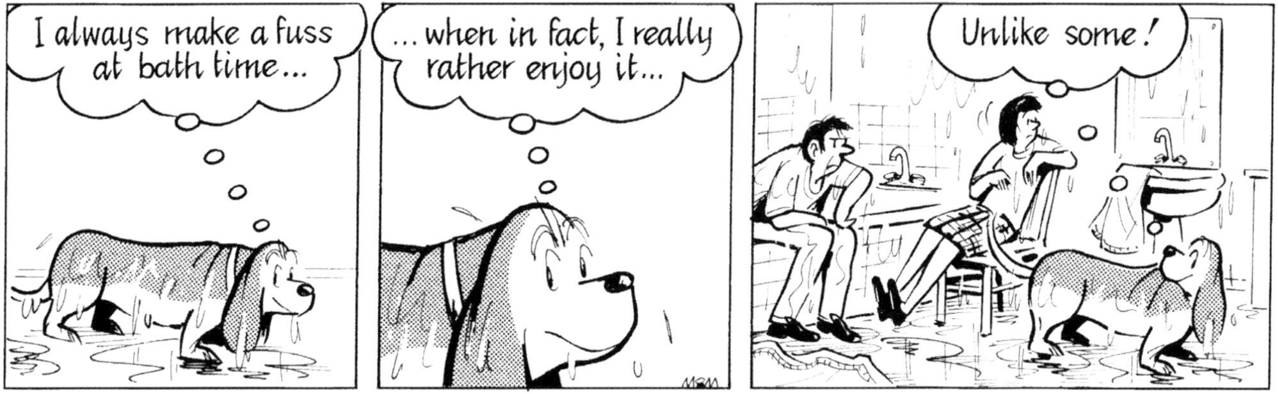
I always make a fuss at bath time...
...when in fact, I really rather enjoy it...
Unlike some!

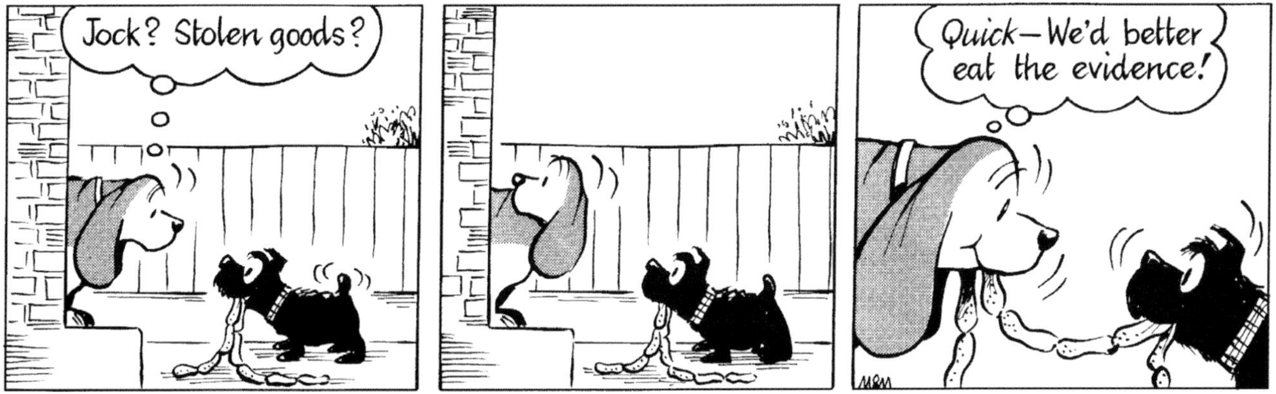
Jock? Stolen goods?
Quick—We'd better eat the evidence!

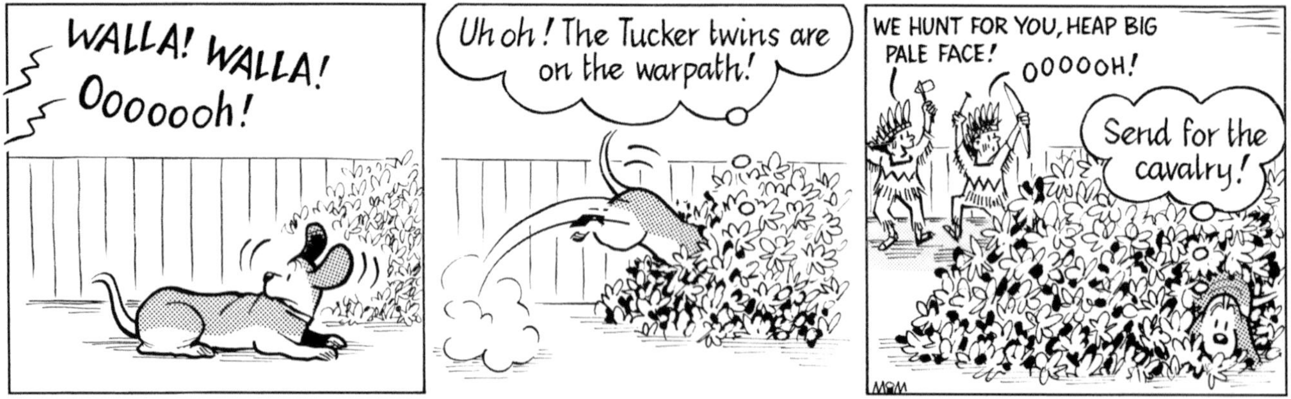
WALLA! WALLA!
Ooooooh!
Uh oh! The Tucker twins are on the warpath!
WE HUNT FOR YOU, HEAP BIG PALE FACE!
OOOOOH!
Send for the cavalry!

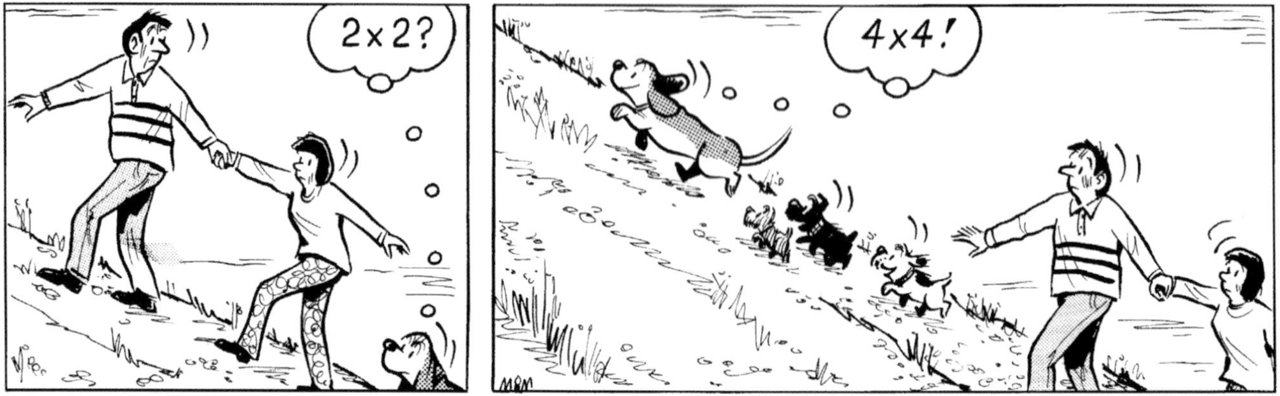
2x2?
4x4!

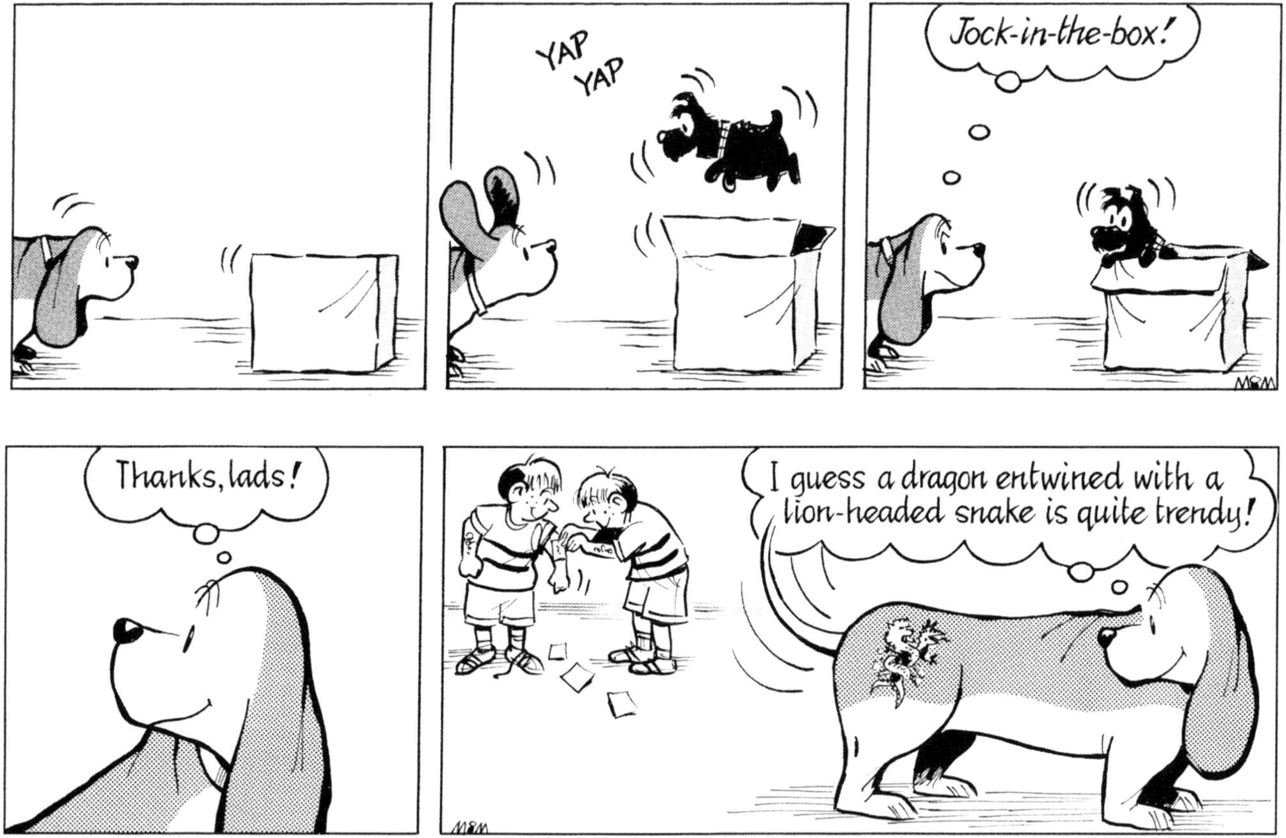
YAP
YAP
Jock-in-the-box!
Thanks, lads!
I guess a dragon entwined with a lion-headed snake is quite trendy!

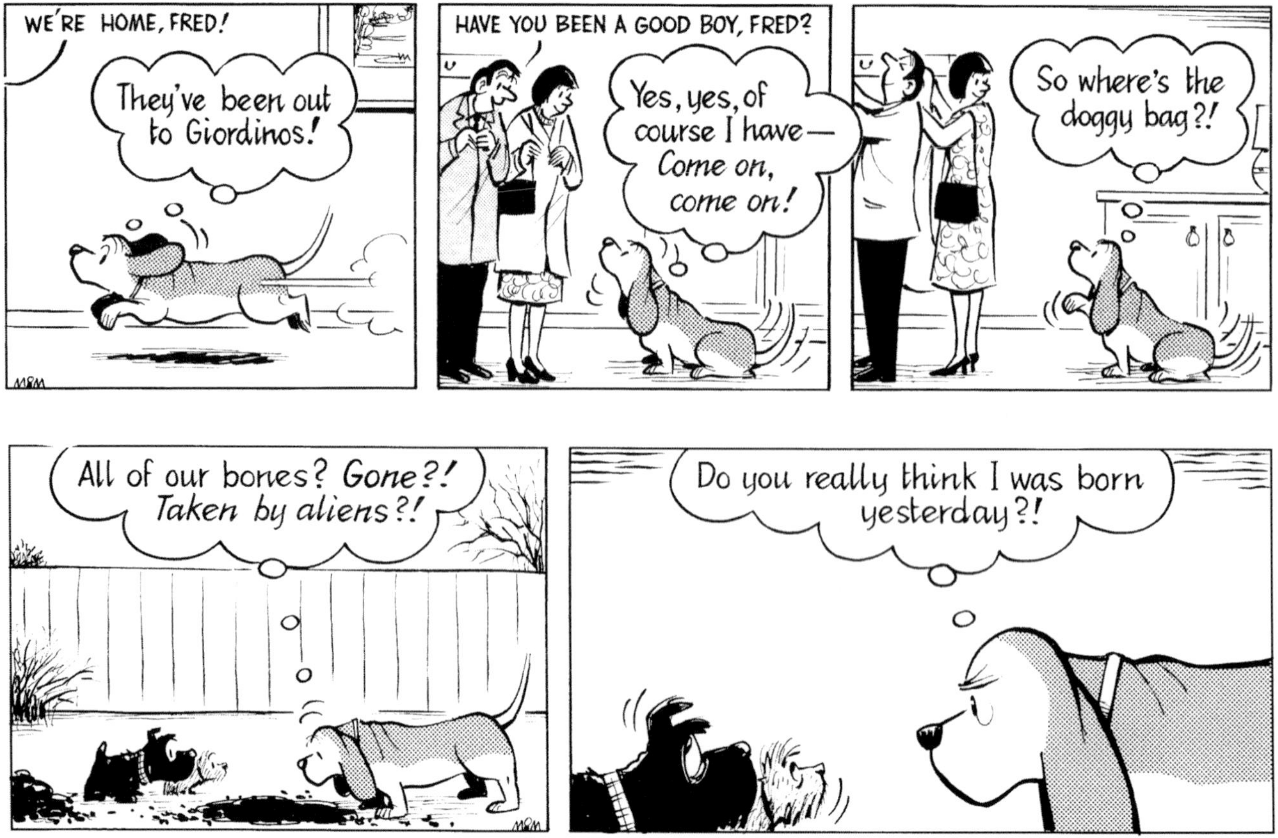
WE'RE HOME, FRED!
They've been out to Giordinos!
HAVE YOU BEEN A GOOD BOY, FRED?
Yes, yes, of course I have— Come on, come on!
So where's the doggy bag?!
All of our bones? Gone?! Taken by aliens?!
Do you really think I was born yesterday?!

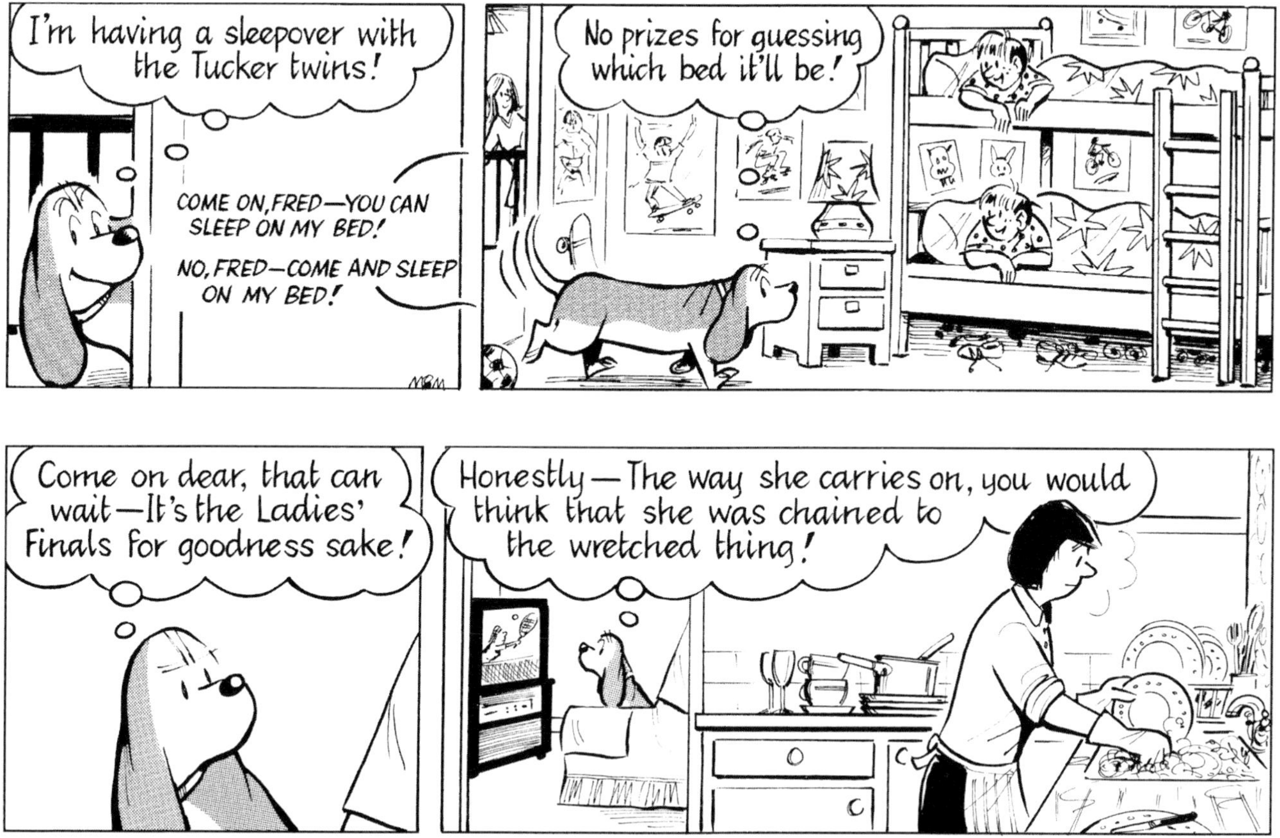
I'm having a sleepover with the Tucker twins!
COME ON, FRED—YOU CAN SLEEP ON MY BED!
NO, FRED—COME AND SLEEP ON MY BED!
No prizes for guessing which bed it'll be!
Come on dear, that can wait—It's the Ladies' Finals for goodness sake!
Honestly—The way she carries on, you would think that she was chained to the wretched thing!

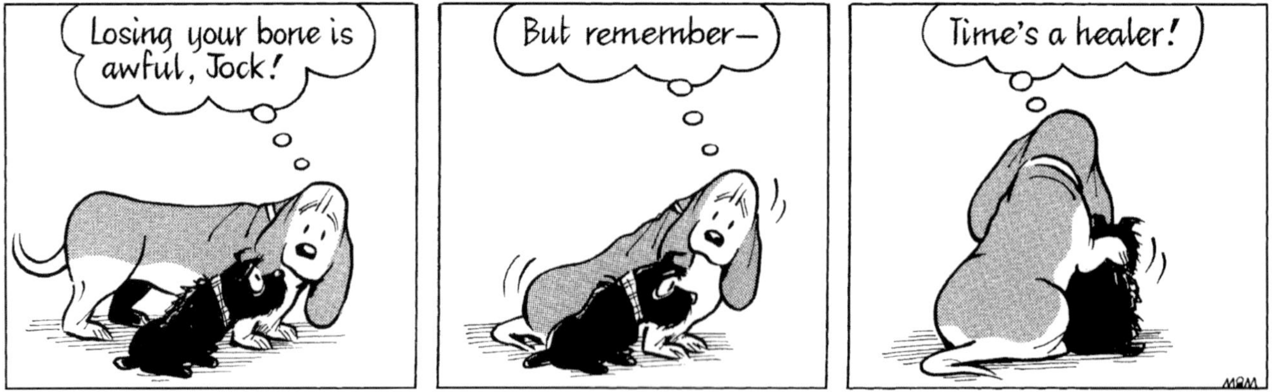
Losing your bone is awful, Jock!
But remember—
Time's a healer!

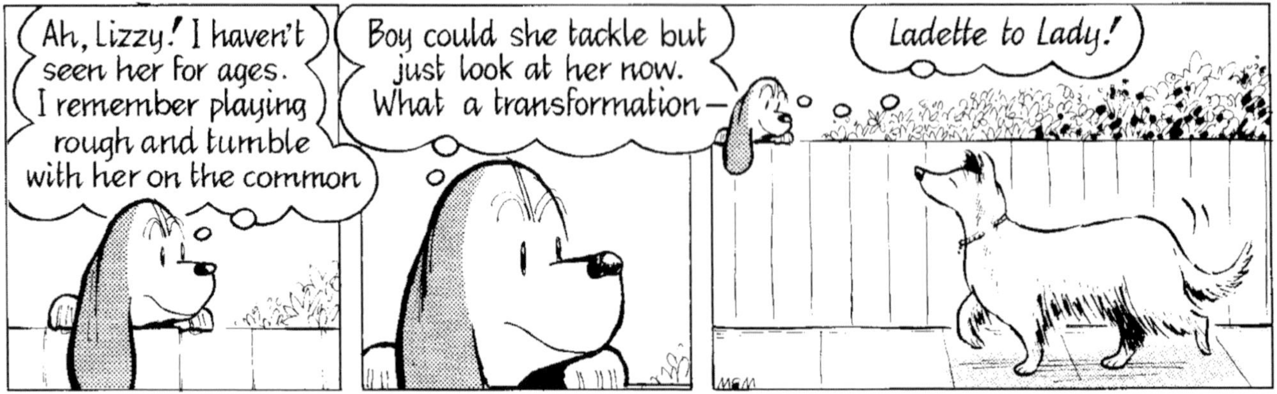
Ah, Lizzy! I haven't seen her for ages. I remember playing rough and tumble with her on the common
Boy could she tackle but just look at her now. What a transformation—
Ladette to Lady!

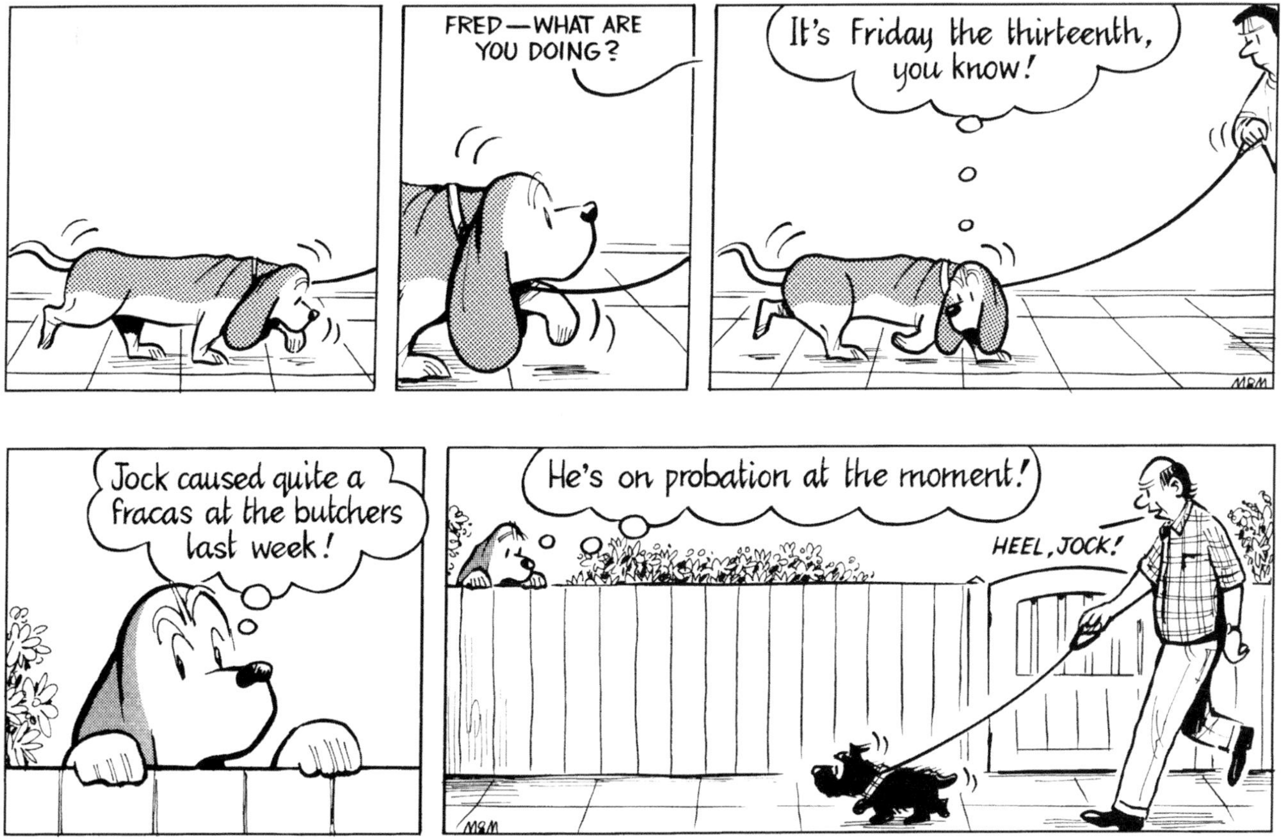
FRED—WHAT ARE YOU DOING?
It's Friday the thirteenth, you know!
Jock caused quite a fracas at the butchers last week!
He's on probation at the moment!
HEEL, JOCK!

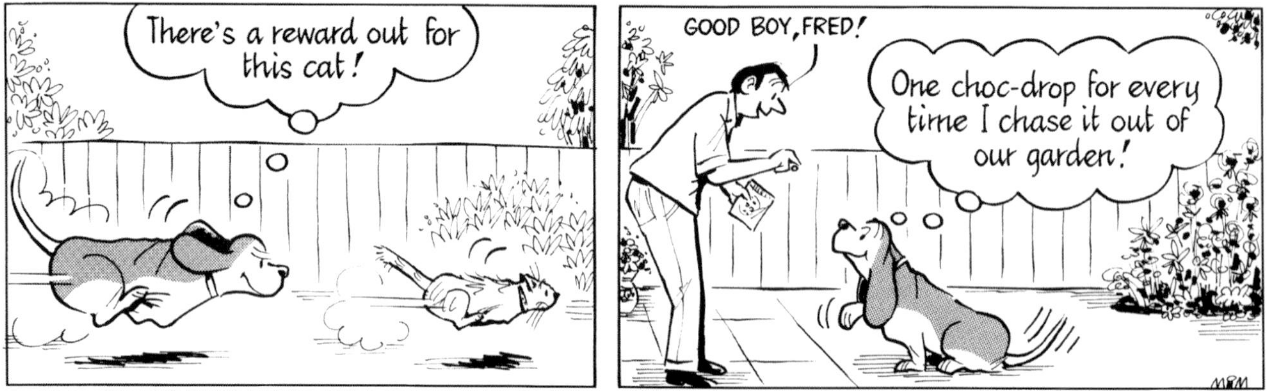
There's a reward out for this cat!
GOOD BOY, FRED!
One choc-drop for every time I chase it out of our garden!

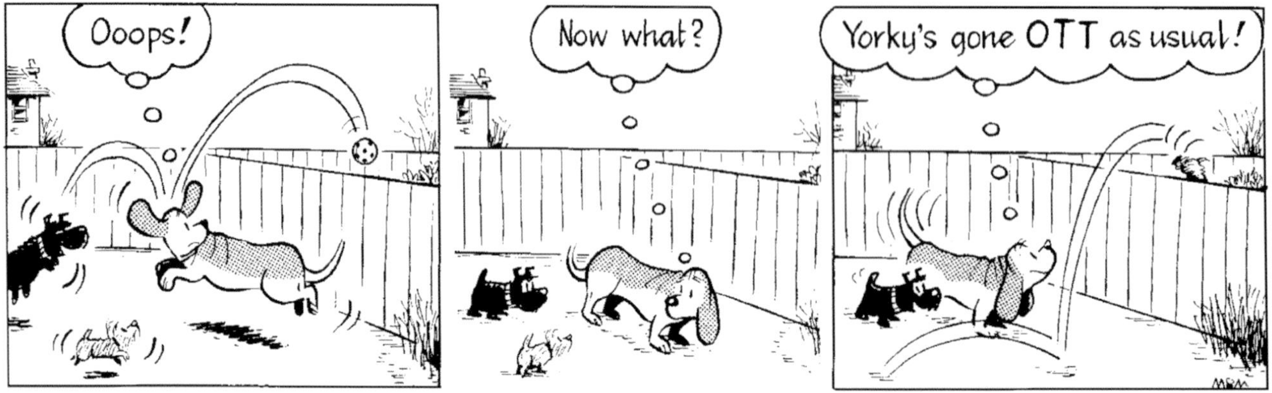
Ooops!
Now what?
Yorky's gone OTT as usual!

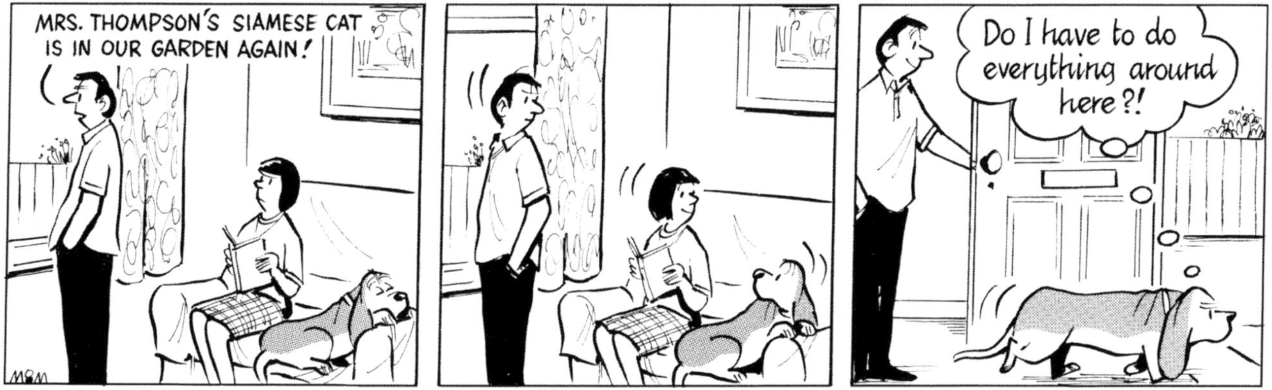
MRS. THOMPSON'S SIAMESE CAT IS IN OUR GARDEN AGAIN!
Do I have to do everything around here?!
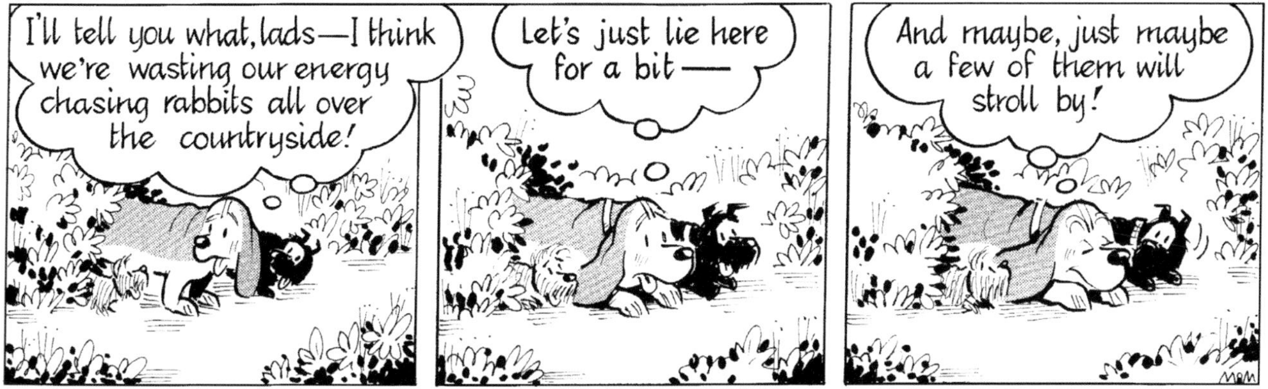
I'll tell you what, lads—I think we're wasting our energy chasing rabbits all over the countryside!
Let's just lie here for a bit—
And maybe, just maybe a few of them will stroll by!

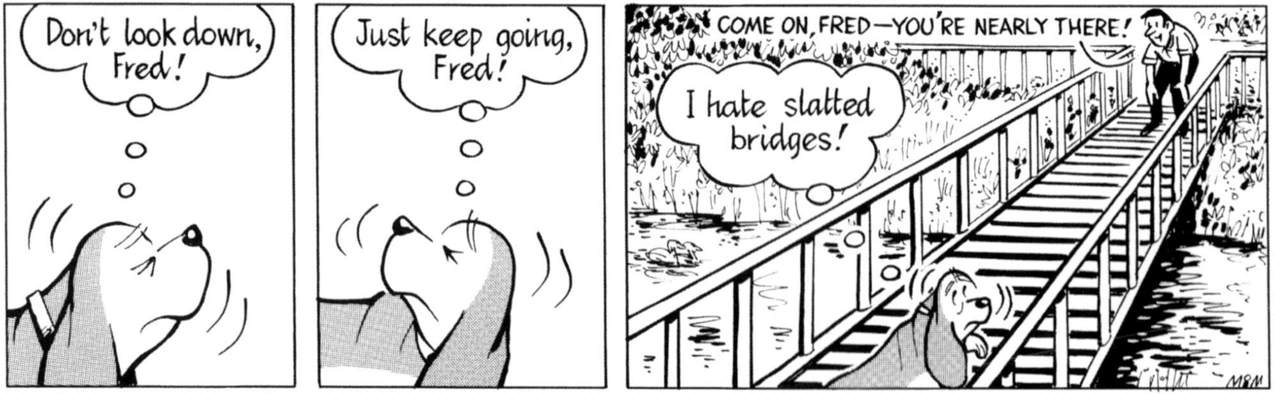
Don't look down, Fred!
Just keep going, Fred!
COME ON, FRED—YOU'RE NEARLY THERE!
I hate slatted bridges!

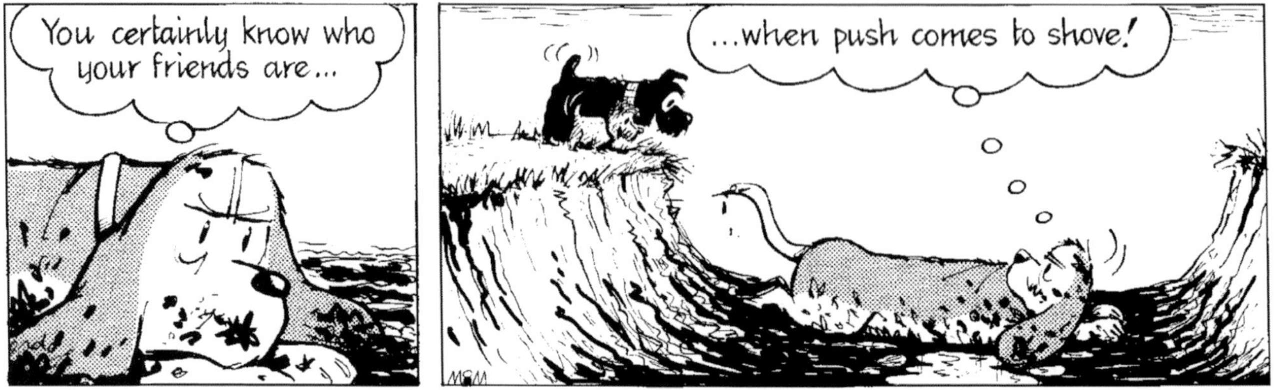
You certainly know who your friends are...
...when push comes to shove!

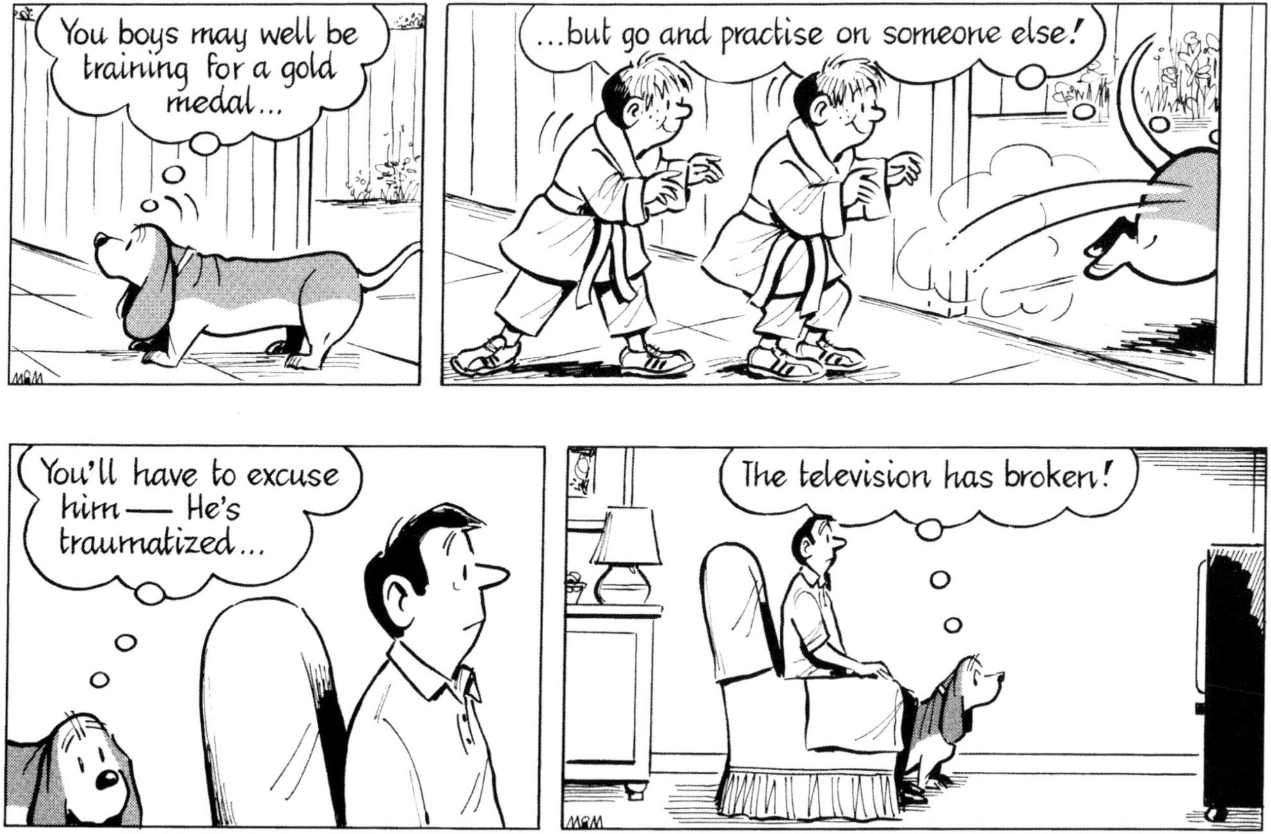
You boys may well be training for a gold medal...
...but go and practise on someone else!
MBM
You'll have to excuse him — He's traumatized...
The television has broken!
MBM

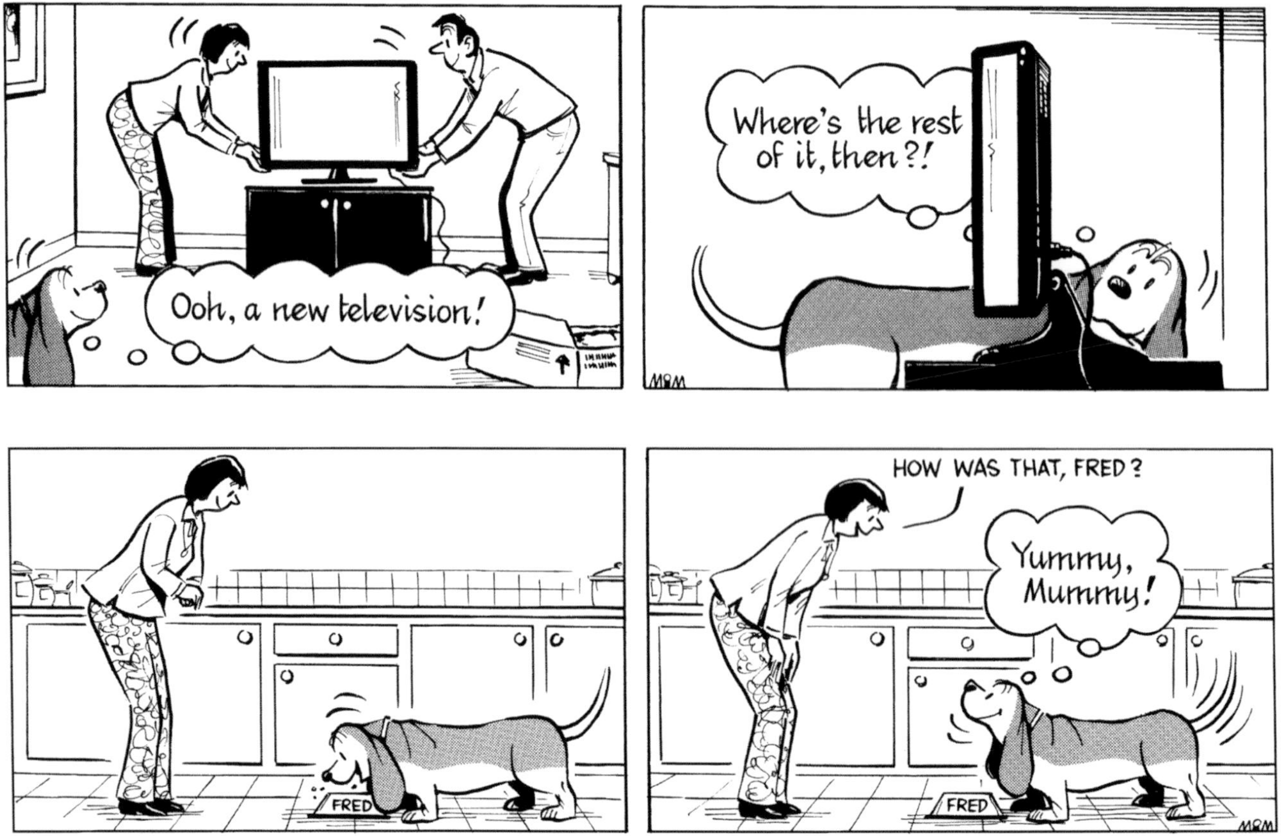
Ooh, a new television!
Where's the rest of it, then?!
FRED
HOW WAS THAT, FRED?
Yummy, Mummy!
FRED

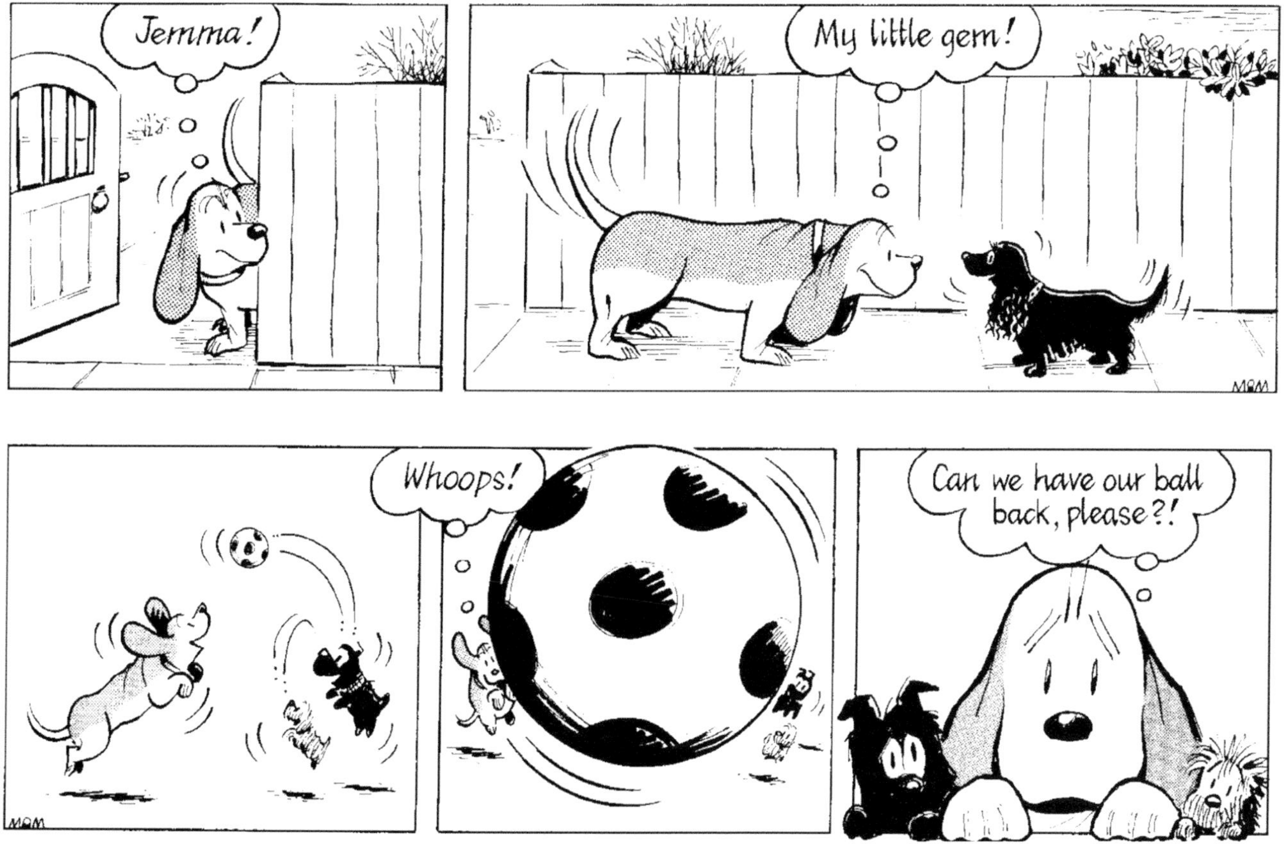
Jemma!
My little gem!
MOM
Whoops!
Can we have our ball back, please?!
MOM

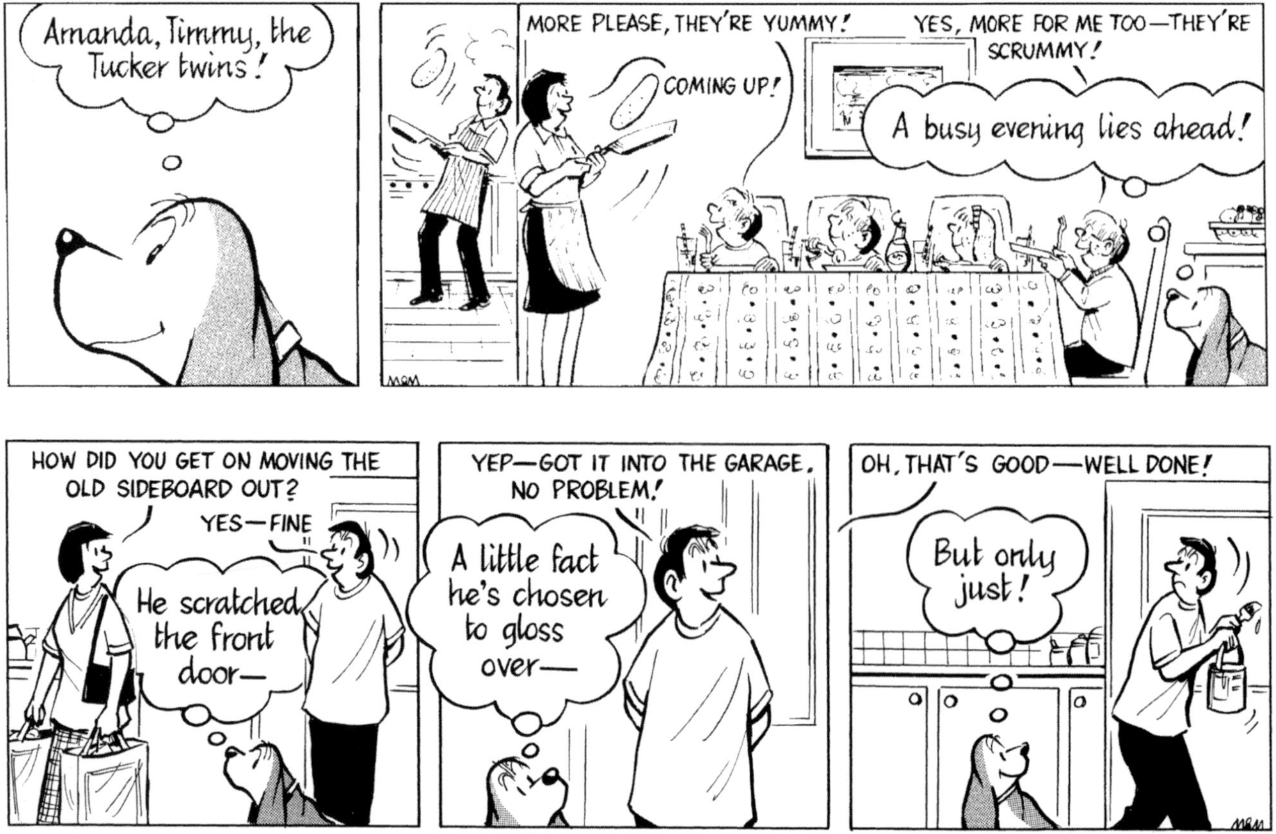
Amanda, Timmy, the Tucker twins!
MORE PLEASE, THEY'RE YUMMY!
COMING UP!
YES, MORE FOR ME TOO—THEY'RE SCRUMMY!
A busy evening lies ahead!
HOW DID YOU GET ON MOVING THE OLD SIDEBOARD OUT?
YES—FINE
He scratched the front door—
YEP—GOT IT INTO THE GARAGE. NO PROBLEM!
A little fact he's chosen to gloss over—
OH, THAT'S GOOD—WELL DONE!
But only just!

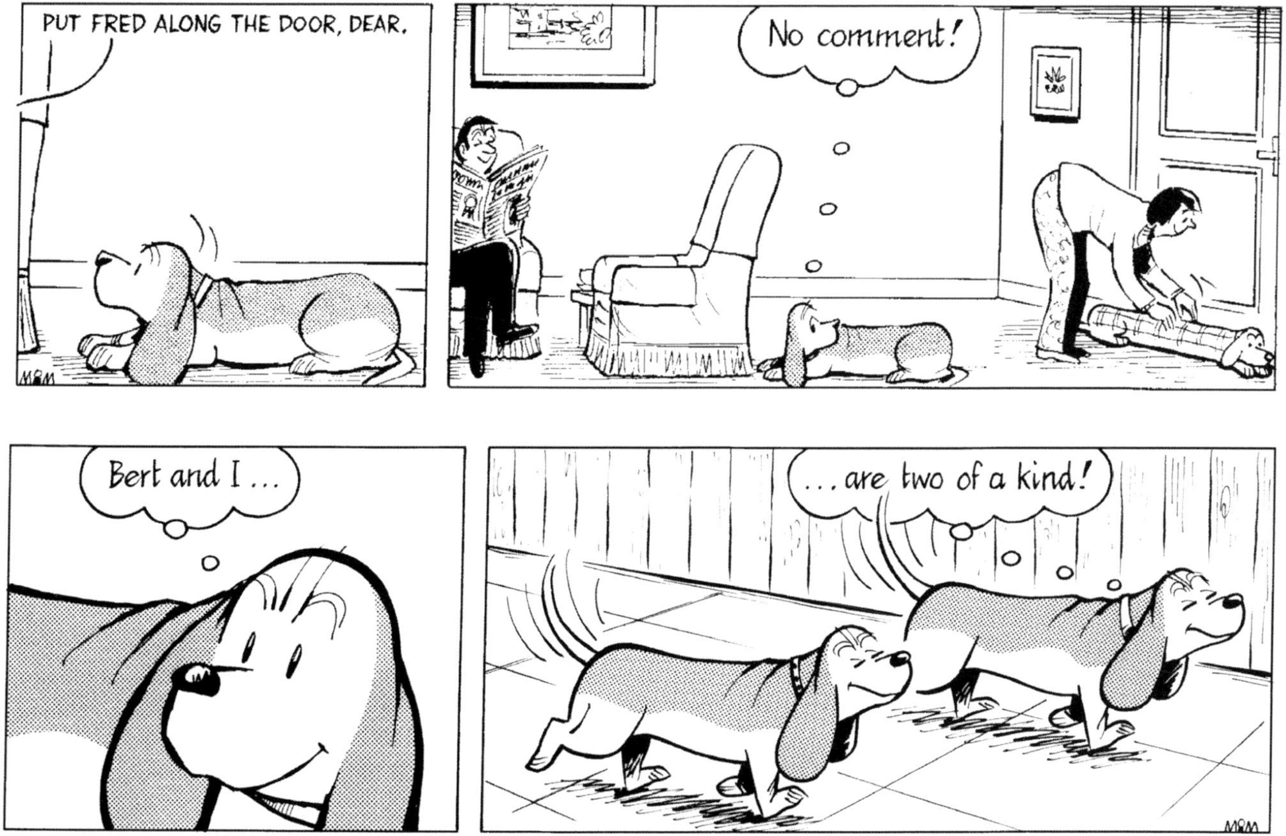
PUT FRED ALONG THE DOOR, DEAR.
No comment!
Bert and I ...
... are two of a kind!

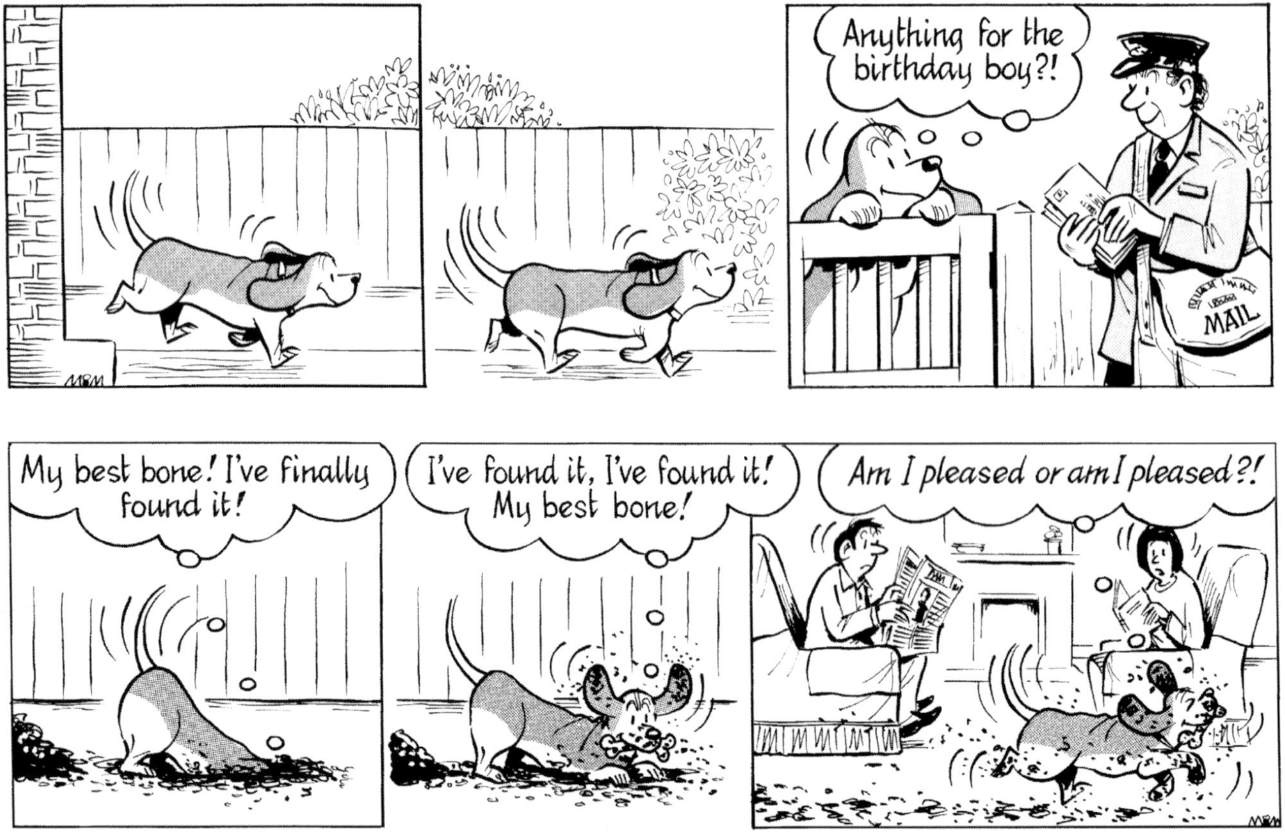
Anything for the birthday boy?!
MAIL
My best bone! I've finally found it!
I've found it, I've found it! My best bone!
Am I pleased or am I pleased?!

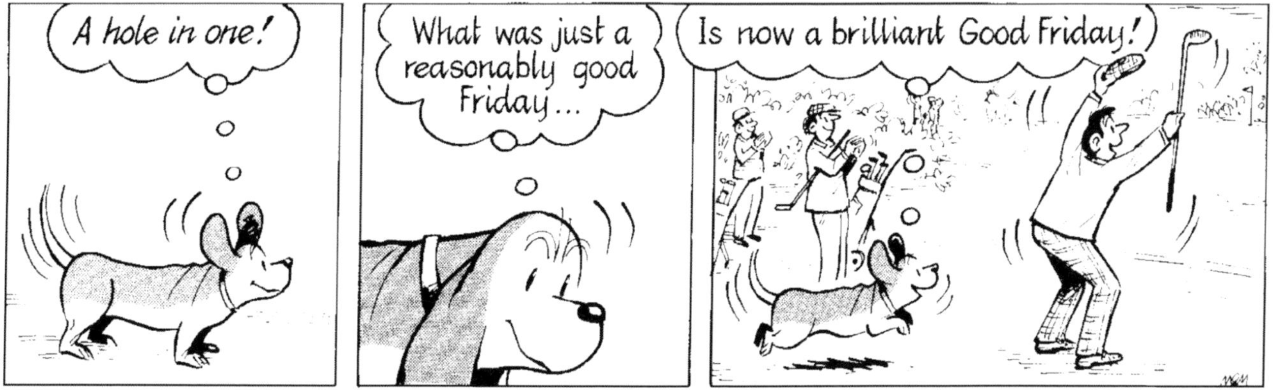
A hole in one!
What was just a reasonably good Friday...
Is now a brilliant Good Friday!
MGM

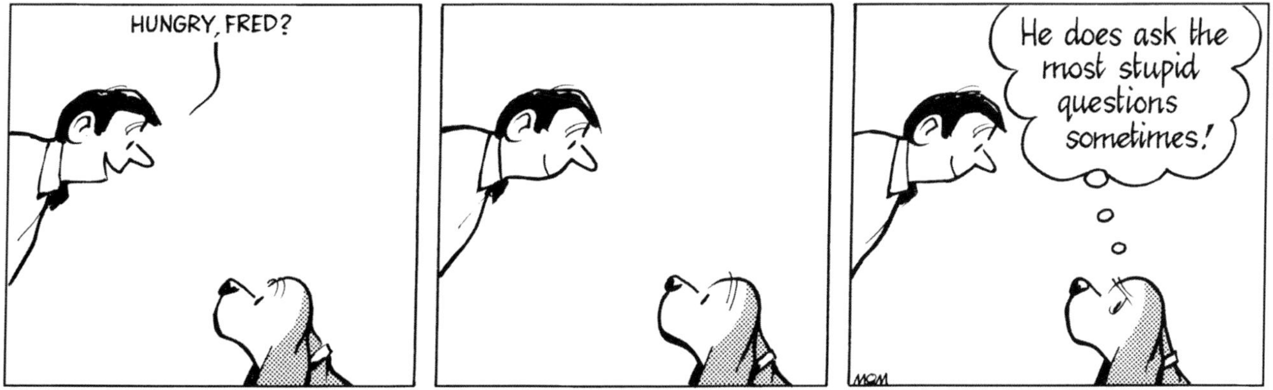
HUNGRY, FRED?
He does ask the most stupid questions sometimes!
MGM

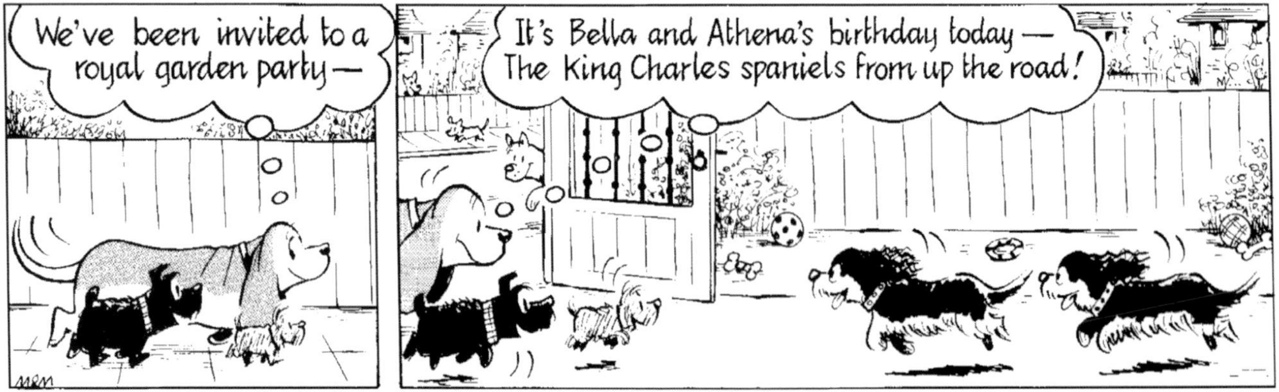
We've been invited to a royal garden party—
It's Bella and Athena's birthday today—The King Charles spaniels from up the road!

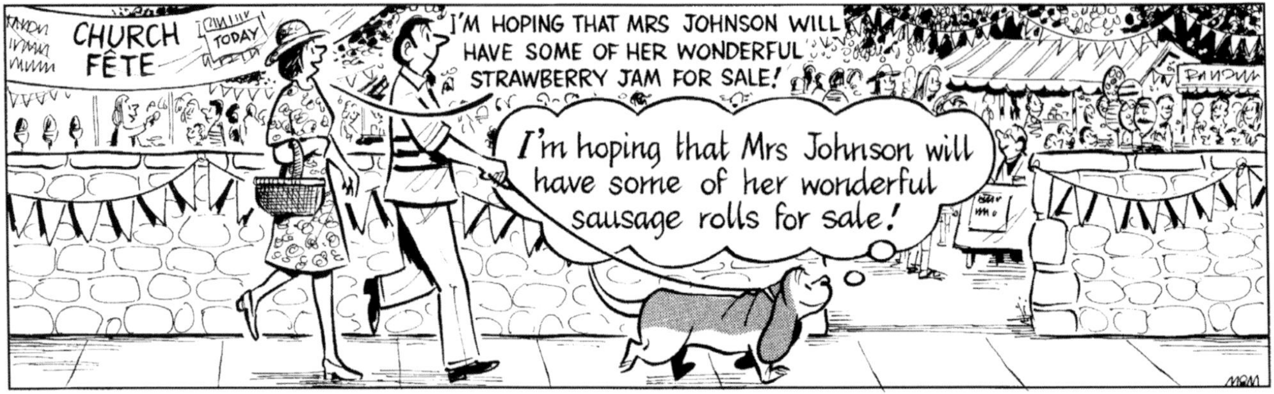
CHURCH FÊTE
TODAY
I'M HOPING THAT MRS JOHNSON WILL HAVE SOME OF HER WONDERFUL STRAWBERRY JAM FOR SALE!
I'm hoping that Mrs Johnson will have some of her wonderful sausage rolls for sale!

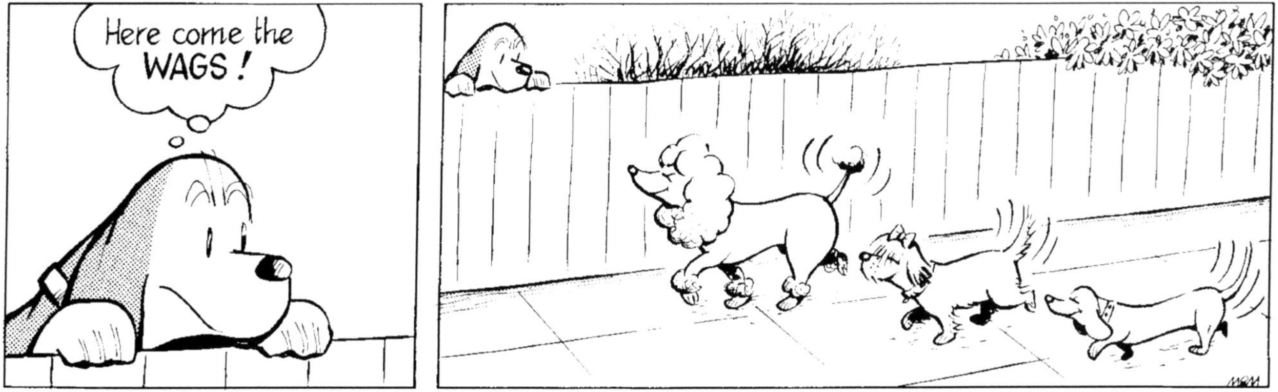
Here come the WAGS!

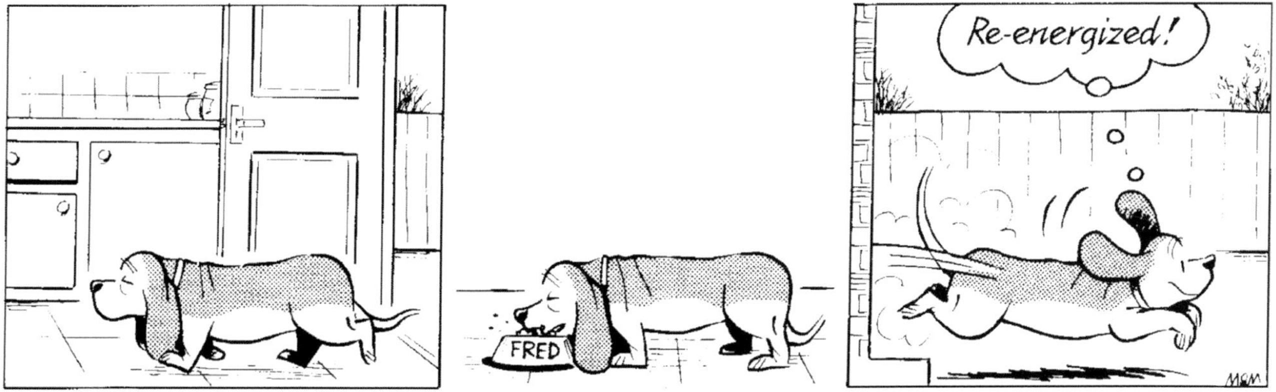
FRED
Re-energized!

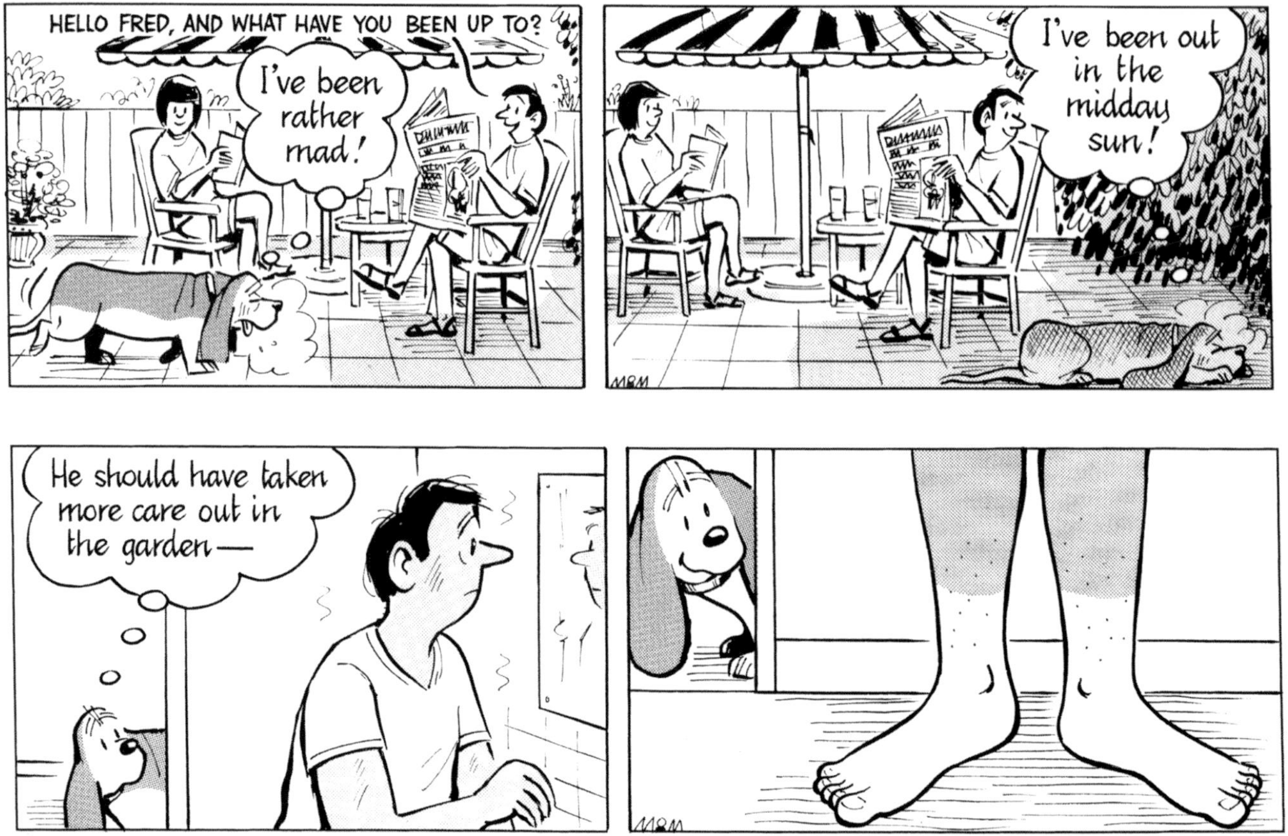
HELLO FRED, AND WHAT HAVE YOU BEEN UP TO?
I've been rather mad!
I've been out in the midday sun!
He should have taken more care out in the garden —

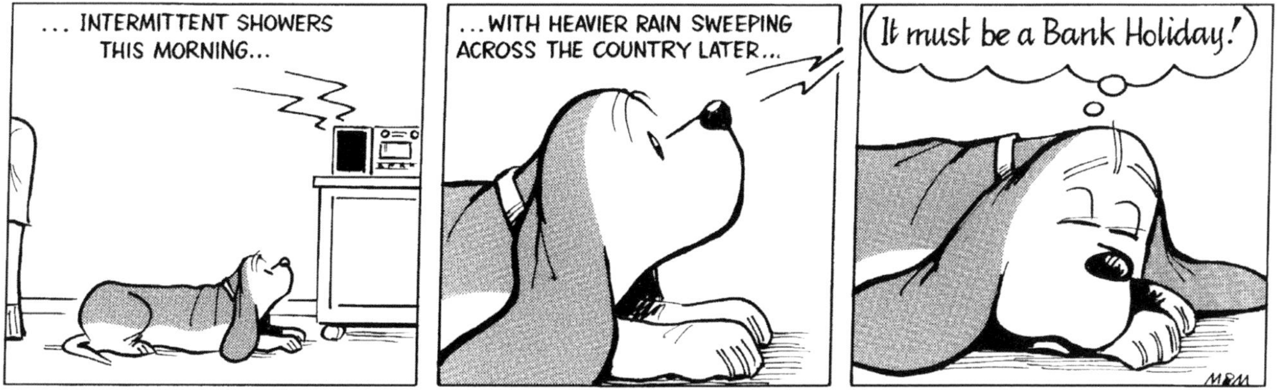
... INTERMITTENT SHOWERS THIS MORNING...
...WITH HEAVIER RAIN SWEEPING ACROSS THE COUNTRY LATER...
It must be a Bank Holiday!
M&M

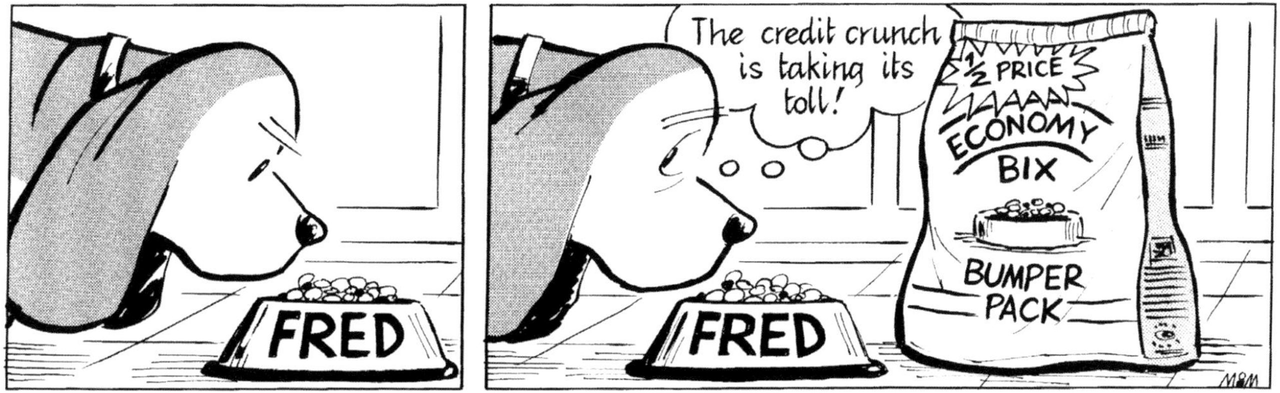
FRED
The credit crunch is taking its toll!
FRED
½ PRICE
ECONOMY
BIX
BUMPER PACK
M&M

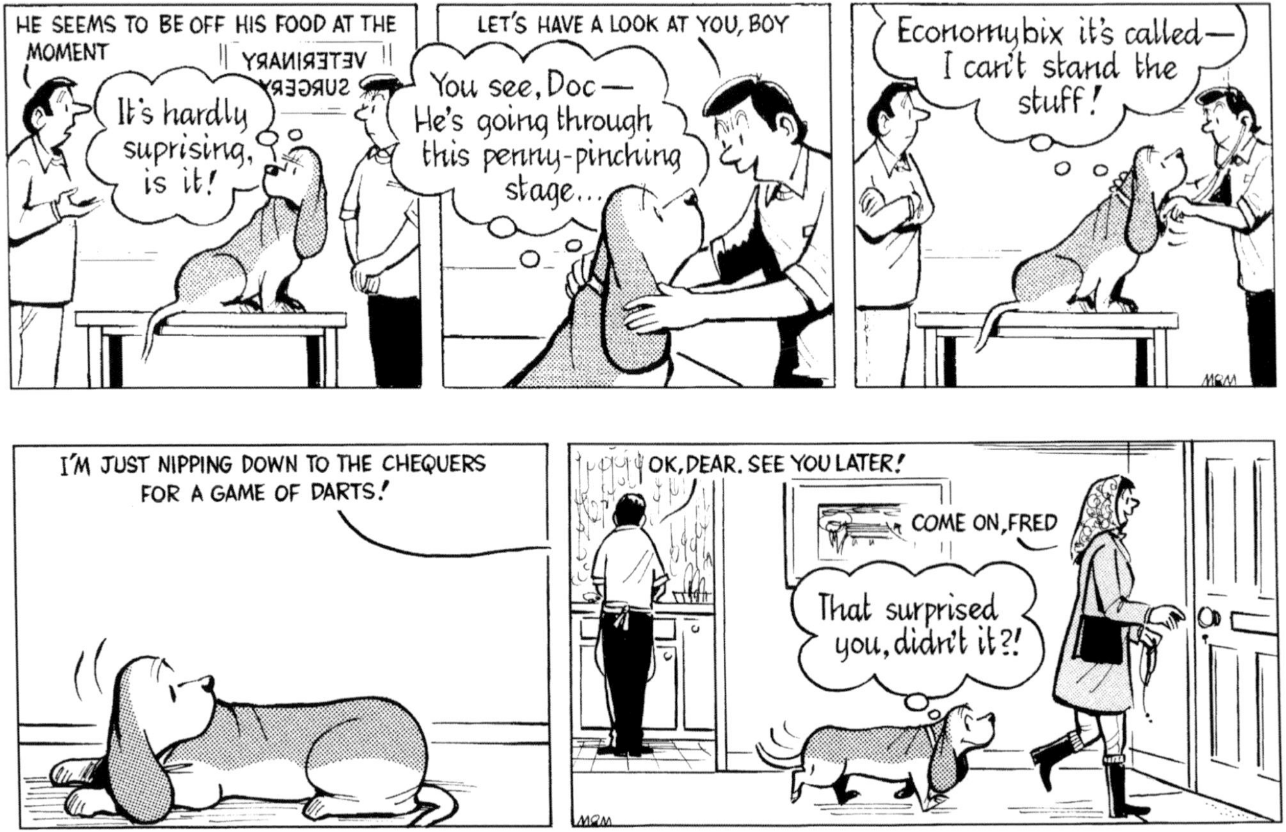
HE SEEMS TO BE OFF HIS FOOD AT THE MOMENT
VETERINARY SURGERY
It's hardly suprising, is it!
LET'S HAVE A LOOK AT YOU, BOY
You see, Doc — He's going through this penny-pinching stage...
Economybix it's called — I can't stand the stuff!
MGM
I'M JUST NIPPING DOWN TO THE CHEQUERS FOR A GAME OF DARTS!
OK, DEAR. SEE YOU LATER!
COME ON, FRED
That surprised you, didn't it?!
MGM

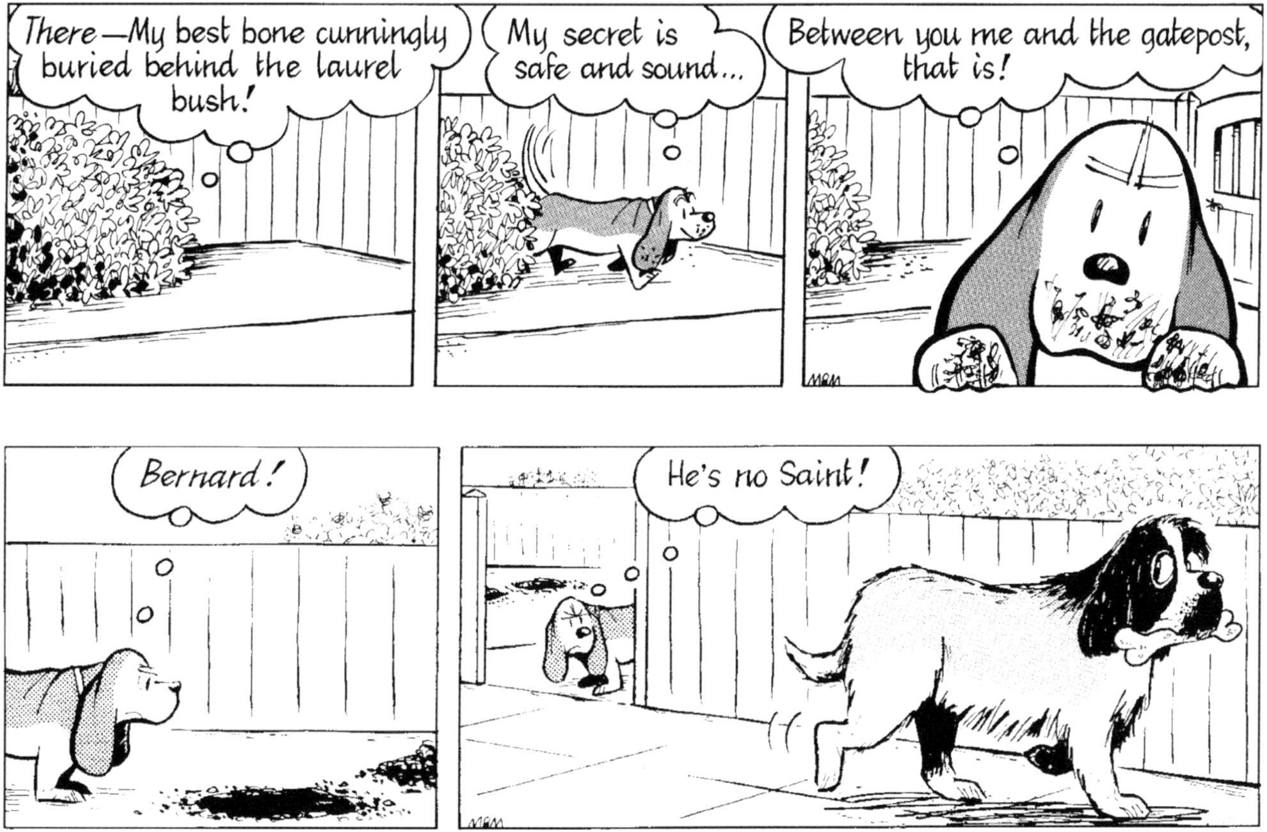
There—My best bone cunningly buried behind the laurel bush!
My secret is safe and sound...
Between you me and the gatepost, that is!
MGM
Bernard!
He's no Saint!
MGM

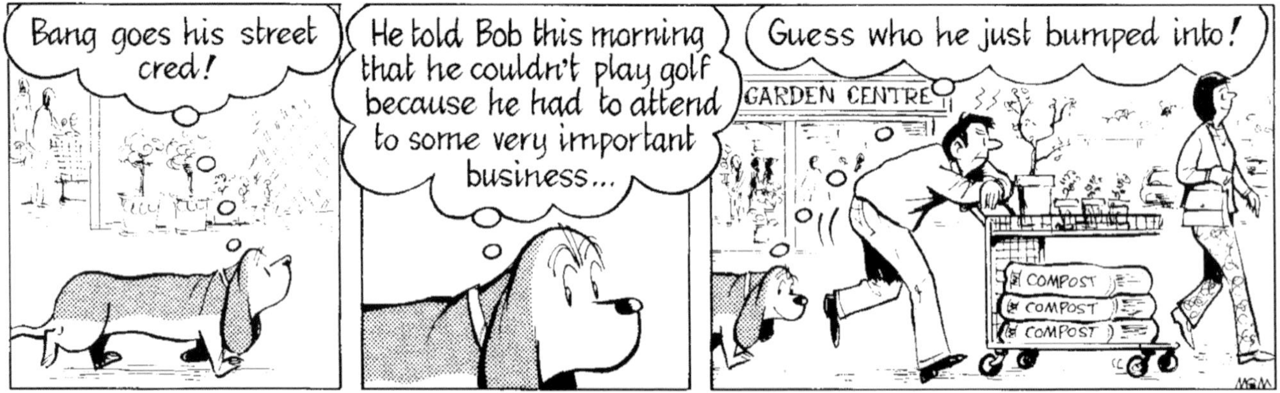

Bang goes his street cred!
He told Bob this morning that he couldn't play golf because he had to attend to some very important business...
Guess who he just bumped into!
GARDEN CENTRE
COMPOST
COMPOST
COMPOST

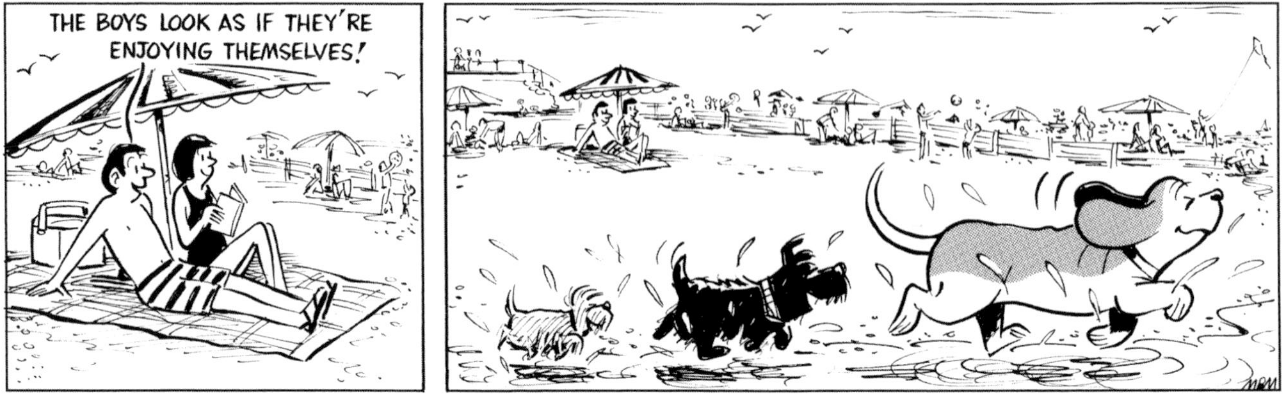

THE BOYS LOOK AS IF THEY'RE ENJOYING THEMSELVES!

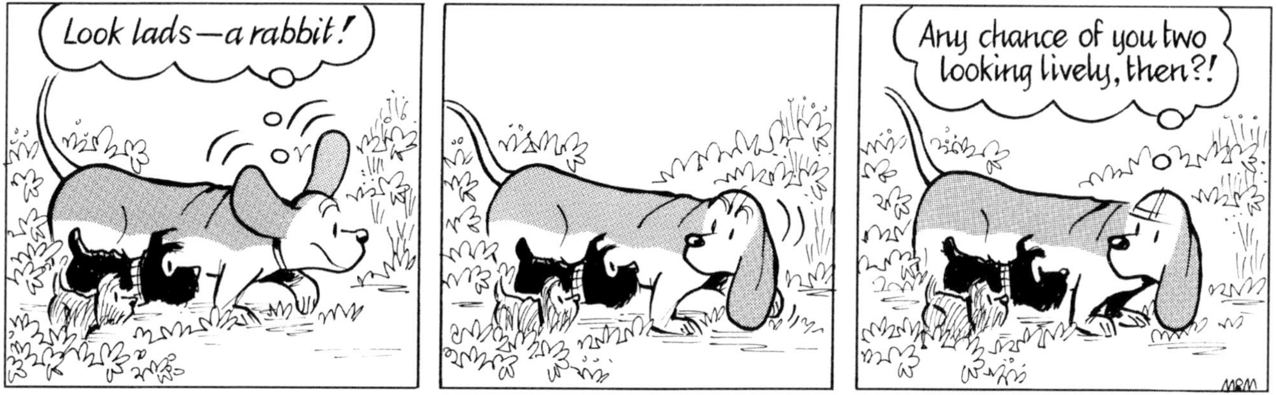
Look lads—a rabbit!
Any chance of you two looking lively, then?!
MRM

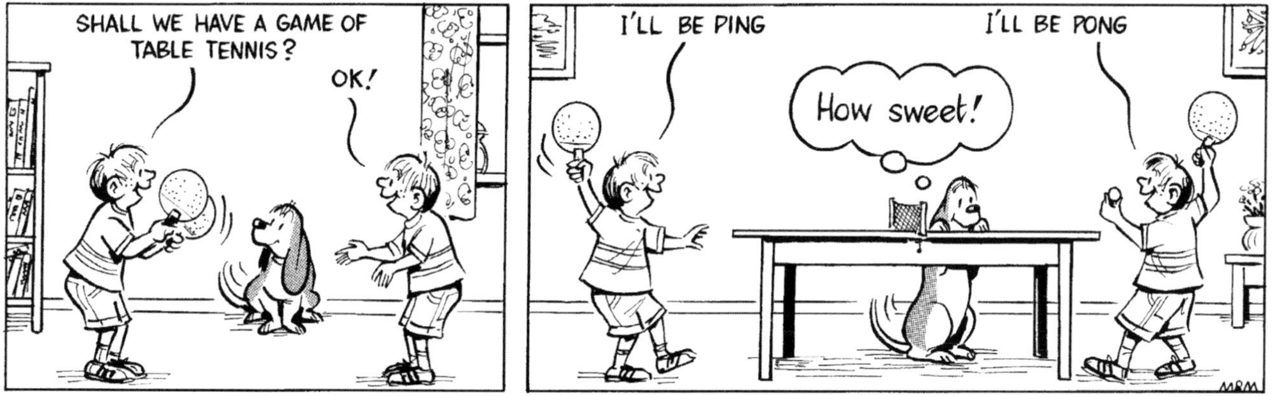
SHALL WE HAVE A GAME OF TABLE TENNIS?
OK!
I'LL BE PING
I'LL BE PONG
How sweet!
MRM

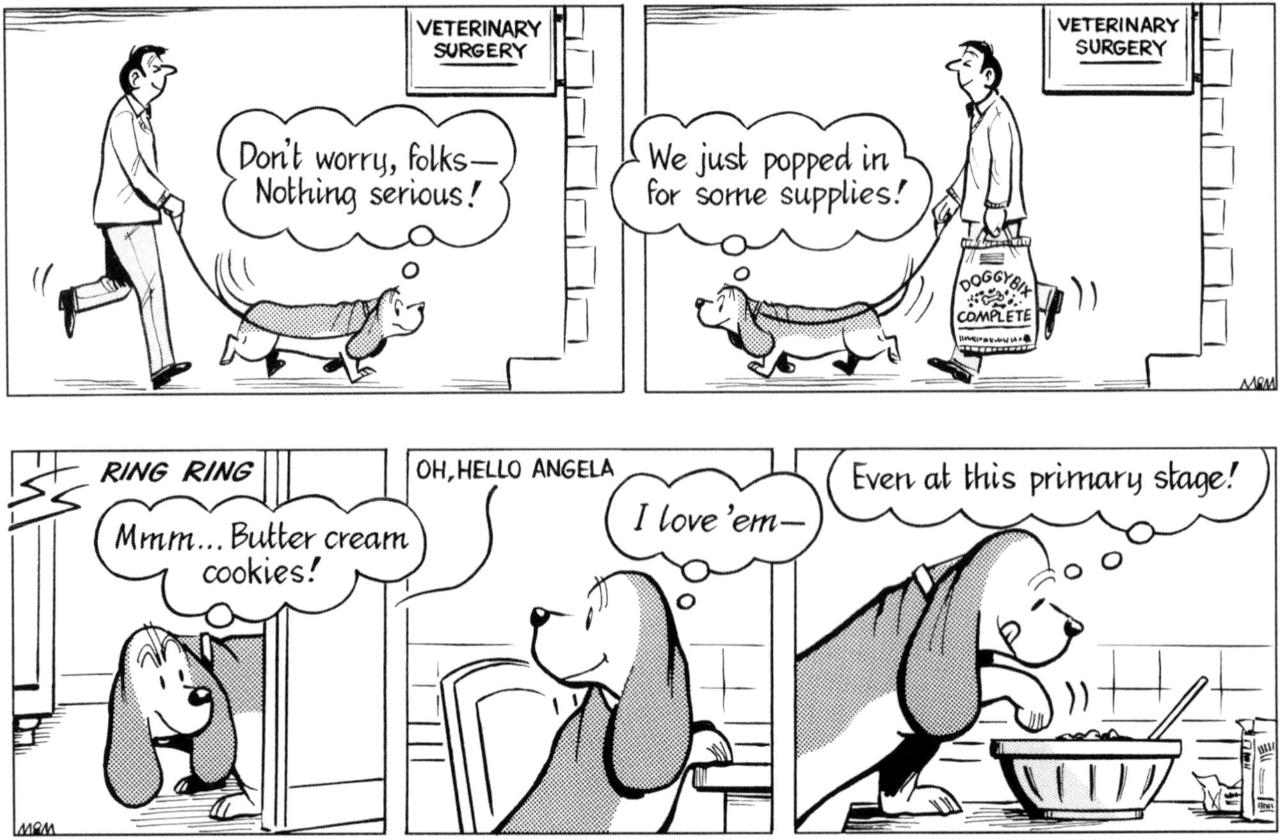
VETERINARY SURGERY
Don't worry, folks— Nothing serious!
VETERINARY SURGERY
We just popped in for some supplies!
DOGGYBIX COMPLETE
RING RING
Mmm... Butter cream cookies!
OH, HELLO ANGELA
I love 'em—
Even at this primary stage!

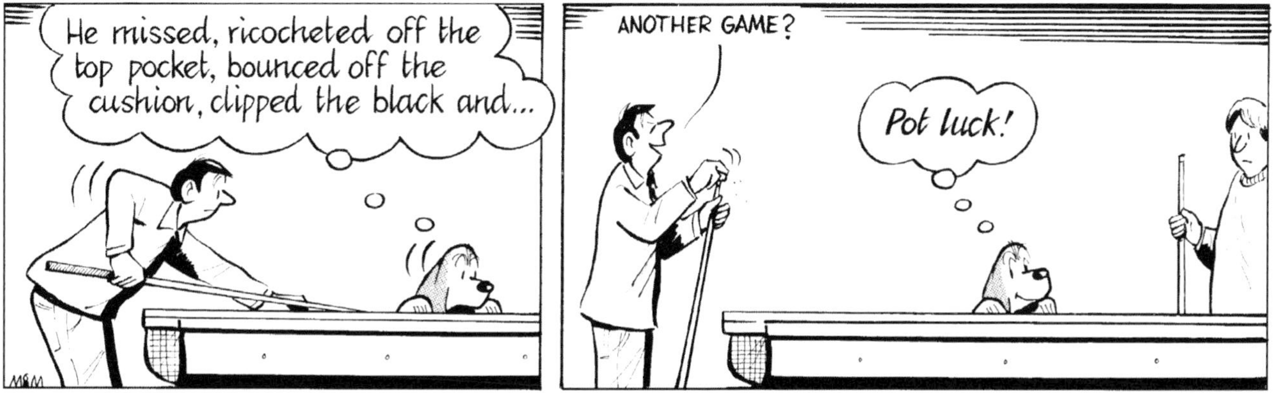
He missed, ricocheted off the top pocket, bounced off the cushion, clipped the black and...
ANOTHER GAME?
Pot luck!

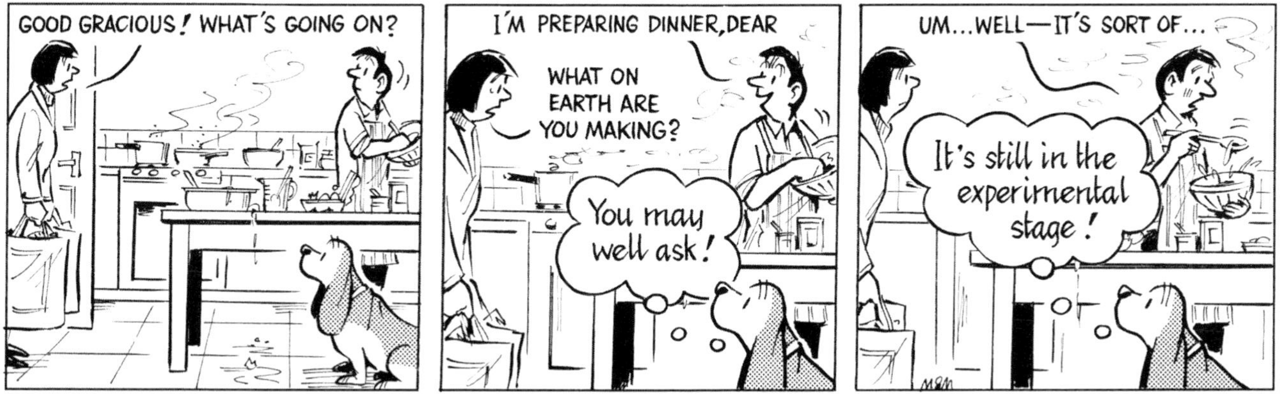
GOOD GRACIOUS! WHAT'S GOING ON?
I'M PREPARING DINNER, DEAR
WHAT ON EARTH ARE YOU MAKING?
You may well ask!
UM...WELL—IT'S SORT OF...
It's still in the experimental stage!

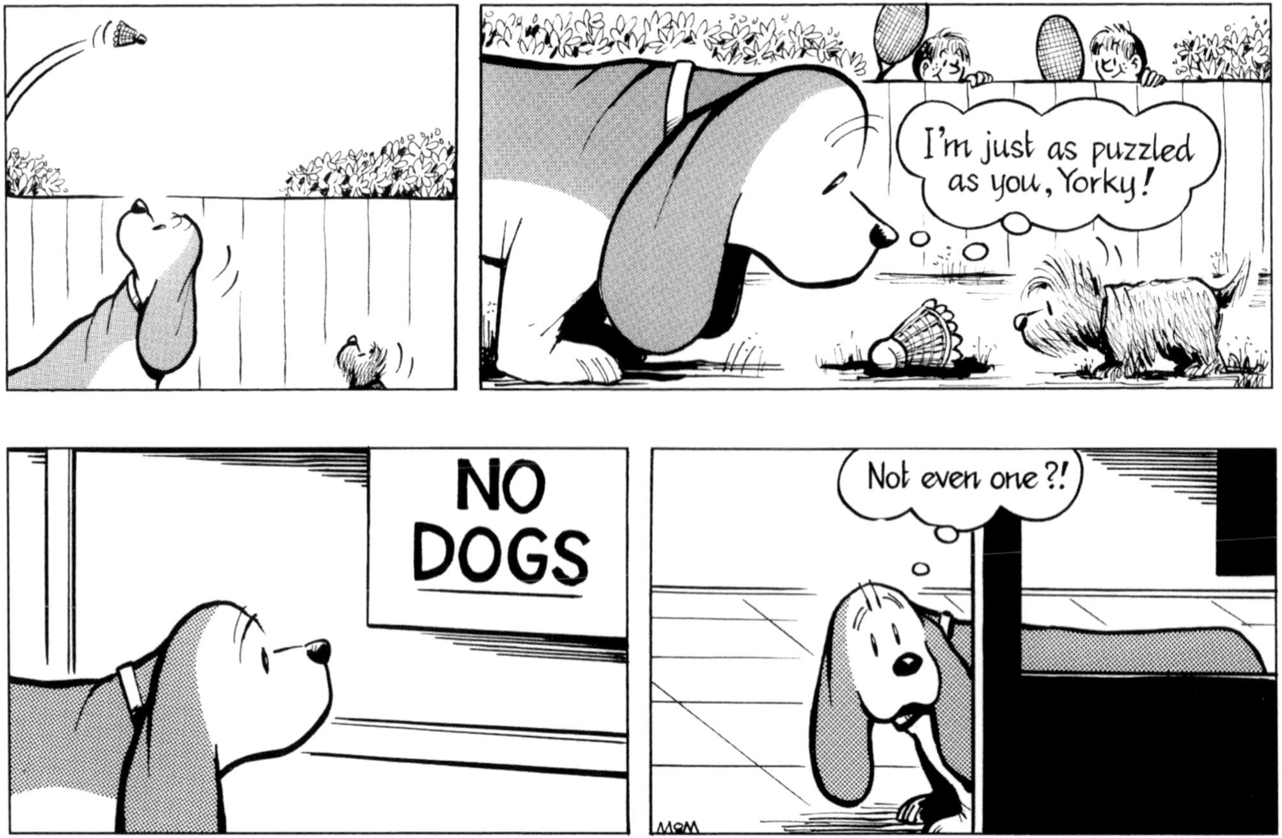
I'm just as puzzled as you, Yorky!
NO DOGS
Not even one?!
M&M

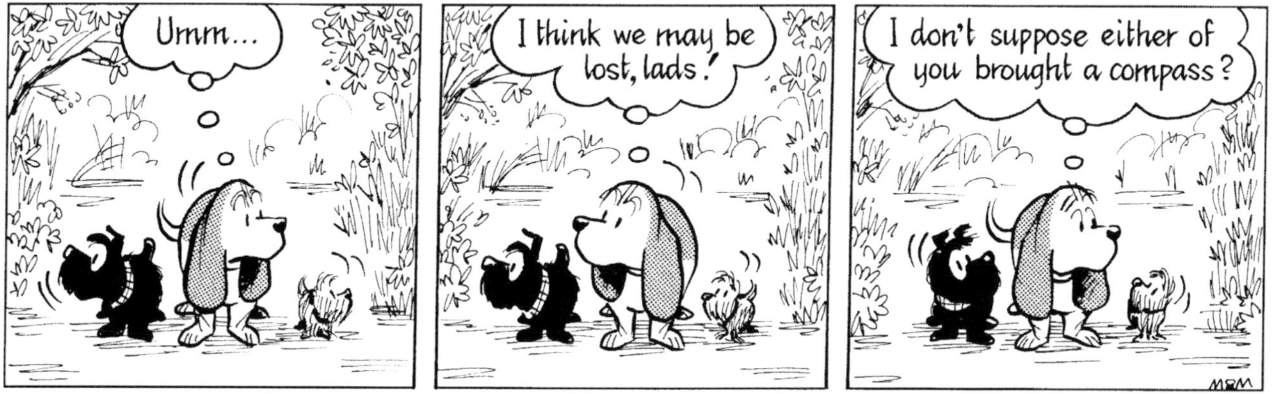
Urnrn...
I think we may be lost, lads!
I don't suppose either of you brought a compass?
M&M

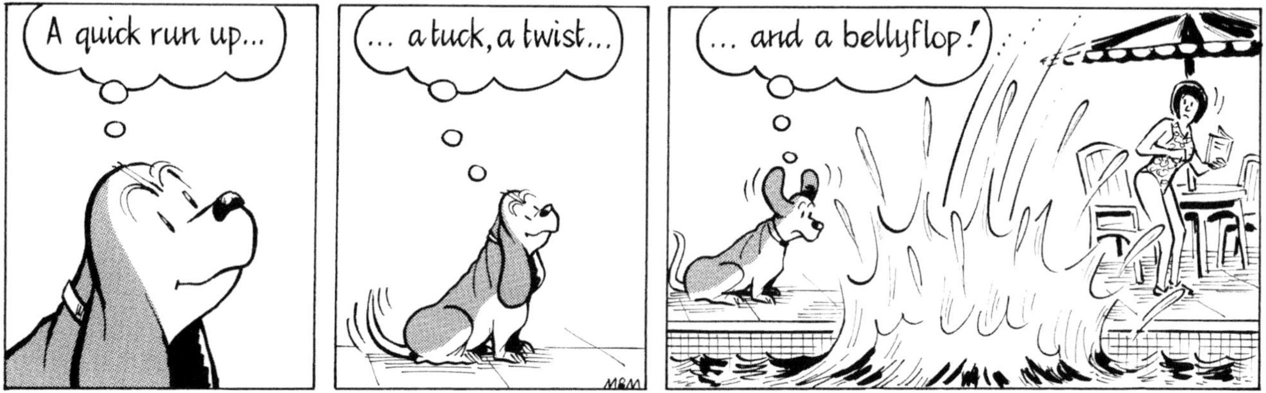
A quick run up...
... a tuck, a twist...
M&M
... and a bellyflop!

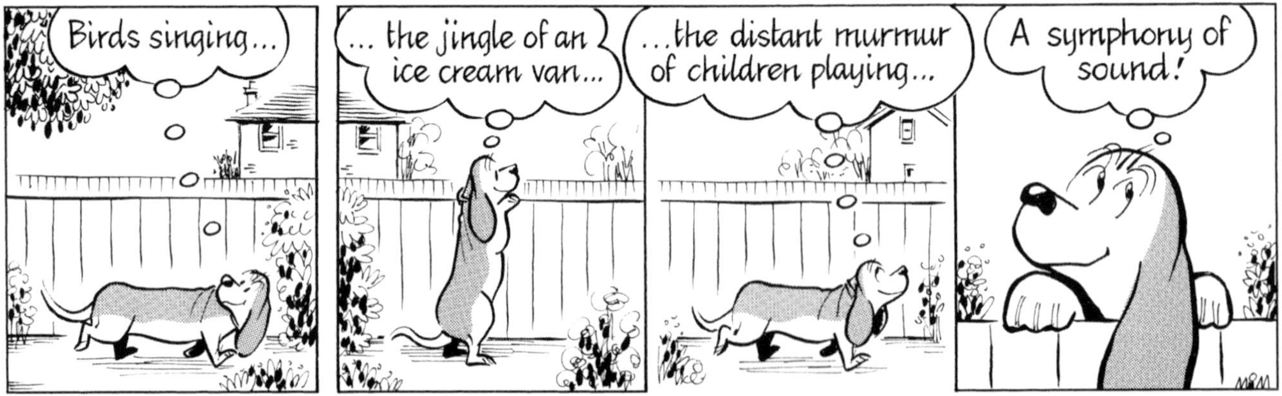
Birds singing...
... the jingle of an ice cream van...
...the distant murmur of children playing...
A symphony of sound!

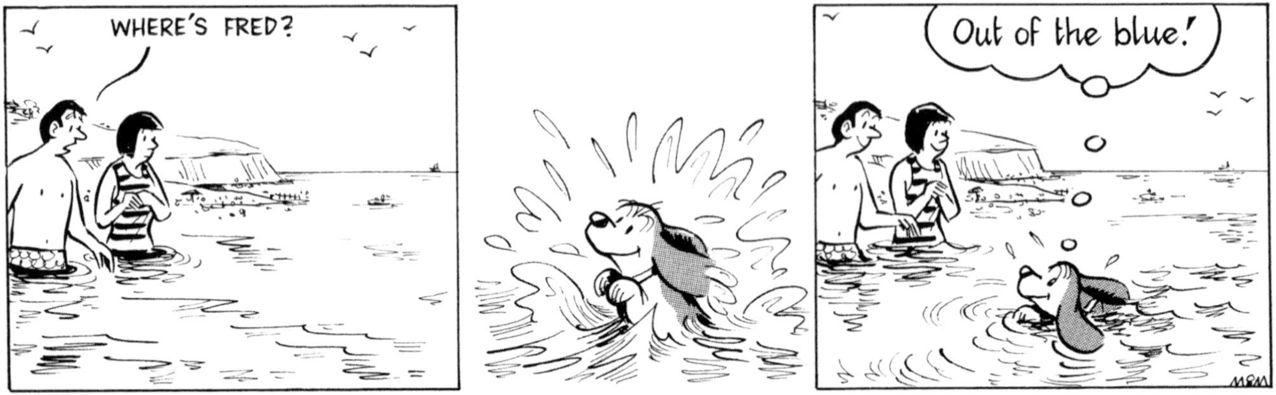
WHERE'S FRED?
Out of the blue!

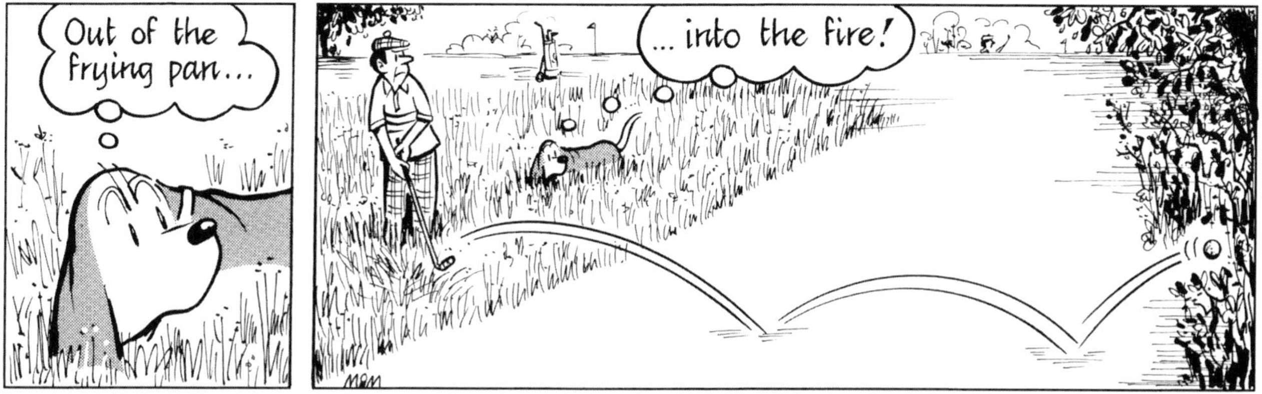
Out of the frying pan...
... into the fire!

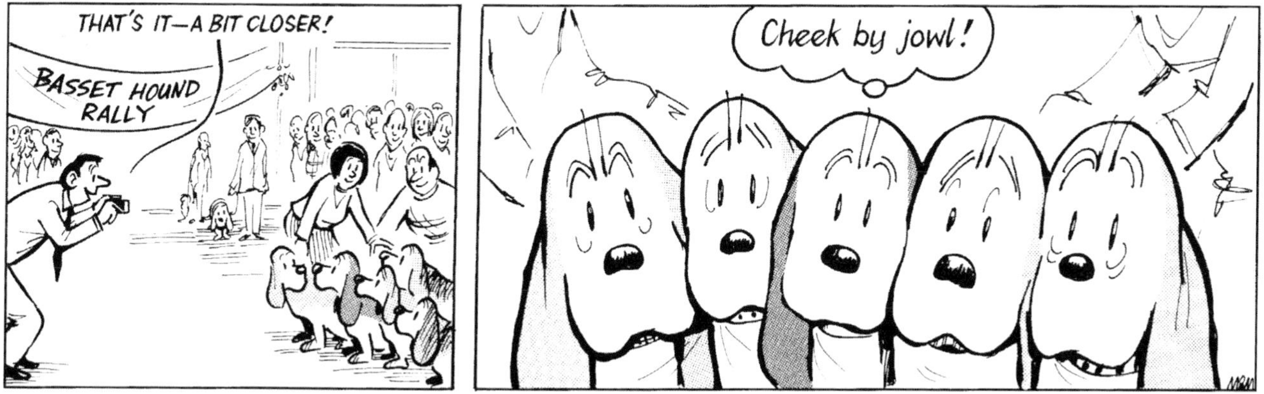
THAT'S IT—A BIT CLOSER!
BASSET HOUND RALLY
Cheek by jowl!

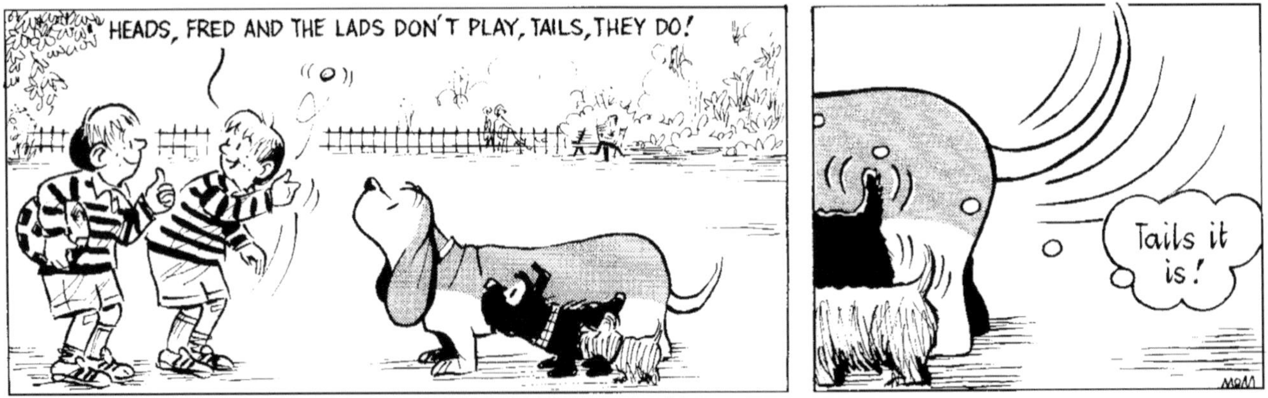
HEADS, FRED AND THE LADS DON'T PLAY, TAILS, THEY DO!
Tails it is!
MGM

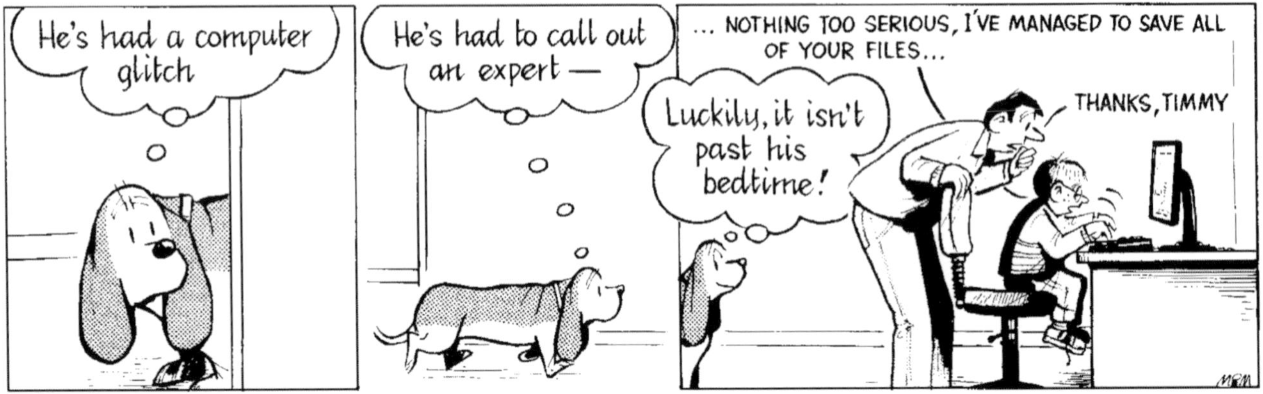
He's had a computer glitch
He's had to call out an expert —
... NOTHING TOO SERIOUS, I'VE MANAGED TO SAVE ALL OF YOUR FILES...
THANKS, TIMMY
Luckily, it isn't past his bedtime!
MGM

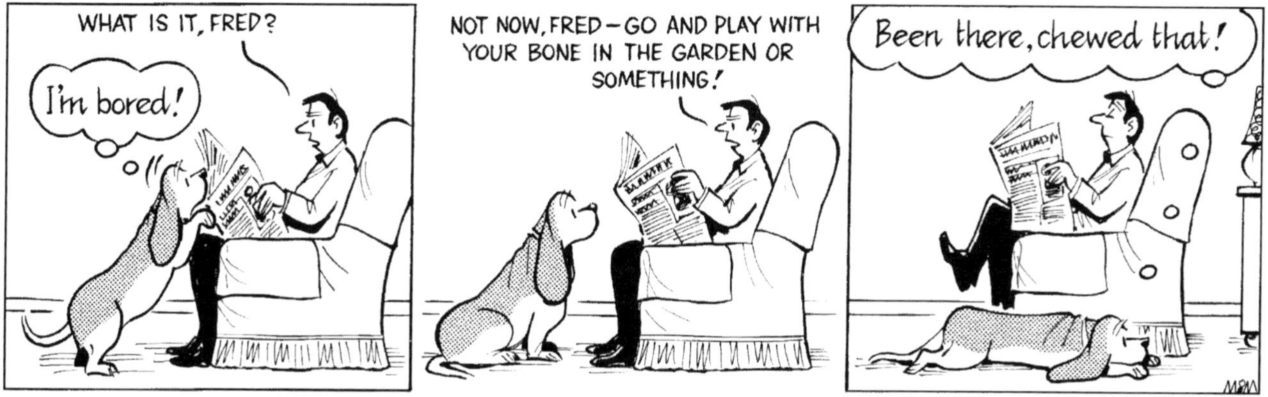
WHAT IS IT, FRED?
I'm bored!
NOT NOW, FRED – GO AND PLAY WITH YOUR BONE IN THE GARDEN OR SOMETHING!
Been there, chewed that!
MGM

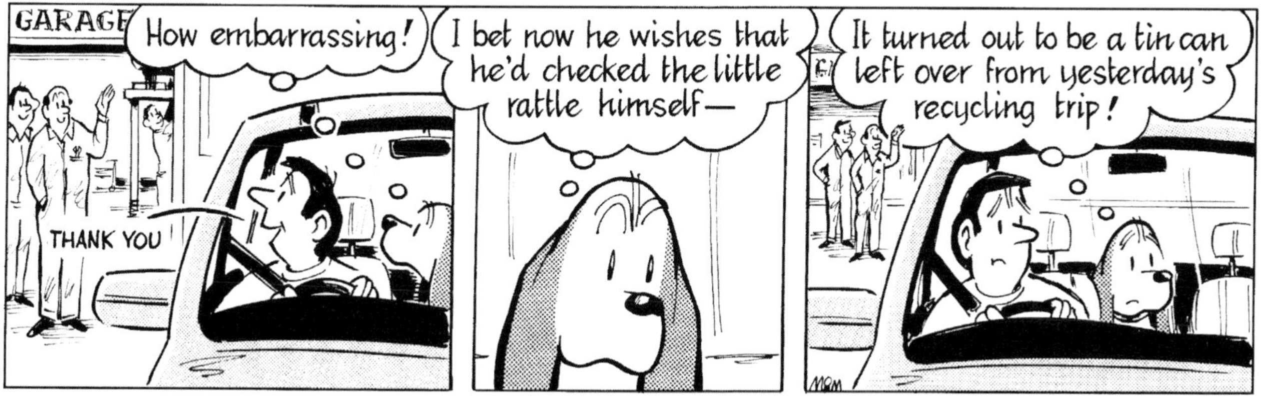
GARAGE
How embarrassing!
THANK YOU
I bet now he wishes that he'd checked the little rattle himself—
It turned out to be a tin can left over from yesterday's recycling trip!
MGM

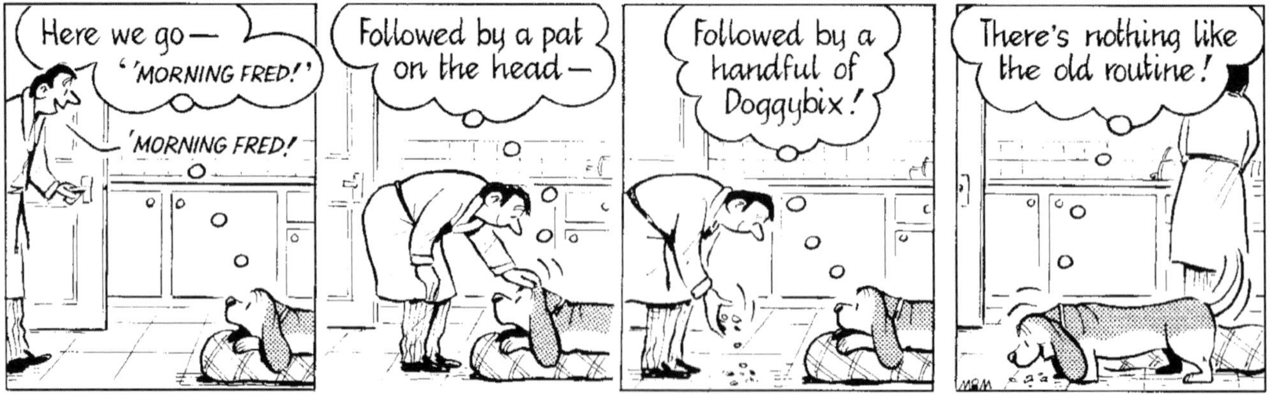
Here we go— '' 'MORNING FRED!''
'MORNING FRED!
Followed by a pat on the head—
Followed by a handful of Doggybix!
There's nothing like the old routine!

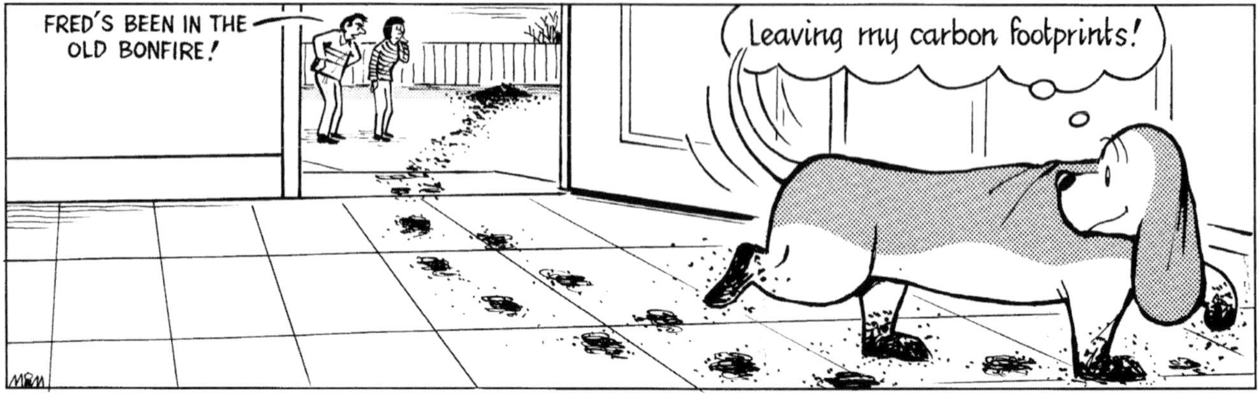
FRED'S BEEN IN THE OLD BONFIRE!
Leaving my carbon footprints!

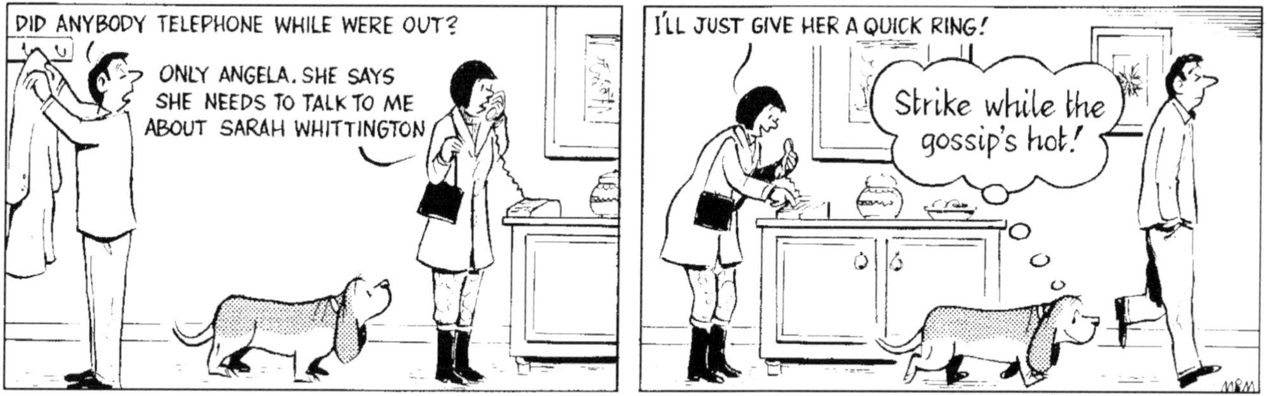
DID ANYBODY TELEPHONE WHILE WERE OUT?
ONLY ANGELA. SHE SAYS SHE NEEDS TO TALK TO ME ABOUT SARAH WHITTINGTON
I'LL JUST GIVE HER A QUICK RING!
Strike while the gossip's hot!
M&M

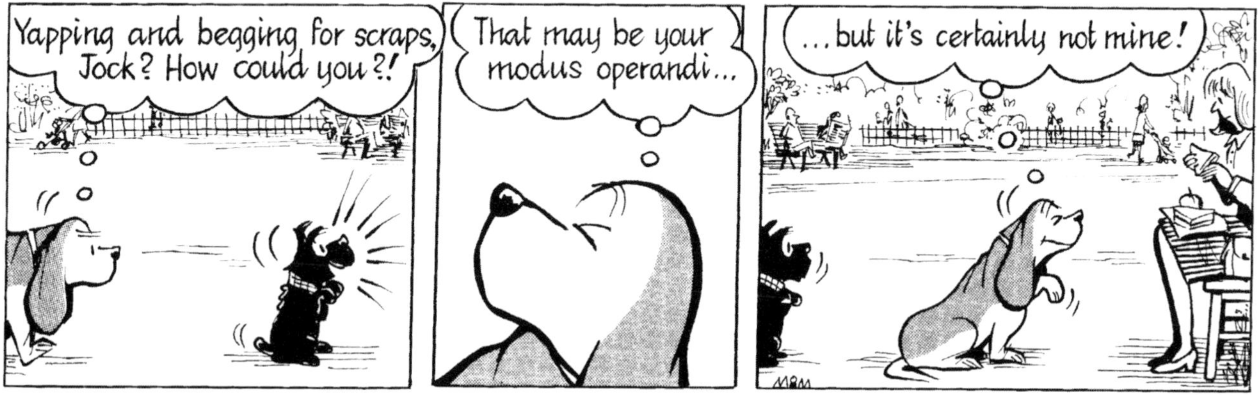
Yapping and begging for scraps, Jock? How could you?!
That may be your modus operandi...
...but it's certainly not mine!
M&M

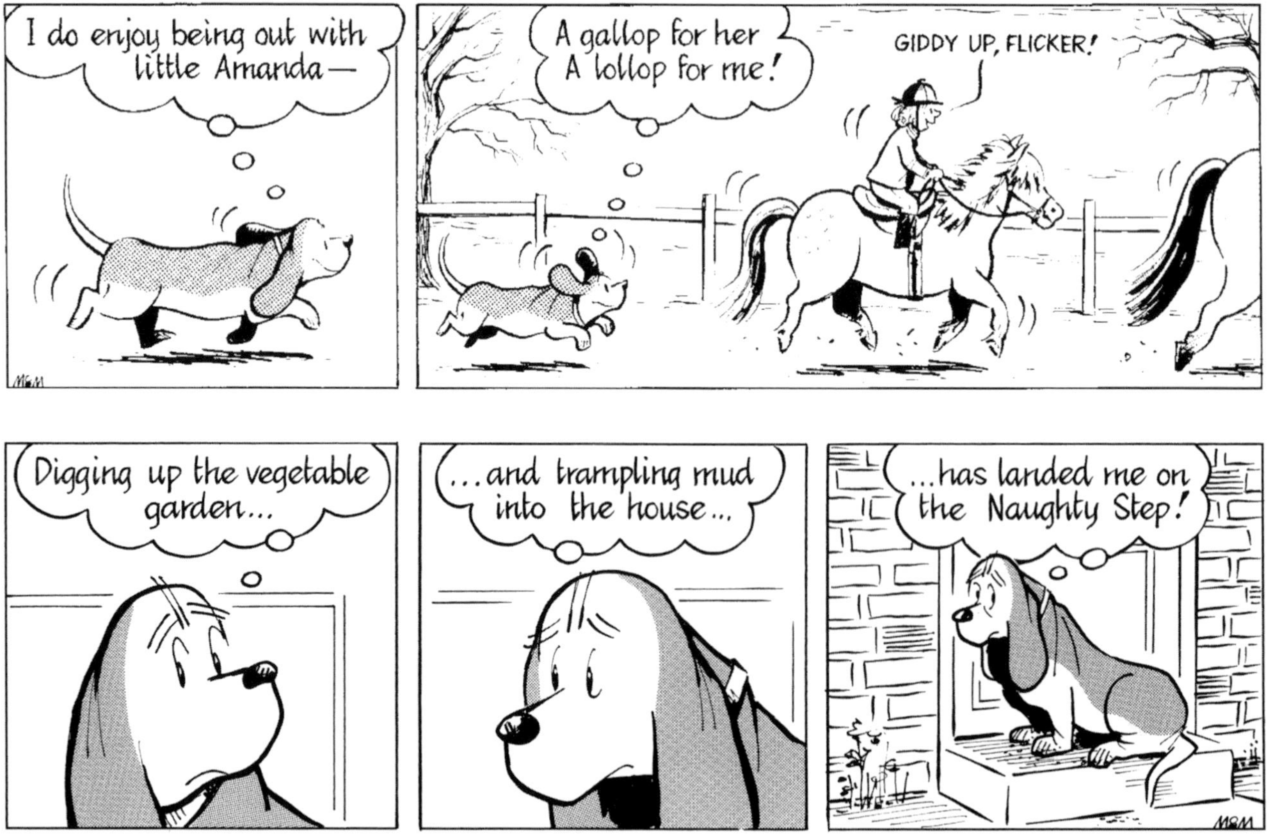
I do enjoy being out with little Amanda—
A gallop for her A lollop for me!
GIDDY UP, FLICKER!
Digging up the vegetable garden...
...and trampling mud into the house...
...has landed me on the Naughty Step!
MGM

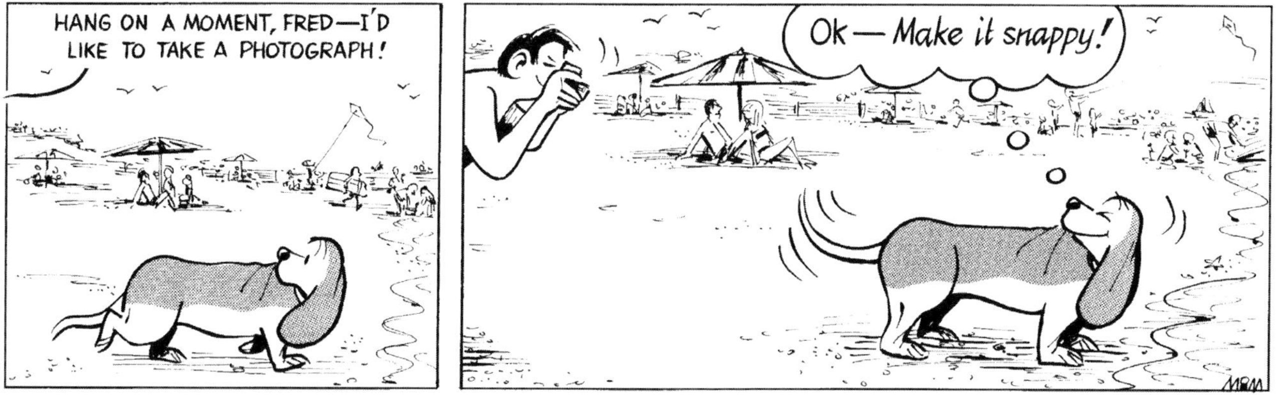
HANG ON A MOMENT, FRED—I'D LIKE TO TAKE A PHOTOGRAPH!
Ok — Make it snappy!

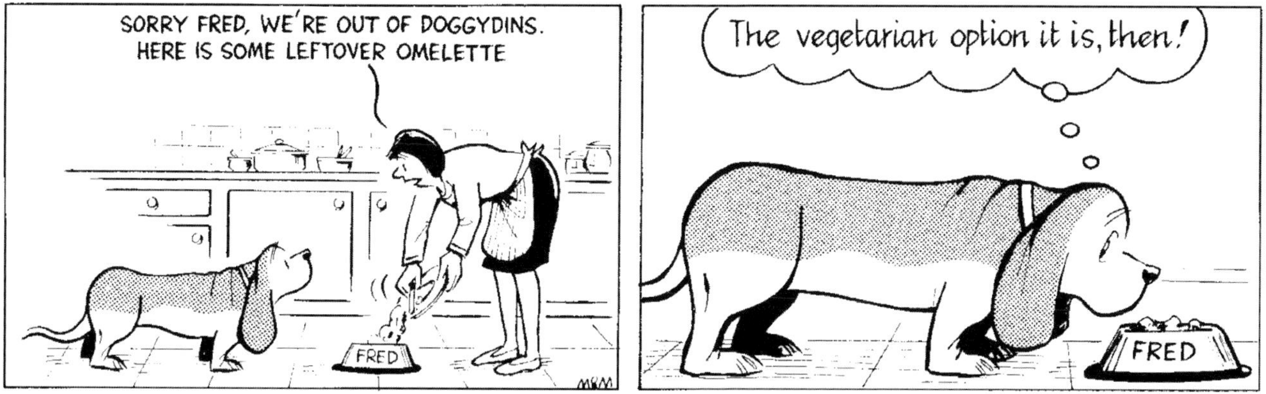
SORRY FRED, WE'RE OUT OF DOGGYDINS. HERE IS SOME LEFTOVER OMELETTE
FRED
The vegetarian option it is, then!
FRED

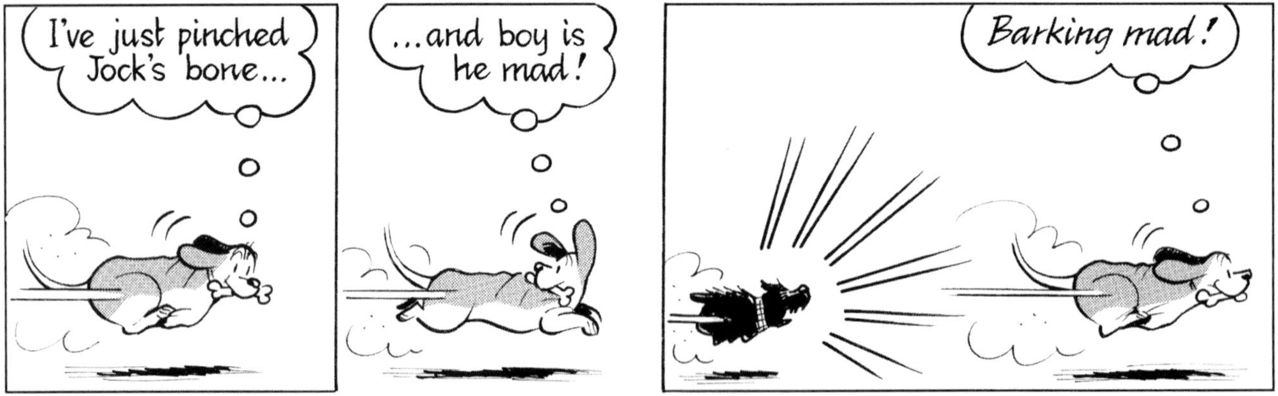
I've just pinched Jock's bone...
...and boy is he mad!
Barking mad!

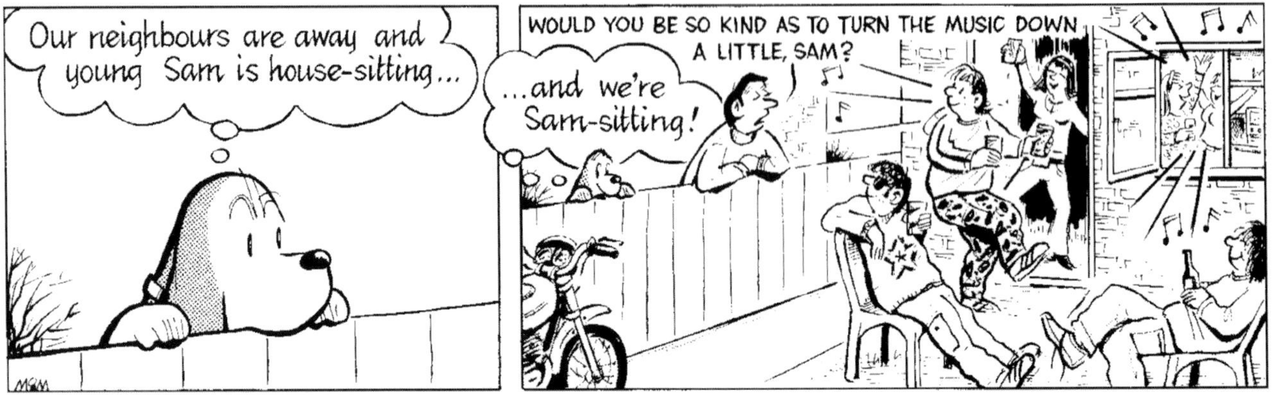
Our neighbours are away and young Sam is house-sitting...
...and we're Sam-sitting!
WOULD YOU BE SO KIND AS TO TURN THE MUSIC DOWN A LITTLE, SAM?

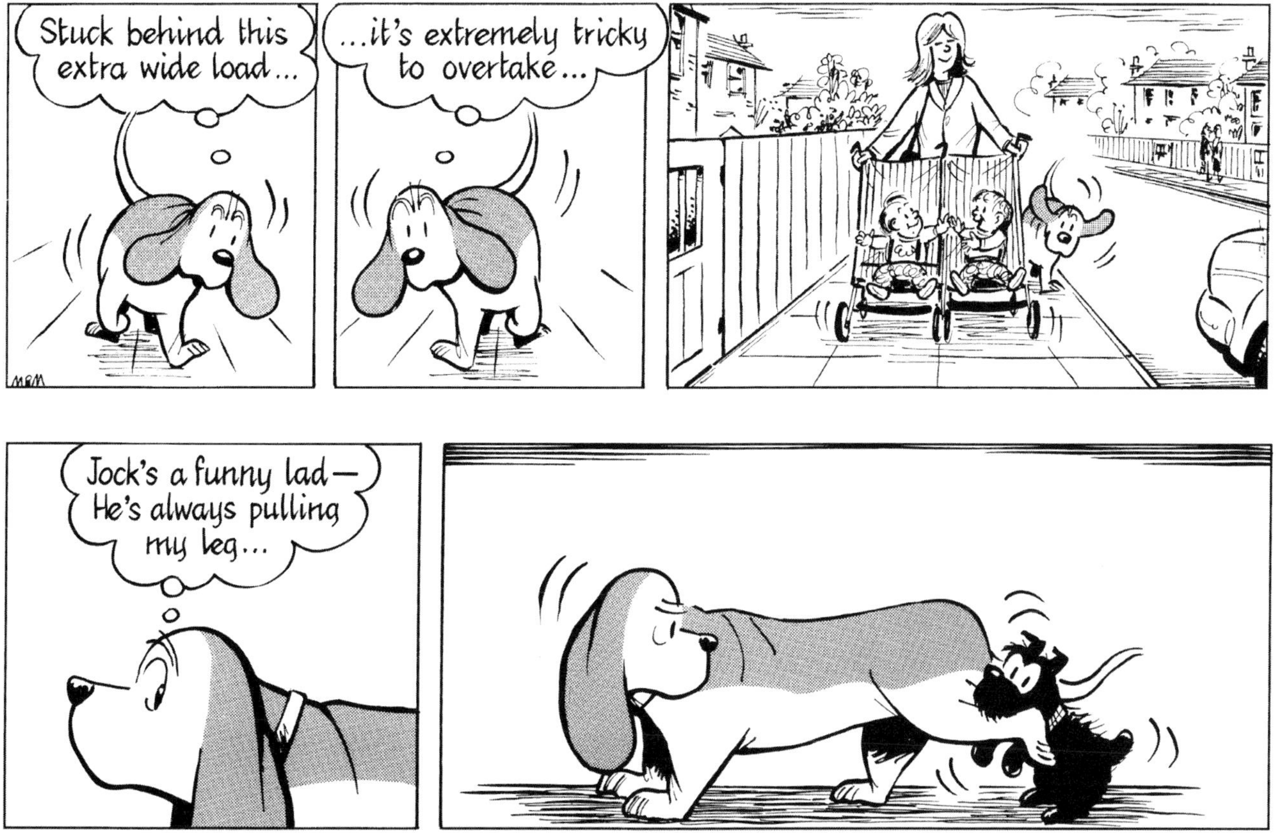
Stuck behind this extra wide load...
...it's extremely tricky to overtake...
Jock's a funny lad— He's always pulling my leg...

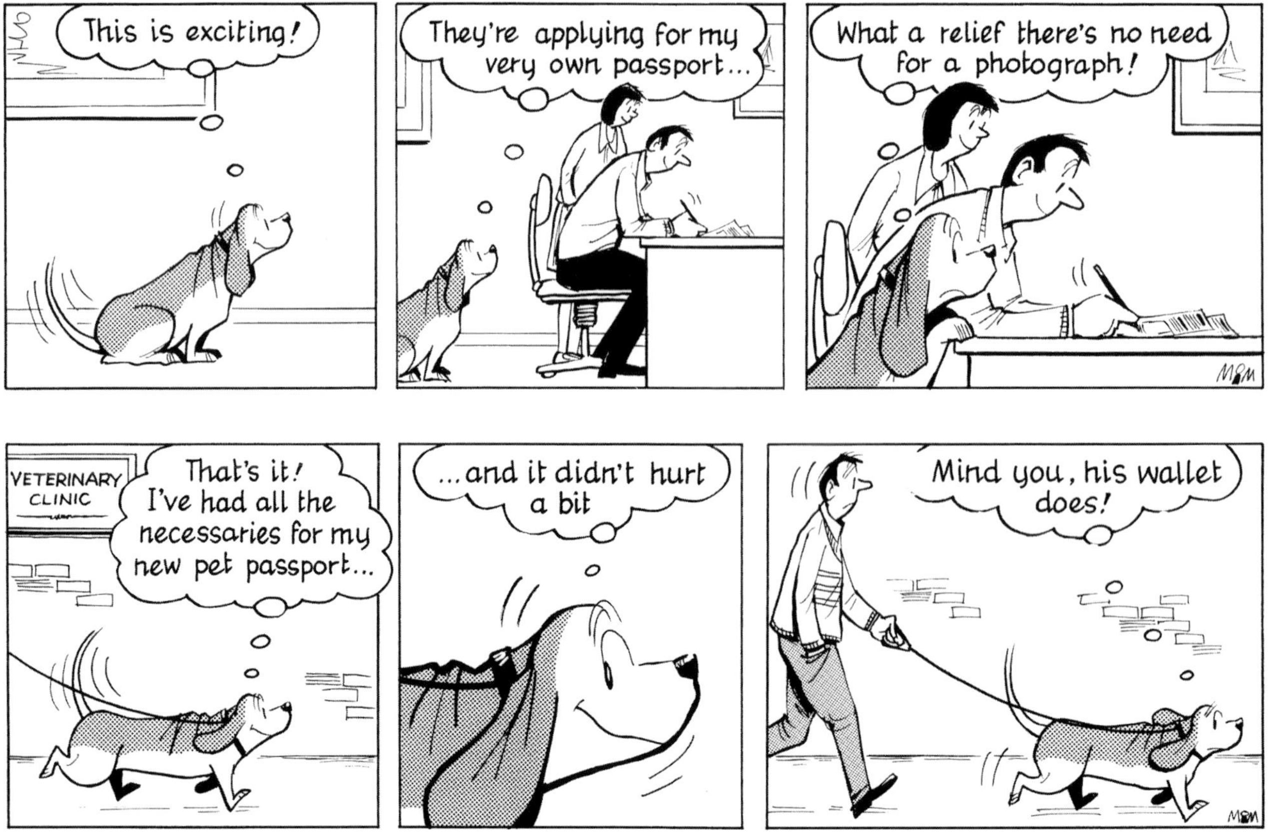
This is exciting!
They're applying for my very own passport...
What a relief there's no need for a photograph!
MGM
VETERINARY CLINIC
That's it! I've had all the necessaries for my new pet passport...
...and it didn't hurt a bit
Mind you, his wallet does!
MGM

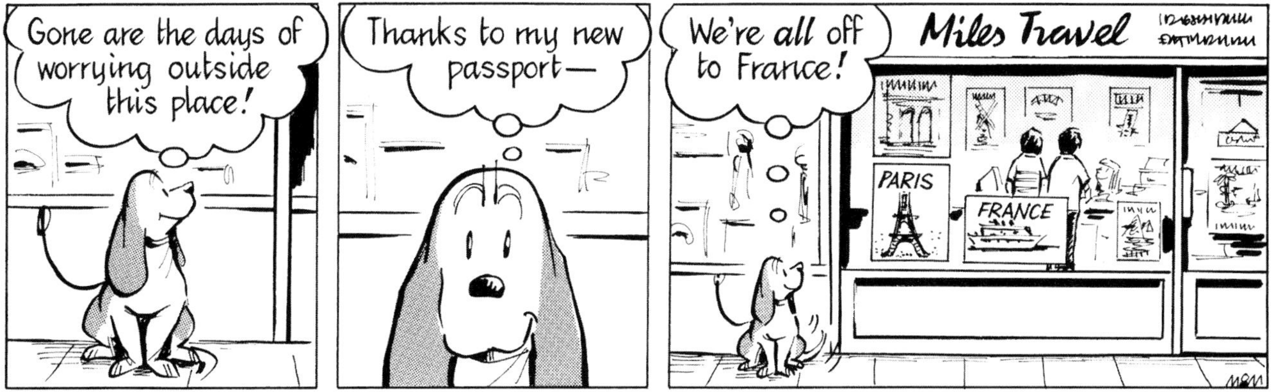
Gone are the days of worrying outside this place!
Thanks to my new passport—
We're *all* off to France!
Miles Travel
PARIS
FRANCE

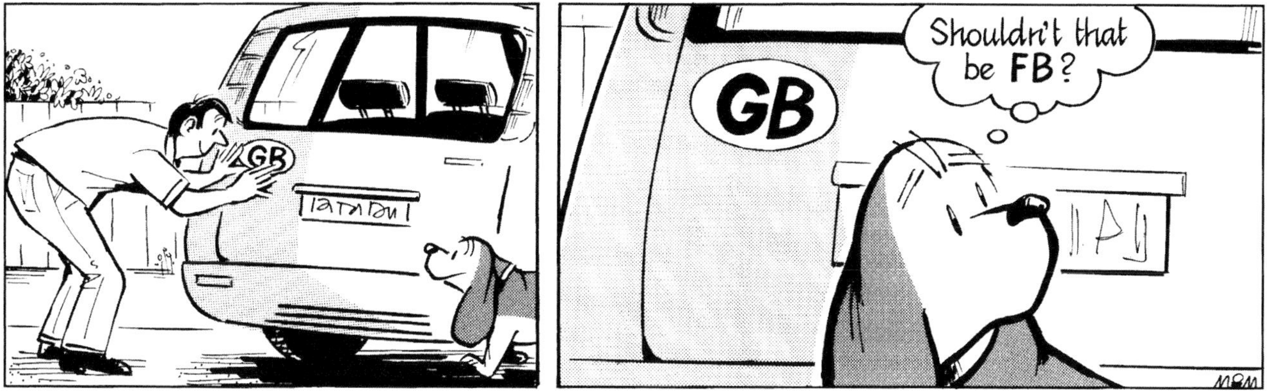
GB
GB
Shouldn't that be **FB**?

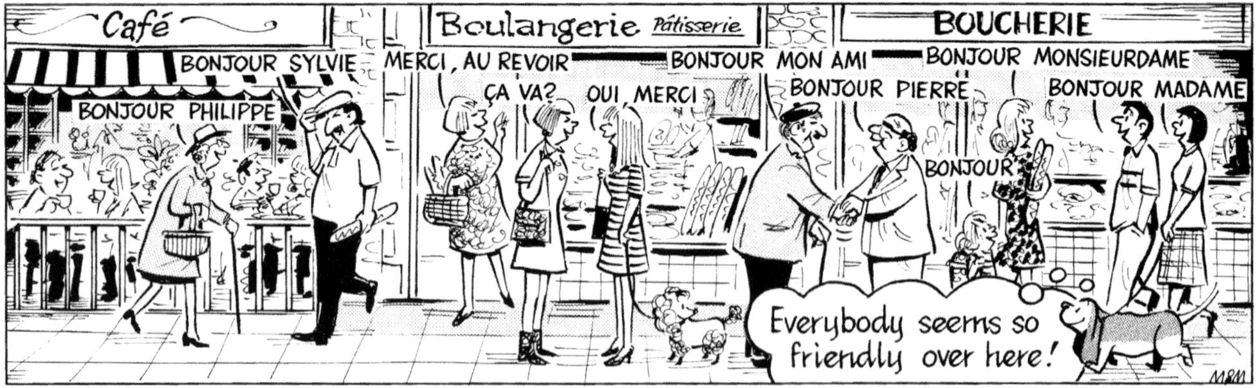
Café
Boulangerie
Pâtisserie
BOUCHERIE
BONJOUR SYLVIE
MERCI, AU REVOIR
BONJOUR MON AMI
BONJOUR MONSIEURDAME
BONJOUR PHILIPPE
ÇA VA?
OUI, MERCI
BONJOUR PIERRE
BONJOUR MADAME
BONJOUR
Everybody seems so friendly over here!
M&M

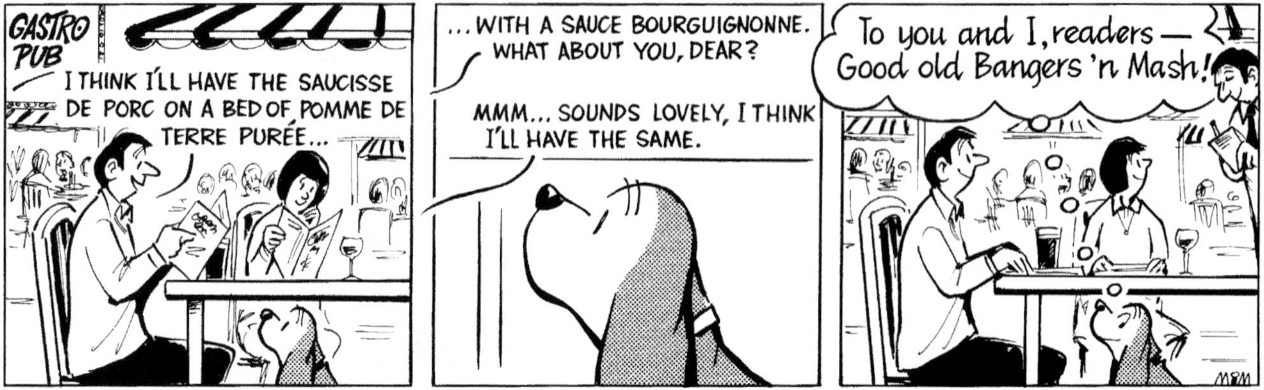
GASTRO PUB
I THINK I'LL HAVE THE SAUCISSE DE PORC ON A BED OF POMME DE TERRE PURÉE...
...WITH A SAUCE BOURGUIGNONNE. WHAT ABOUT YOU, DEAR?
MMM... SOUNDS LOVELY, I THINK I'LL HAVE THE SAME.
To you and I, readers — Good old Bangers 'n Mash!
M&M

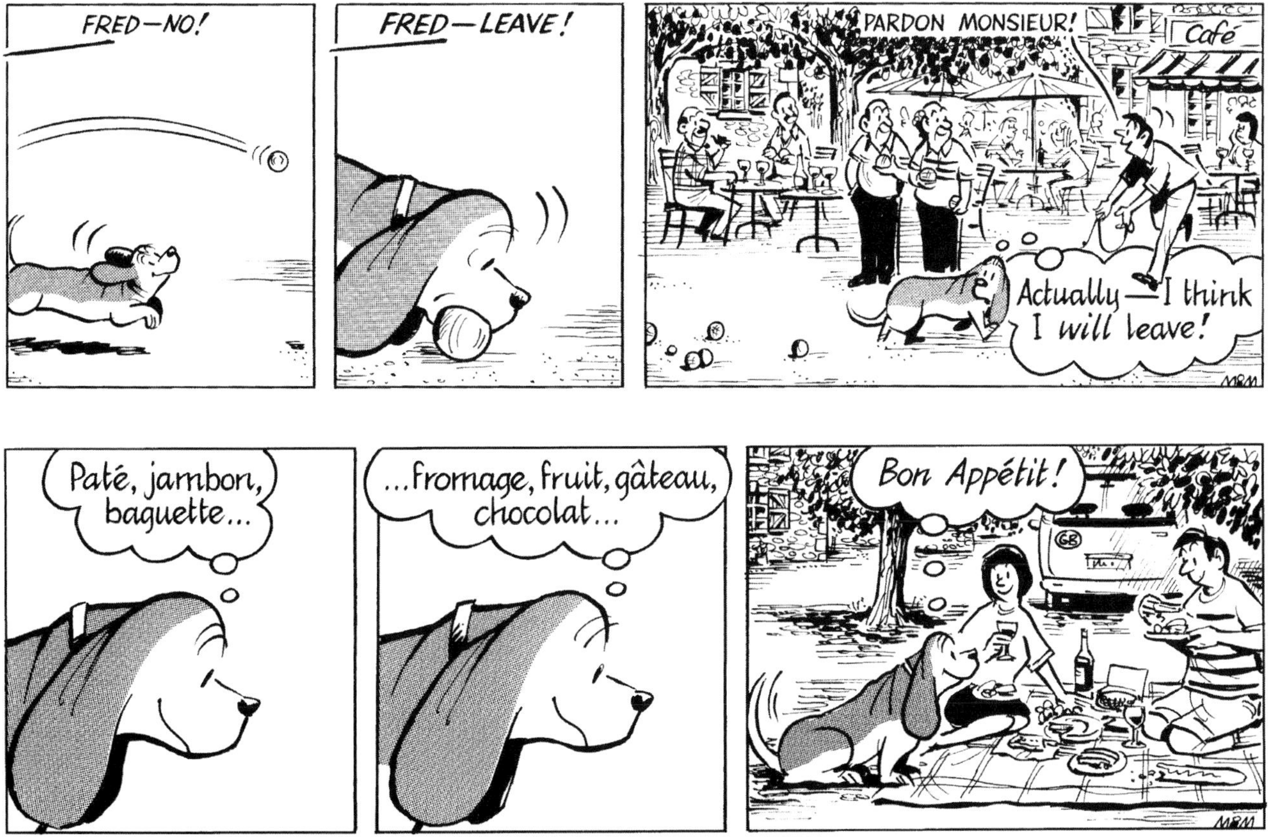
FRED—NO!
FRED—LEAVE!
PARDON MONSIEUR!
Café
Actually—I think I will leave!
Paté, jambon, baguette...
...fromage, fruit, gâteau, chocolat...
GB
Bon Appétit!

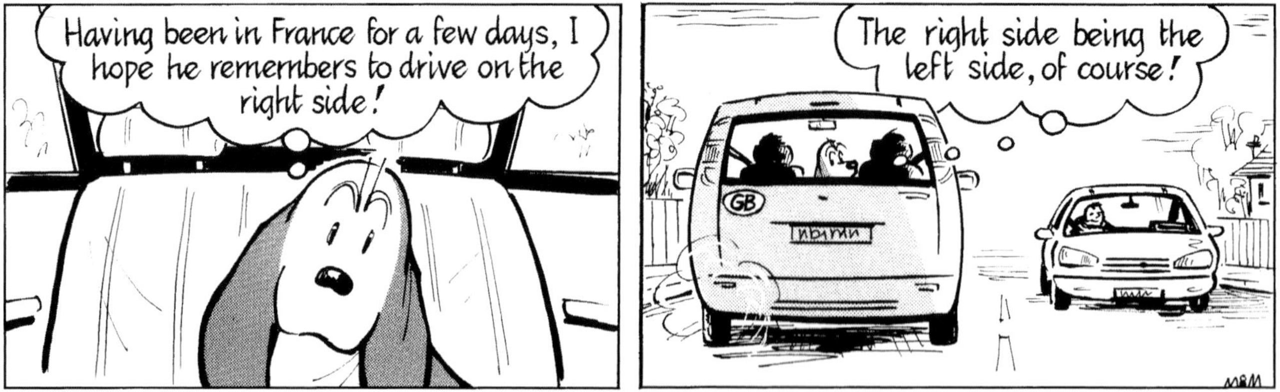
Having been in France for a few days, I hope he remembers to drive on the right side!
The right side being the left side, of course!
GB

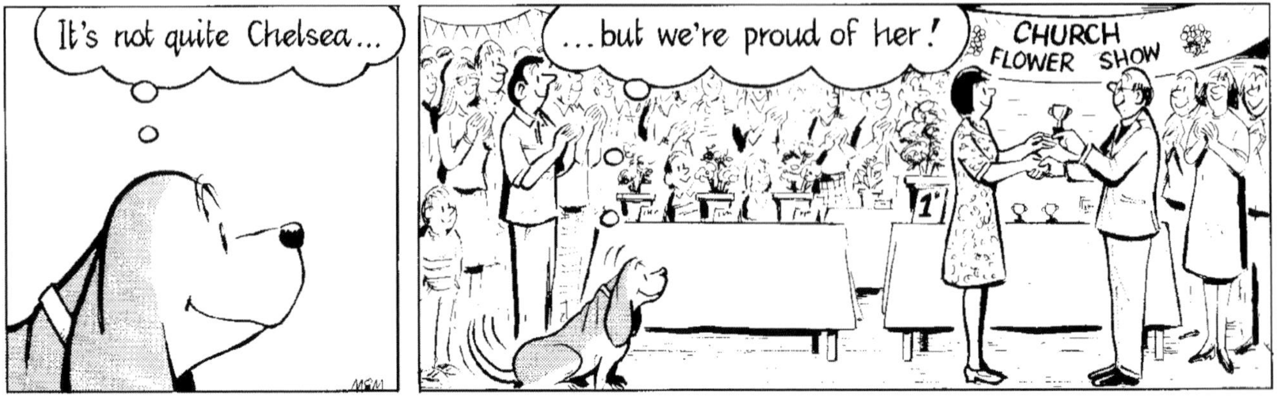
It's not quite Chelsea...
...but we're proud of her!
CHURCH FLOWER SHOW

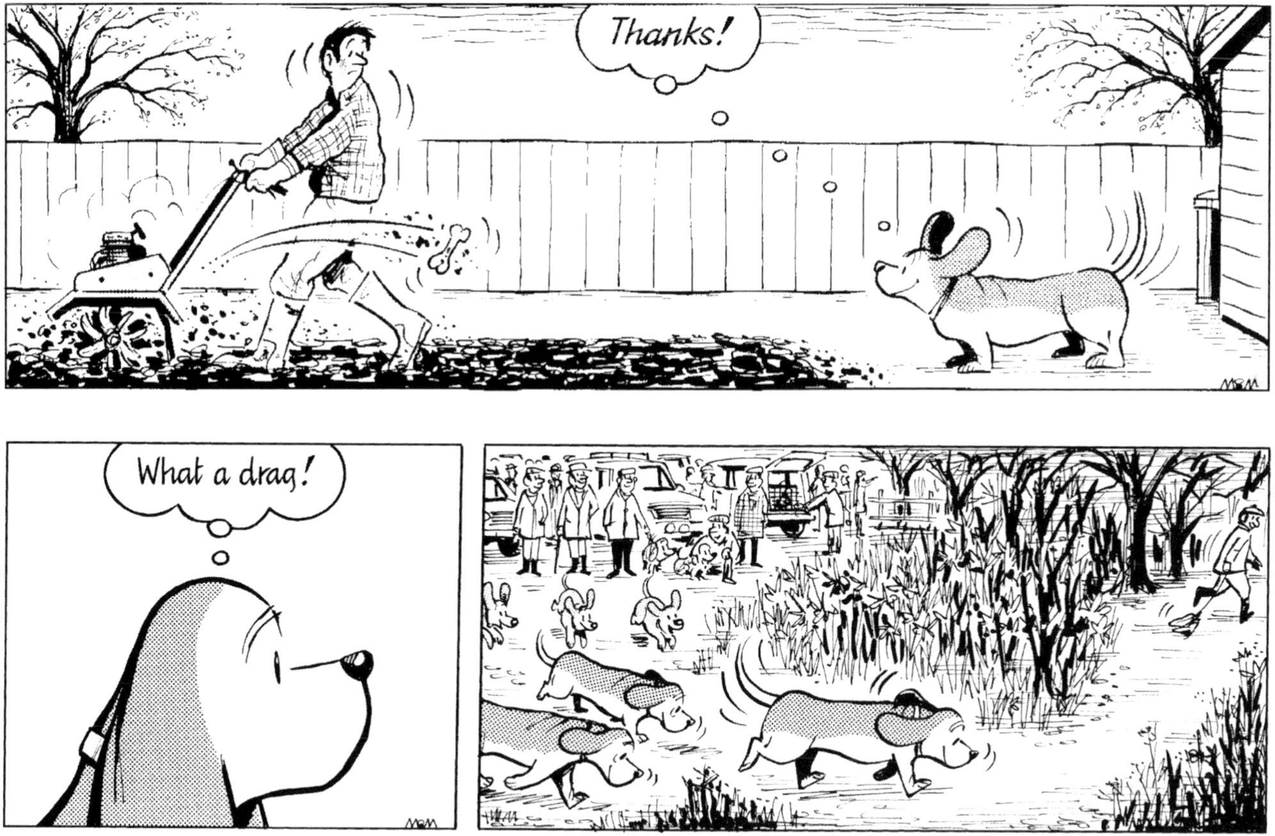
Thanks!
What a drag!

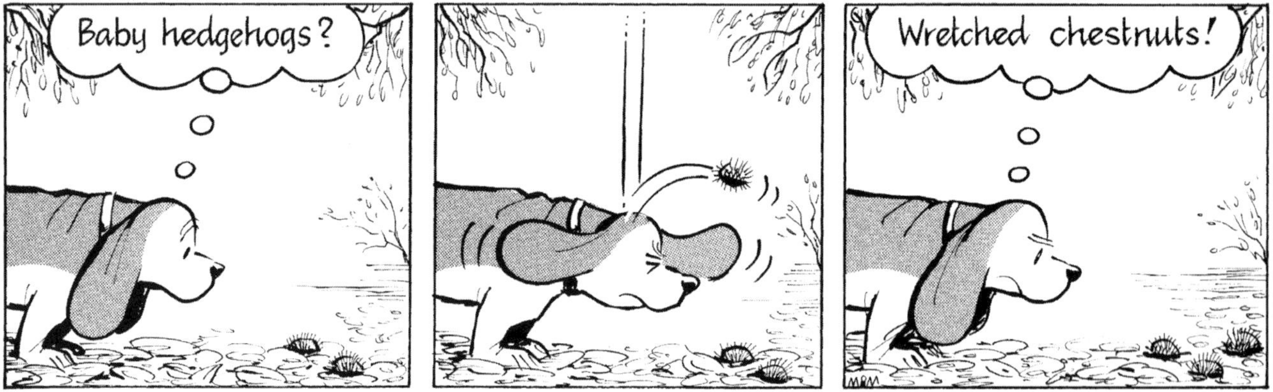
Baby hedgehogs?
Wretched chestnuts!

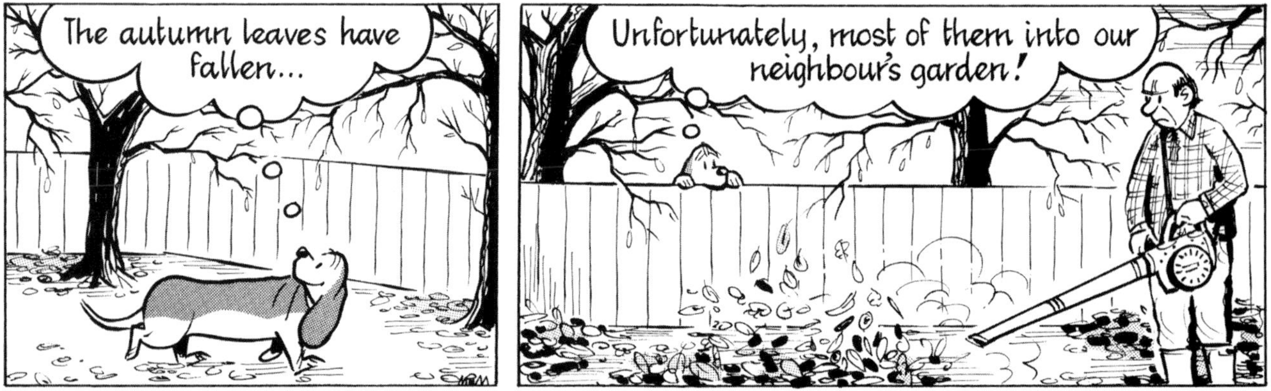
The autumn leaves have fallen...
Unfortunately, most of them into our neighbour's garden!

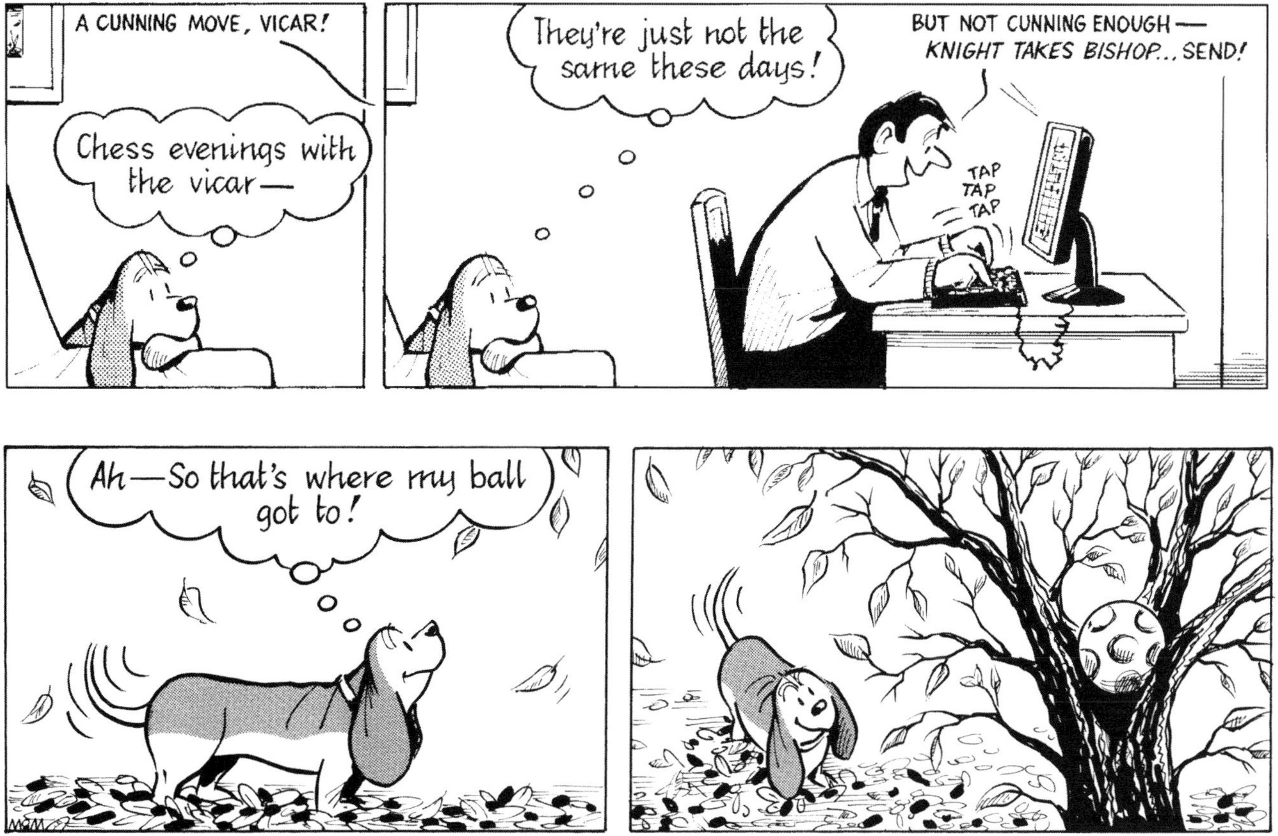
A CUNNING MOVE, VICAR!
Chess evenings with the vicar—
They're just not the same these days!
BUT NOT CUNNING ENOUGH— KNIGHT TAKES BISHOP... SEND!
TAP TAP TAP
Ah—So that's where my ball got to!

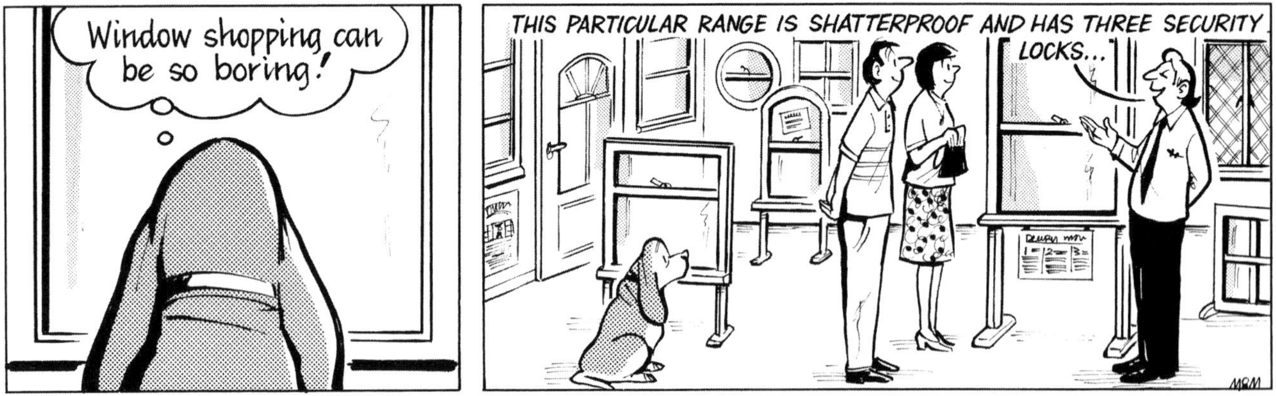
Window shopping can be so boring!
THIS PARTICULAR RANGE IS SHATTERPROOF AND HAS THREE SECURITY LOCKS...

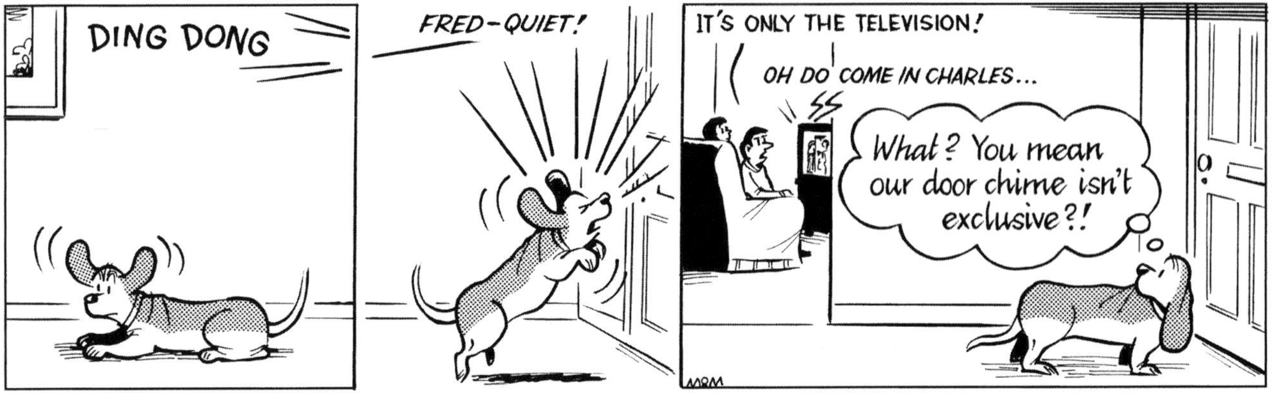
DING DONG
FRED – QUIET!
IT'S ONLY THE TELEVISION!
OH DO COME IN CHARLES...
What? You mean our door chime isn't exclusive?!

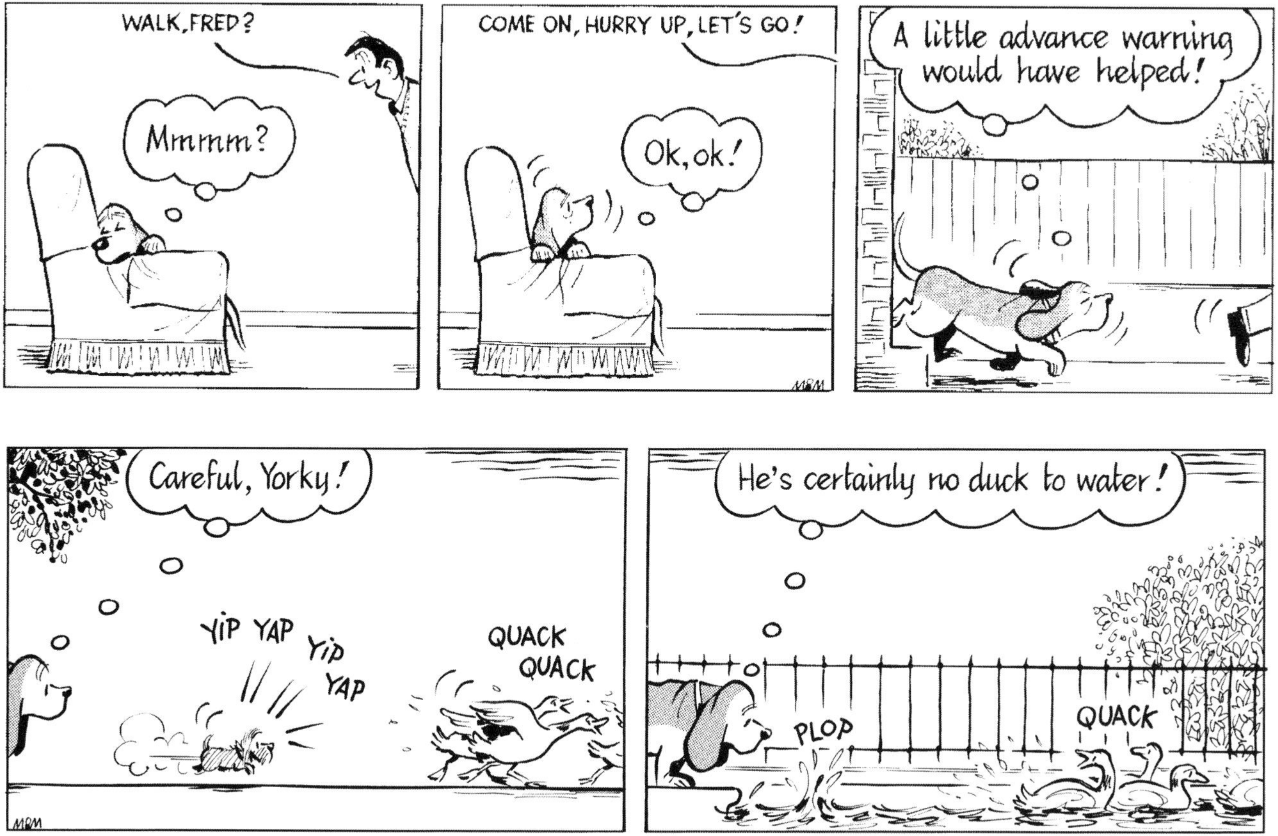
WALK, FRED?
Mmmmm?
COME ON, HURRY UP, LET'S GO!
Ok, ok!
A little advance warning would have helped!
Careful, Yorky!
YIP YAP
YIP YAP
QUACK QUACK
He's certainly no duck to water!
PLOP
QUACK

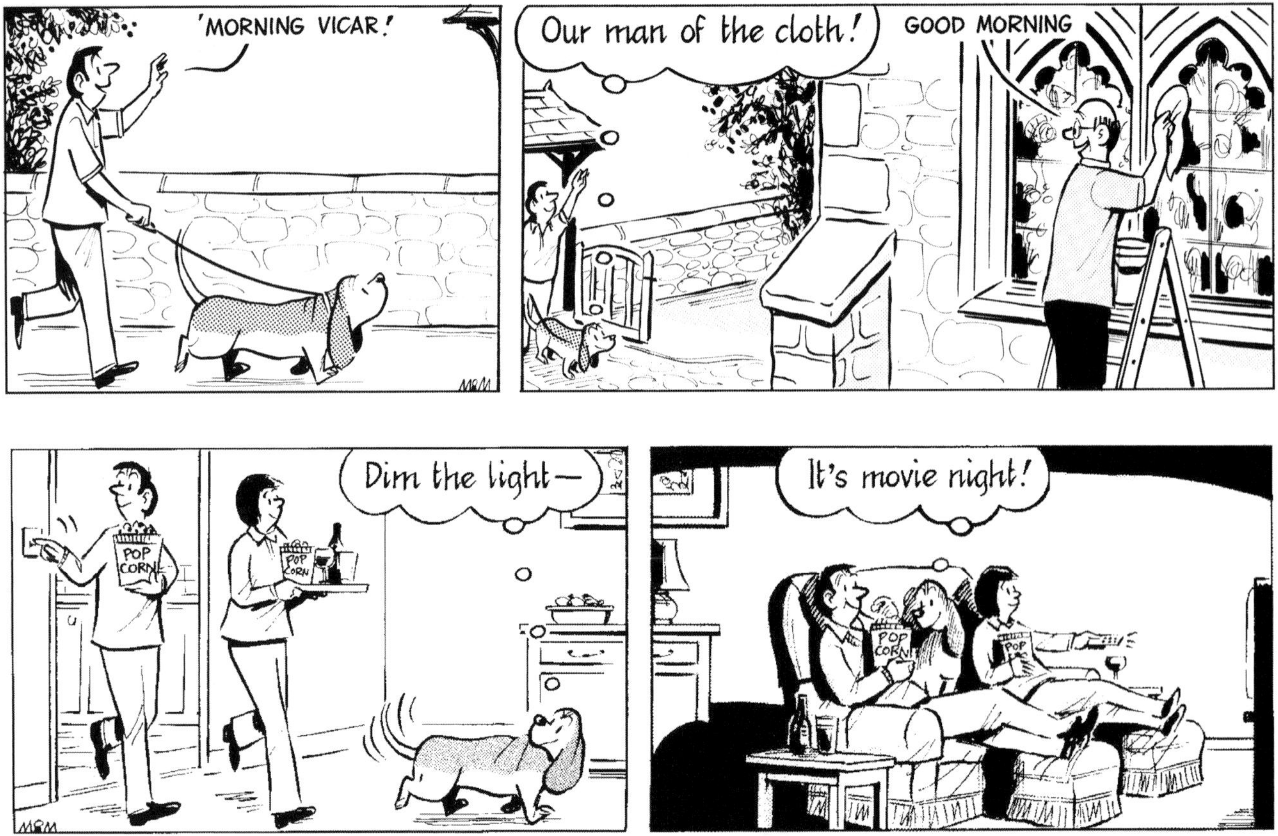
'MORNING VICAR!
Our man of the cloth!
GOOD MORNING
Dim the light—
It's movie night!

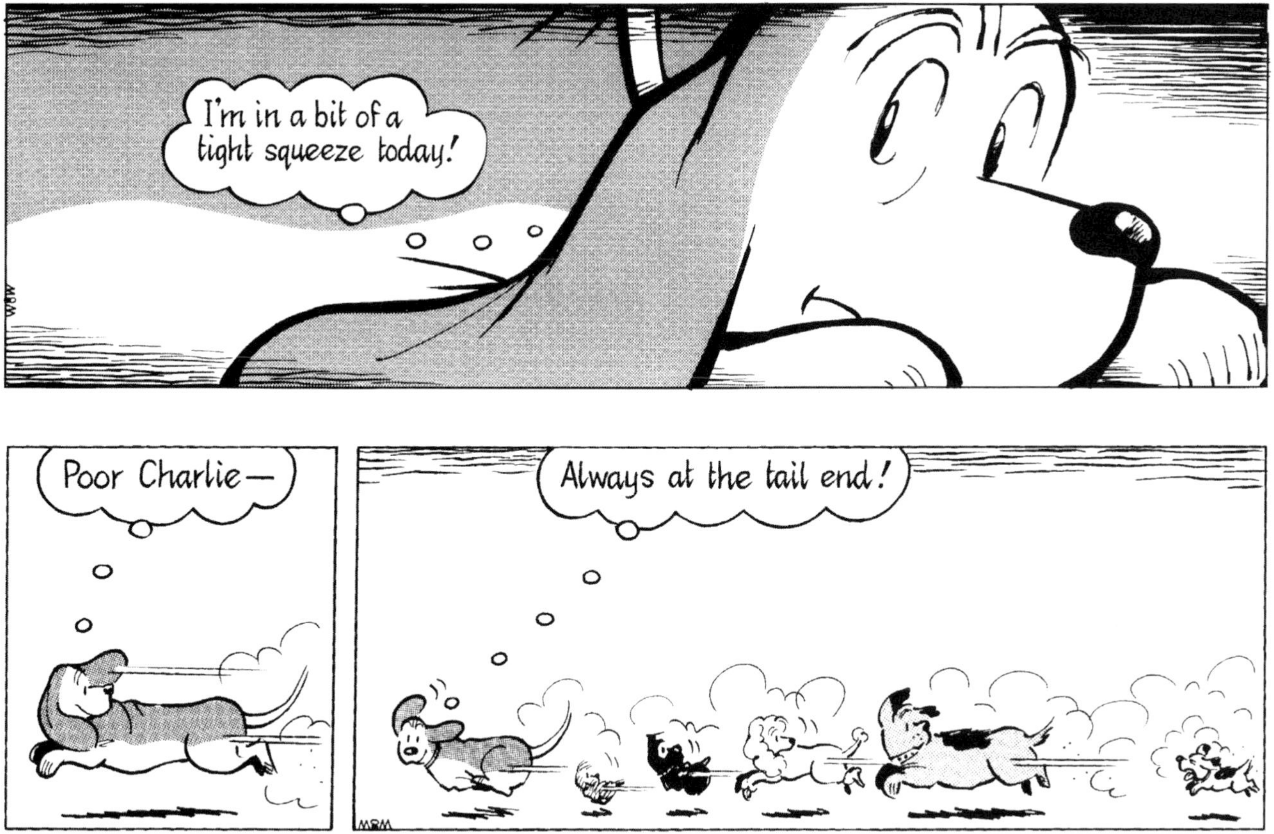
I'm in a bit of a tight squeeze today!
Poor Charlie—
Always at the tail end!

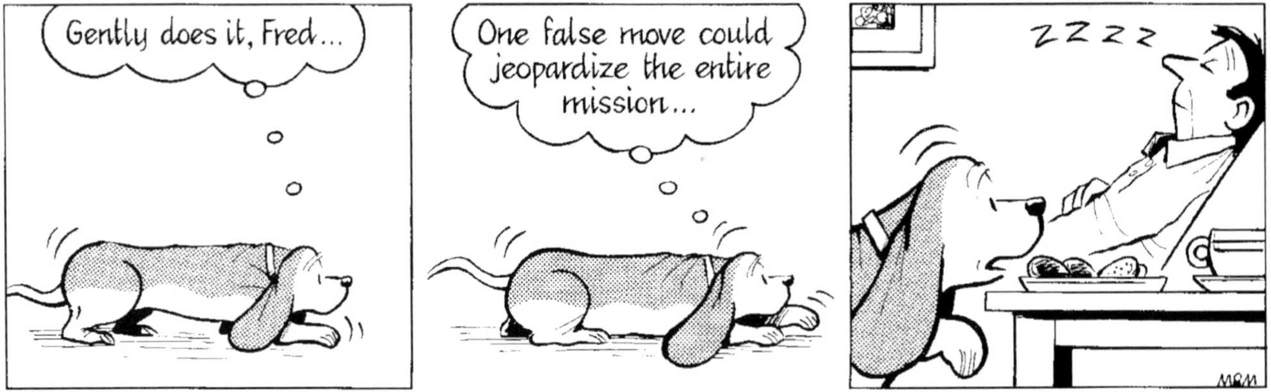

Gently does it, Fred...
One false move could jeopardize the entire mission...
Z Z Z Z

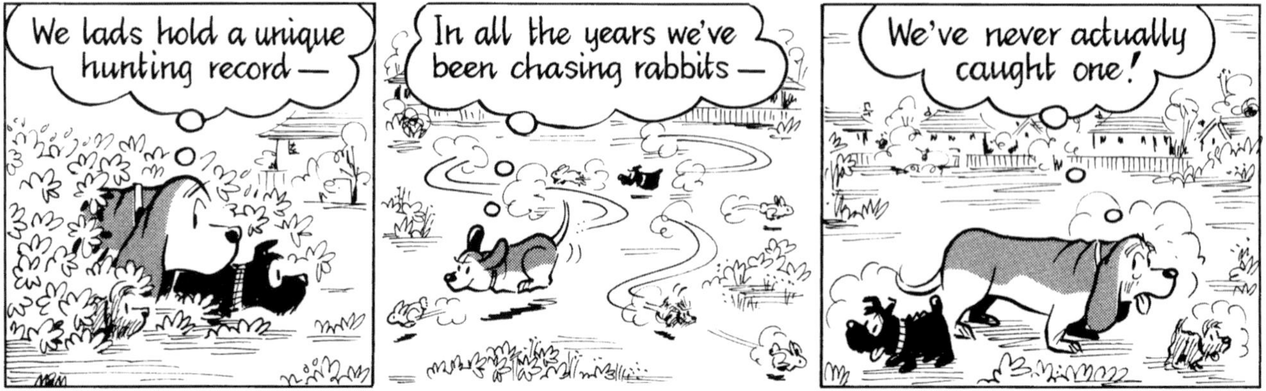

We lads hold a unique hunting record –
In all the years we've been chasing rabbits –
We've never actually caught one!

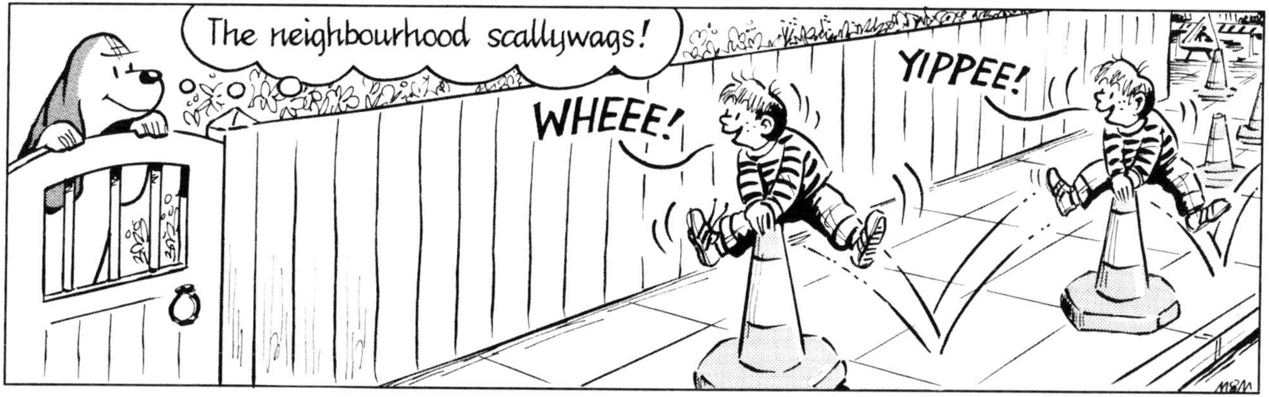
The neighbourhood scallywags!
WHEEE!
YIPPEE!
MSM

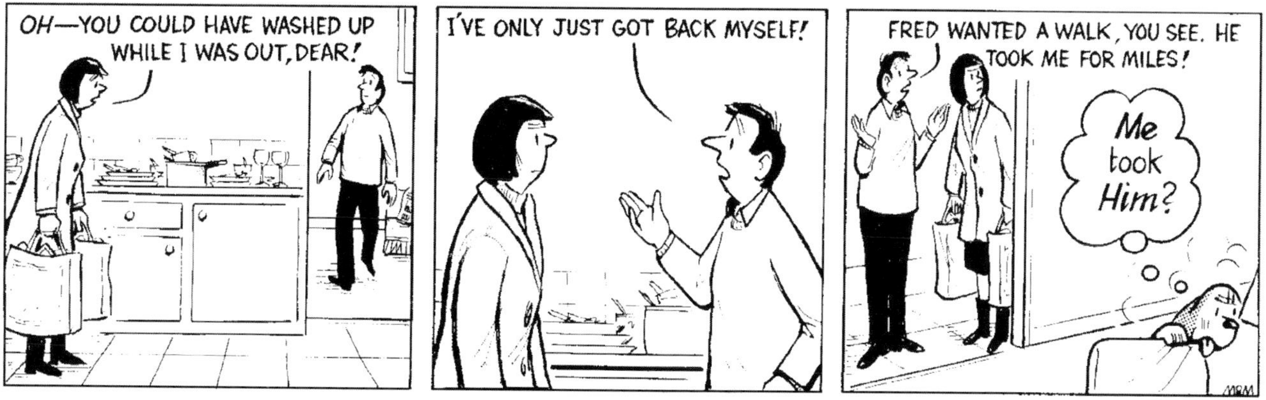
OH—YOU COULD HAVE WASHED UP WHILE I WAS OUT, DEAR!
I'VE ONLY JUST GOT BACK MYSELF!
FRED WANTED A WALK, YOU SEE. HE TOOK ME FOR MILES!
Me took Him?
MSM

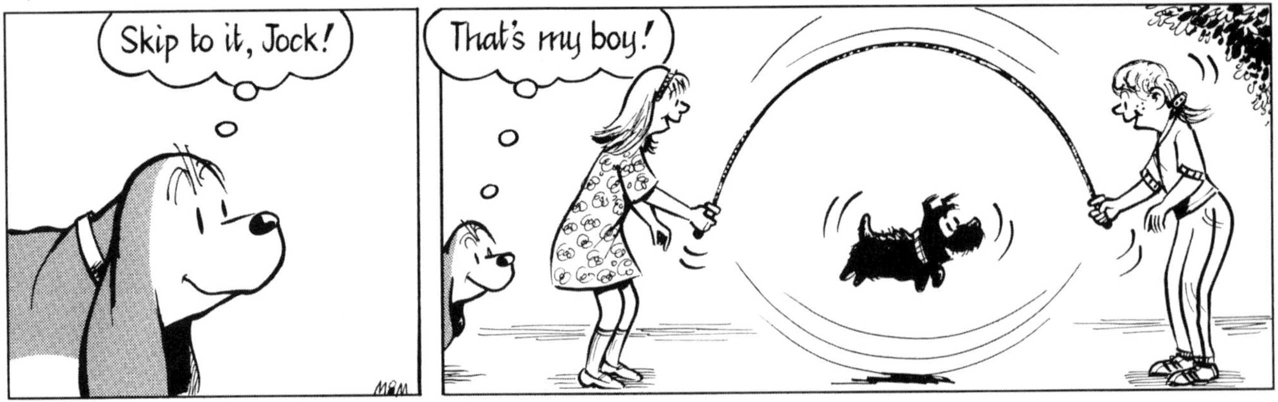
Skip to it, Jock!
That's my boy!

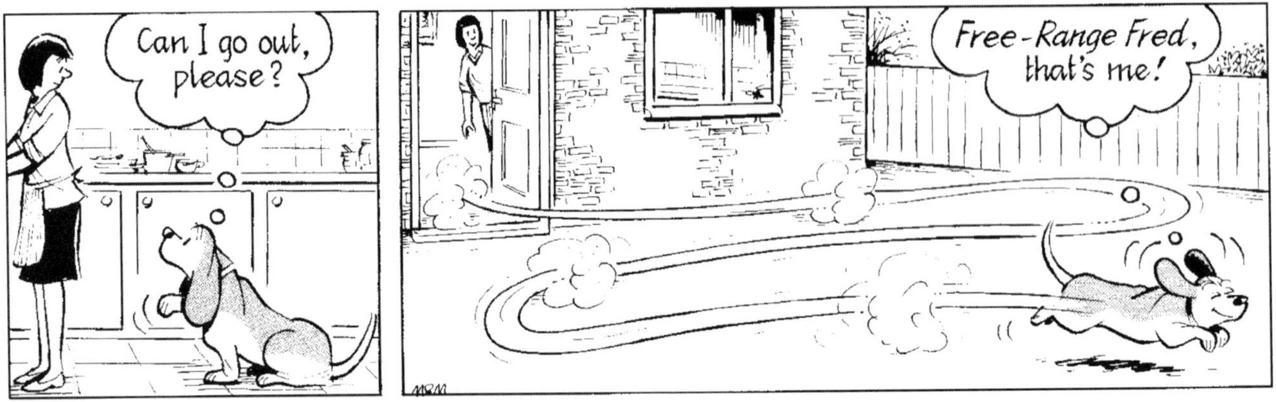
Can I go out, please?
Free-Range Fred, that's me!

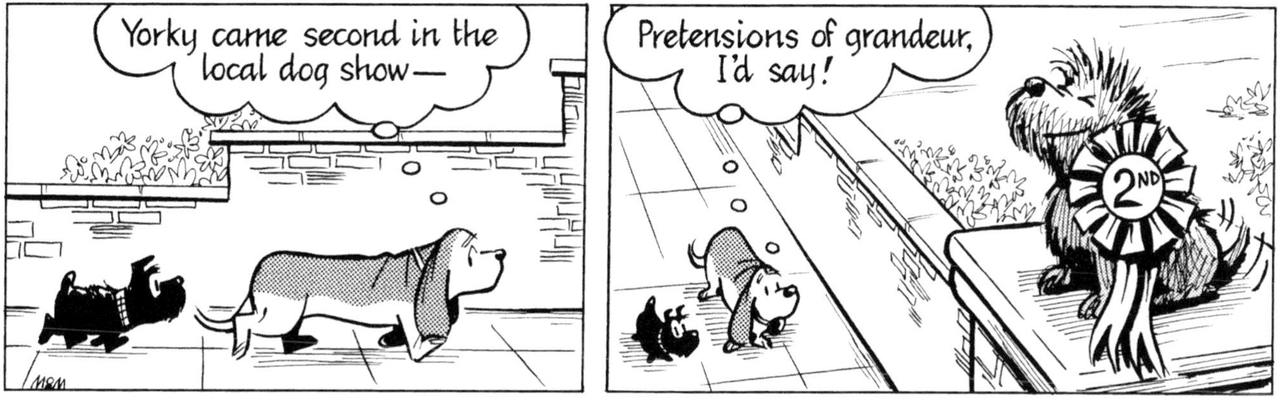
Yorky came second in the local dog show—
Pretensions of grandeur, I'd say!
2ND

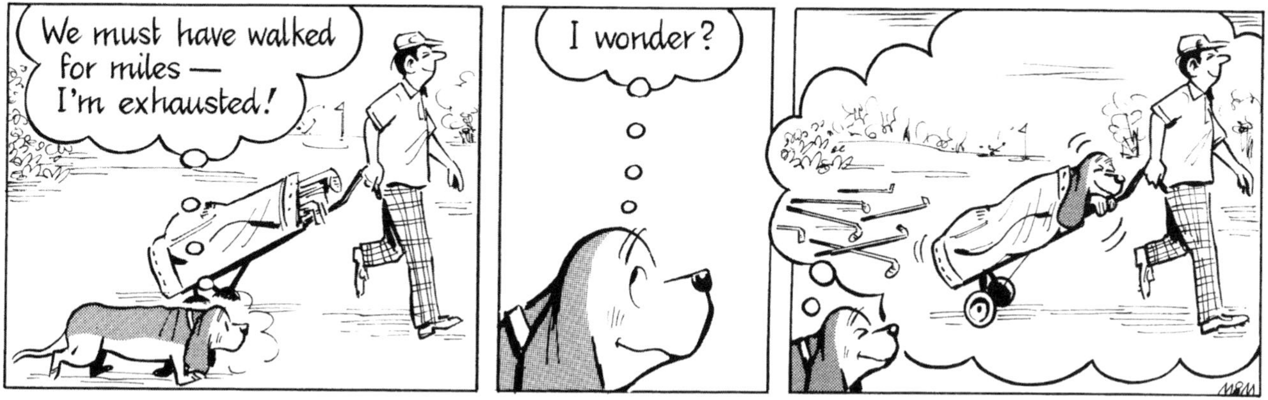
We must have walked for miles — I'm exhausted!
I wonder?

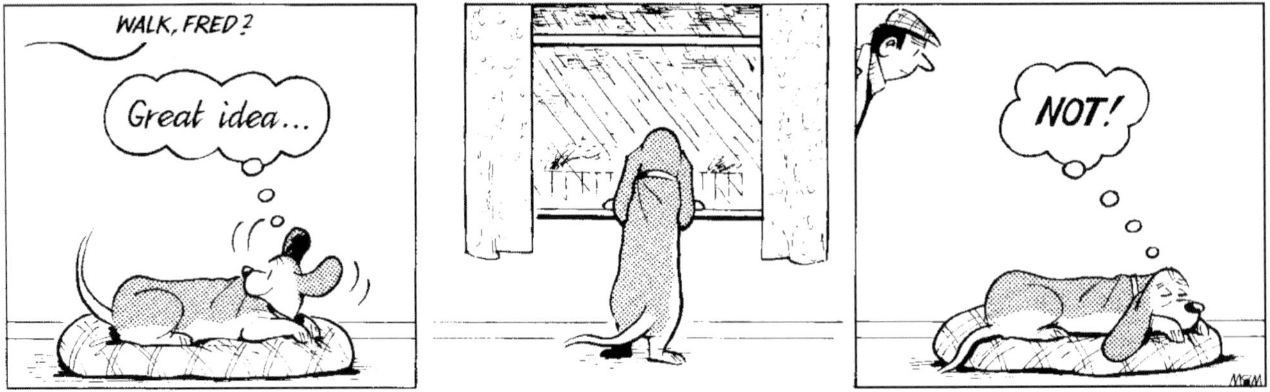
WALK, FRED?
Great idea...
NOT!

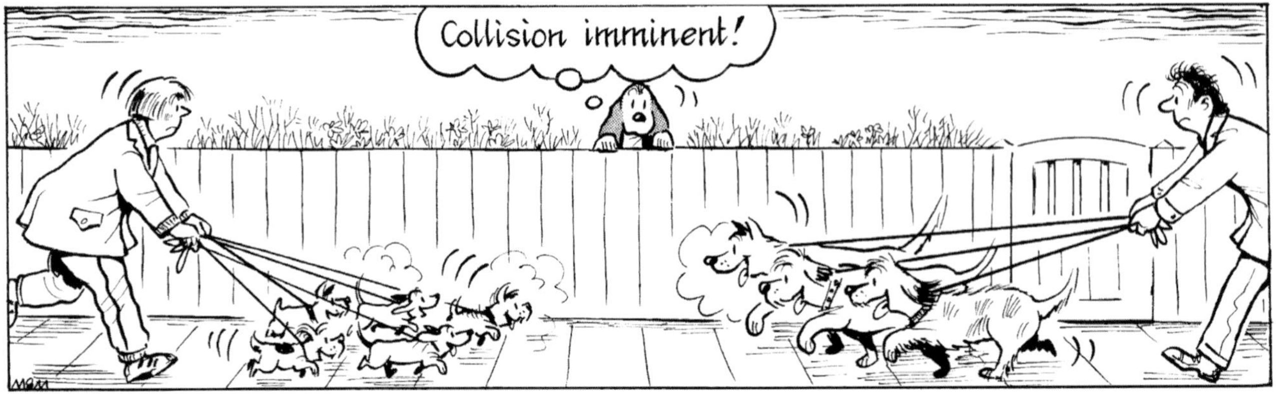
Collision imminent!

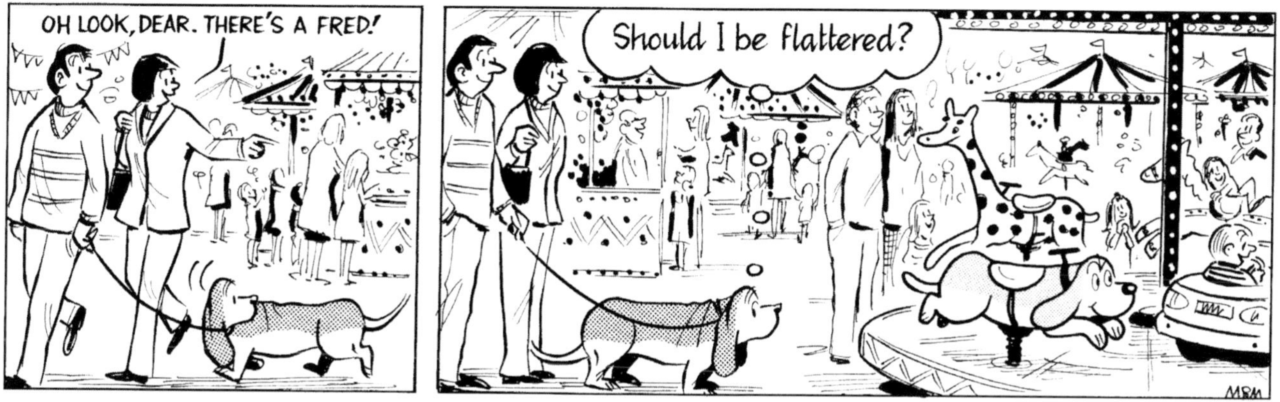
OH LOOK, DEAR. THERE'S A FRED!
Should I be flattered?

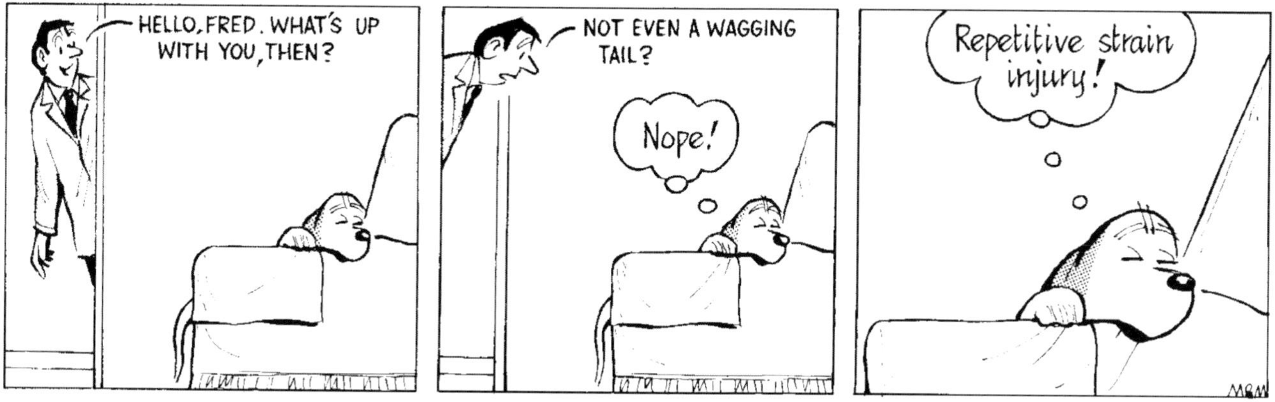
HELLO, FRED. WHAT'S UP WITH YOU, THEN?
NOT EVEN A WAGGING TAIL?
Nope!
Repetitive strain injury!

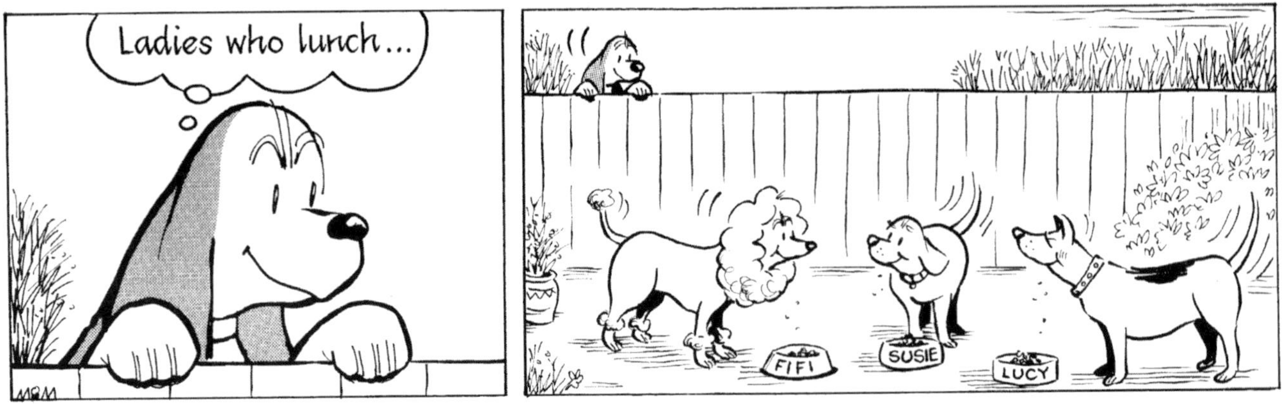
Ladies who lunch...
FIFI
SUSIE
LUCY

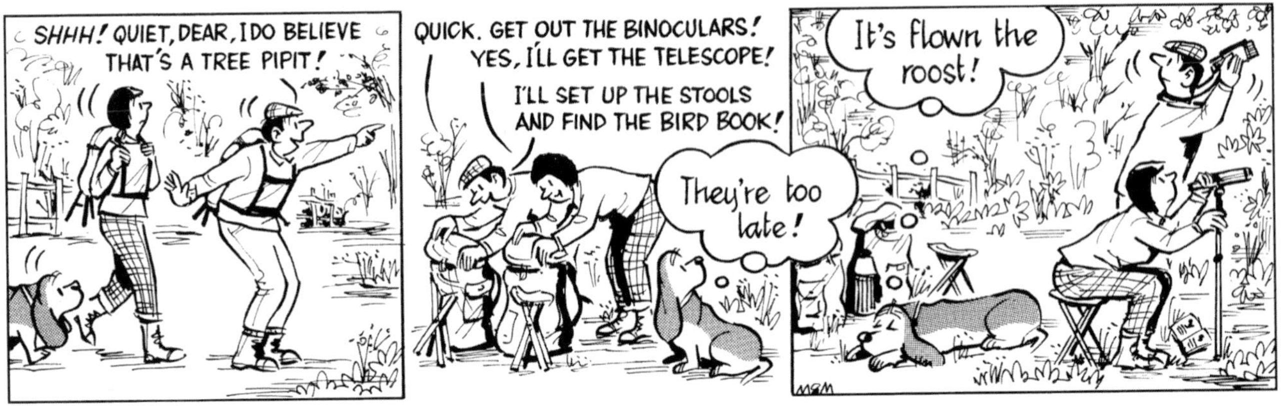
SHHH! QUIET, DEAR, I DO BELIEVE THAT'S A TREE PIPIT!
QUICK. GET OUT THE BINOCULARS!
YES, I'LL GET THE TELESCOPE!
I'LL SET UP THE STOOLS AND FIND THE BIRD BOOK!
They're too late!
It's flown the roost!

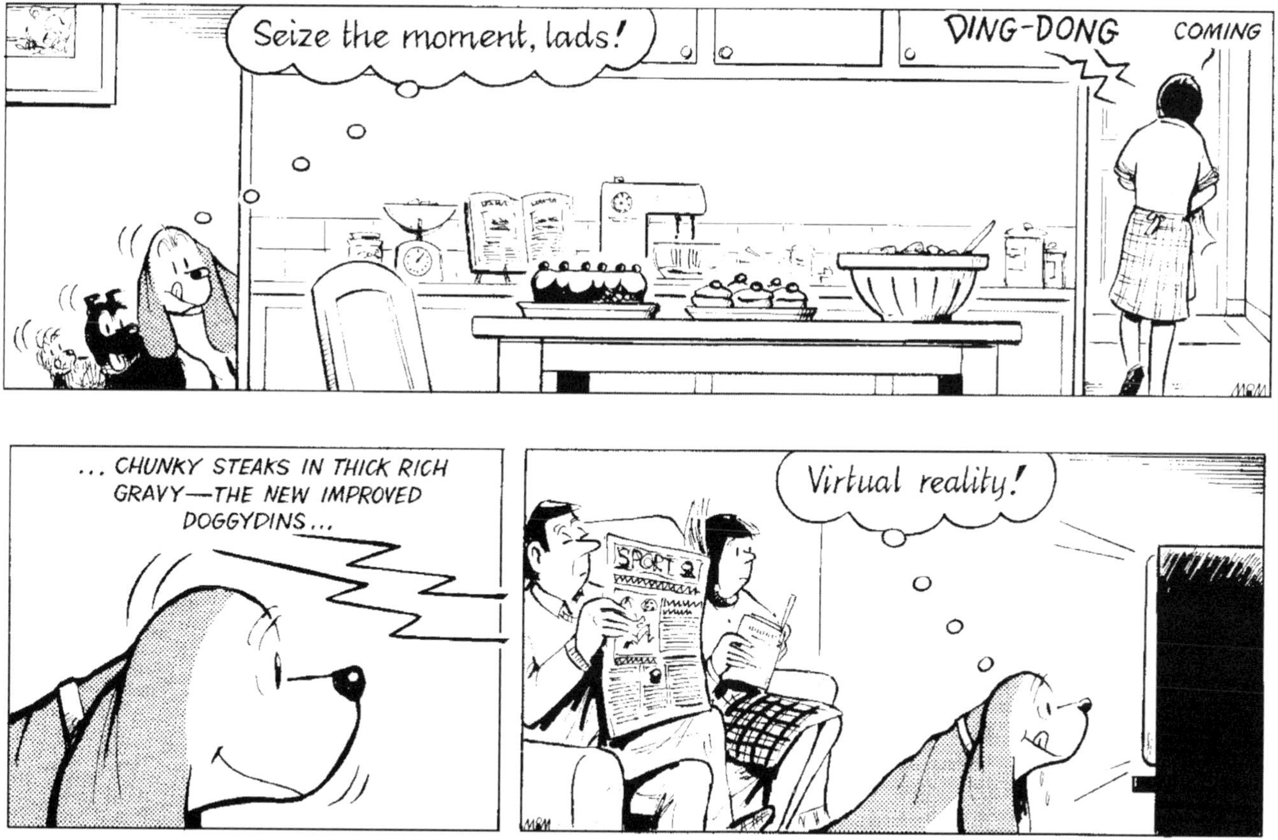
Seize the moment, lads!
DING-DONG
COMING
... CHUNKY STEAKS IN THICK RICH GRAVY—THE NEW IMPROVED DOGGYDINS...
Virtual reality!
SPORT

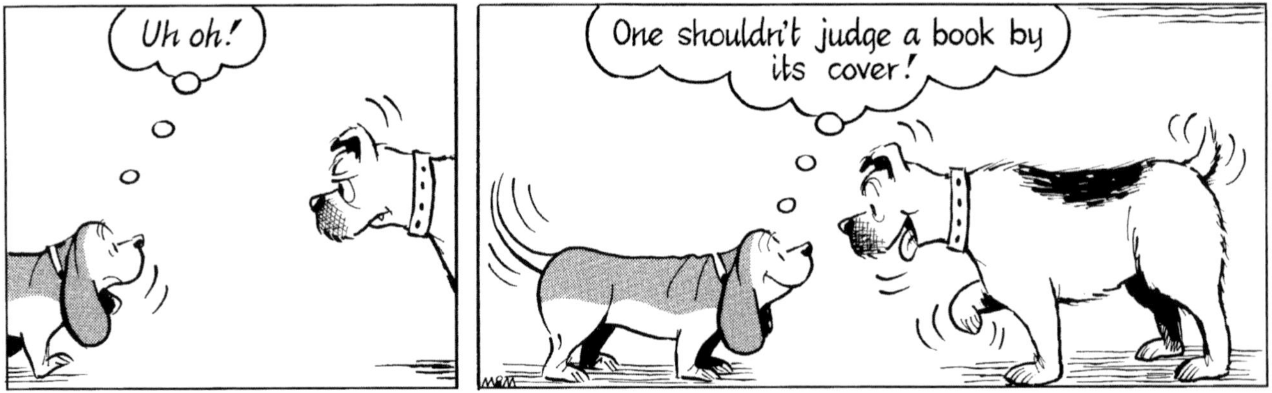
Uh oh!
One shouldn't judge a book by its cover!

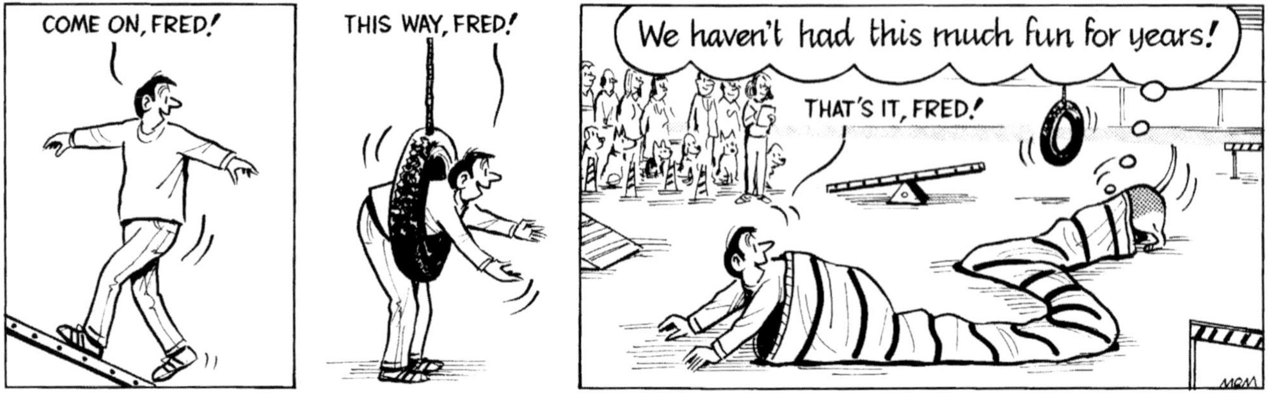
COME ON, FRED!
THIS WAY, FRED!
We haven't had this much fun for years!
THAT'S IT, FRED!

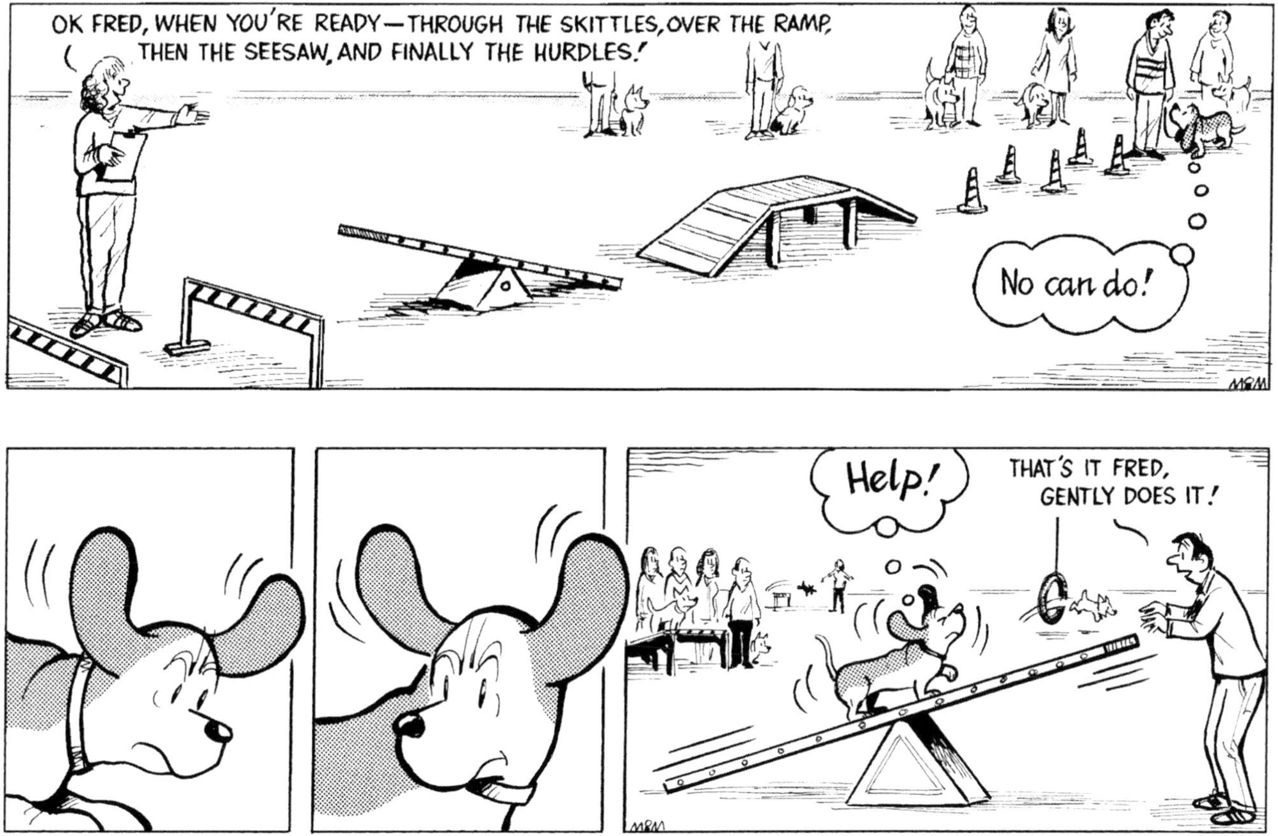
OK FRED, WHEN YOU'RE READY—THROUGH THE SKITTLES, OVER THE RAMP, THEN THE SEESAW, AND FINALLY THE HURDLES!
No can do!
MSM
Help!
THAT'S IT FRED, GENTLY DOES IT!
MSM

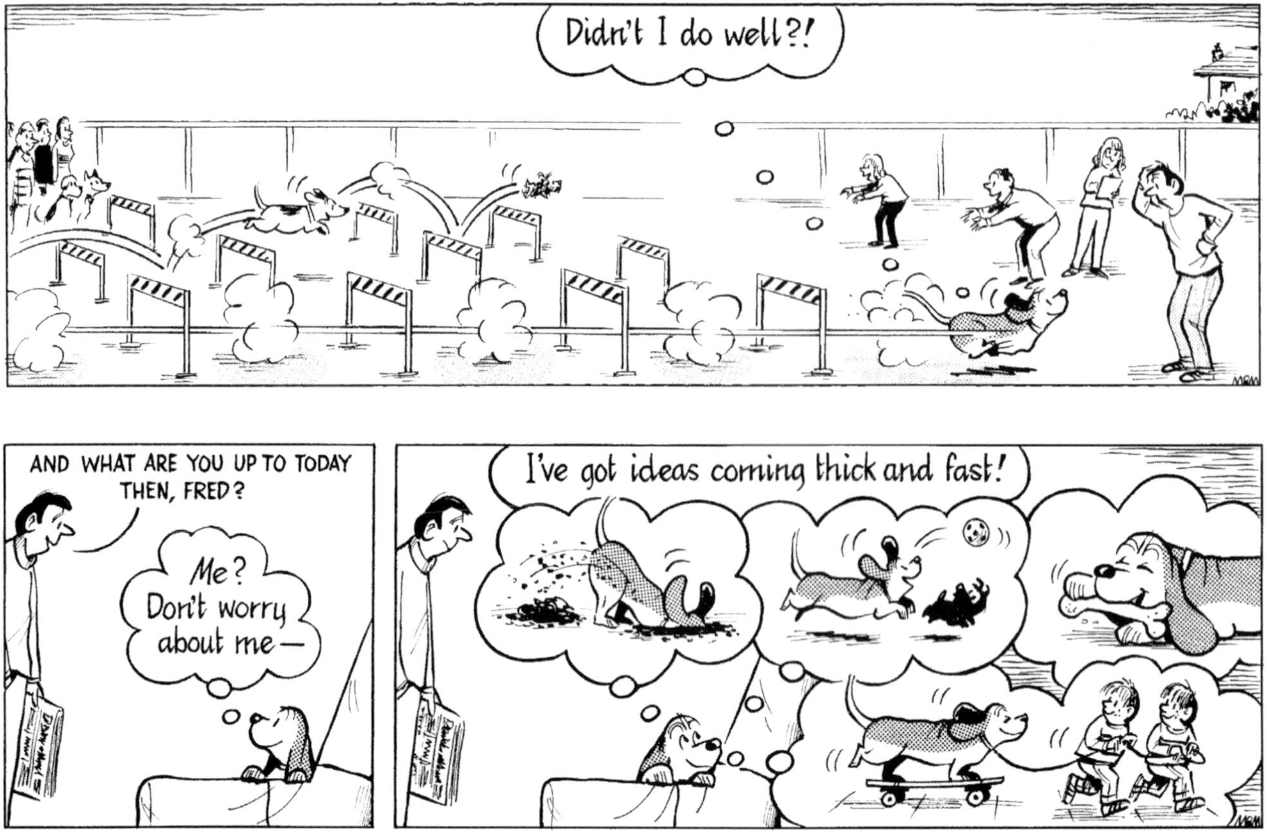

Didn't I do well?!
AND WHAT ARE YOU UP TO TODAY THEN, FRED?
Me? Don't worry about me—
I've got ideas coming thick and fast!

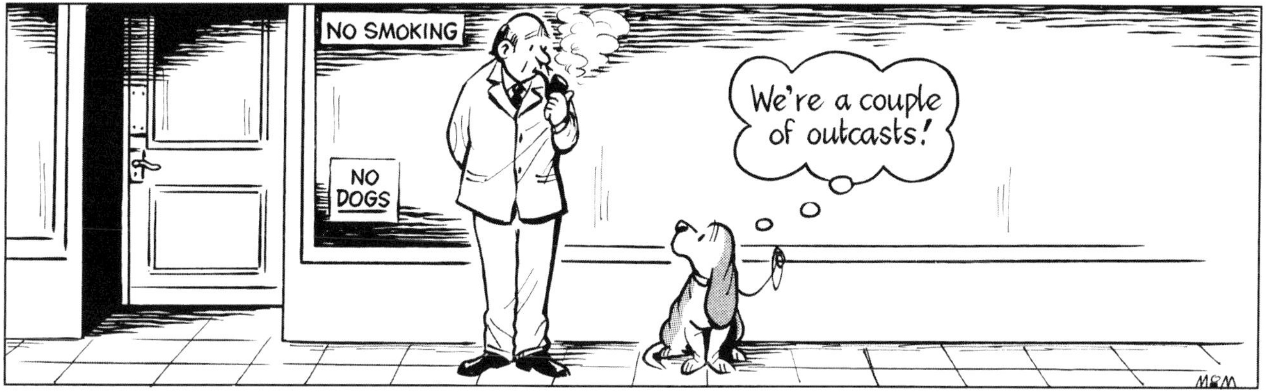
NO SMOKING
NO DOGS
We're a couple of outcasts!

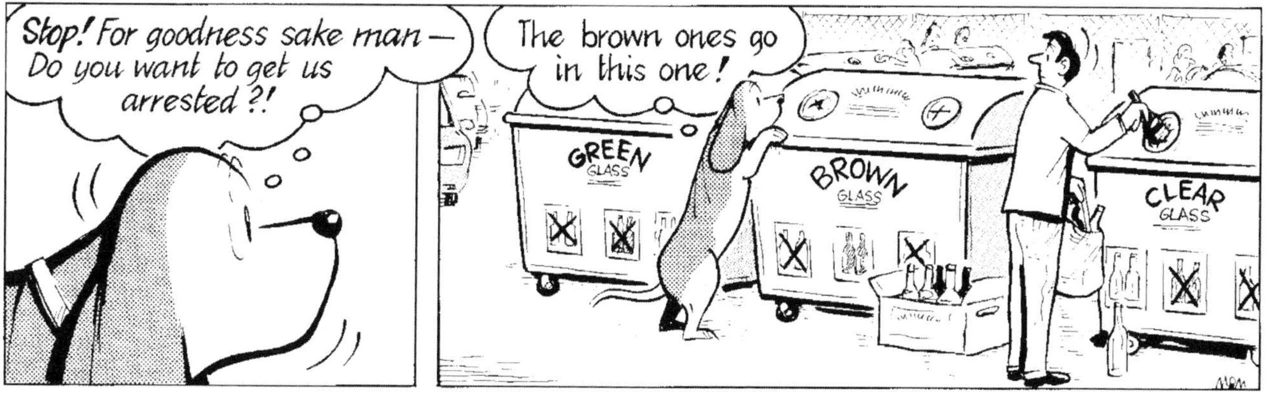
Stop! For goodness sake man — Do you want to get us arrested ?!
The brown ones go in this one!
GREEN GLASS
BROWN GLASS
CLEAR GLASS

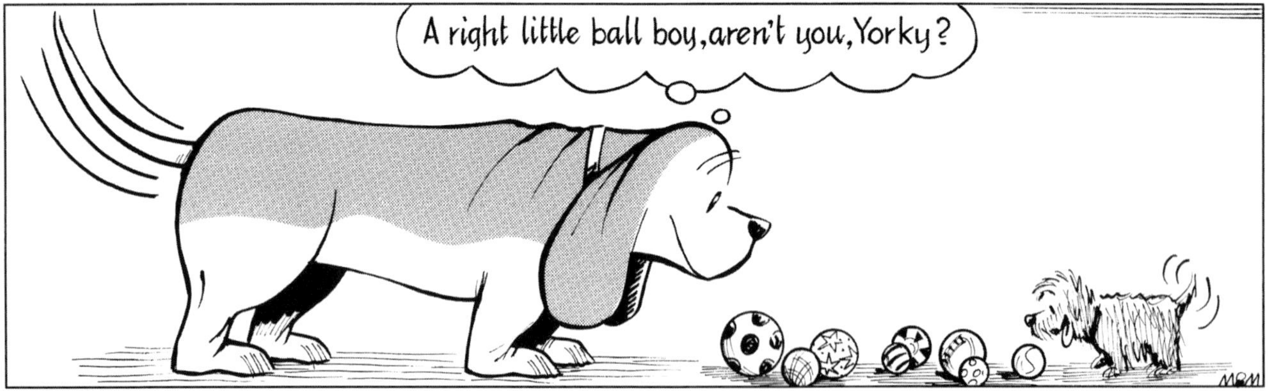
A right little ball boy, aren't you, Yorky?

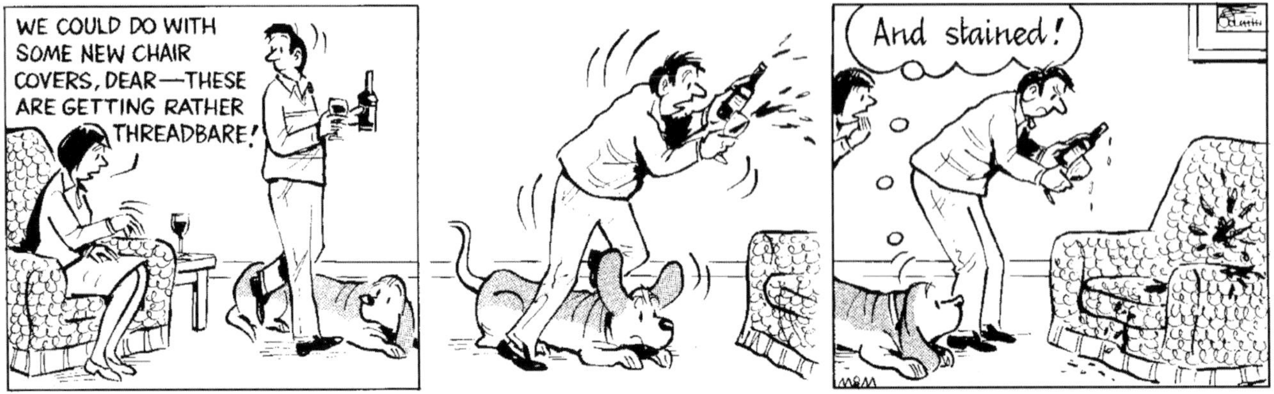
WE COULD DO WITH SOME NEW CHAIR COVERS, DEAR—THESE ARE GETTING RATHER THREADBARE!
And stained!

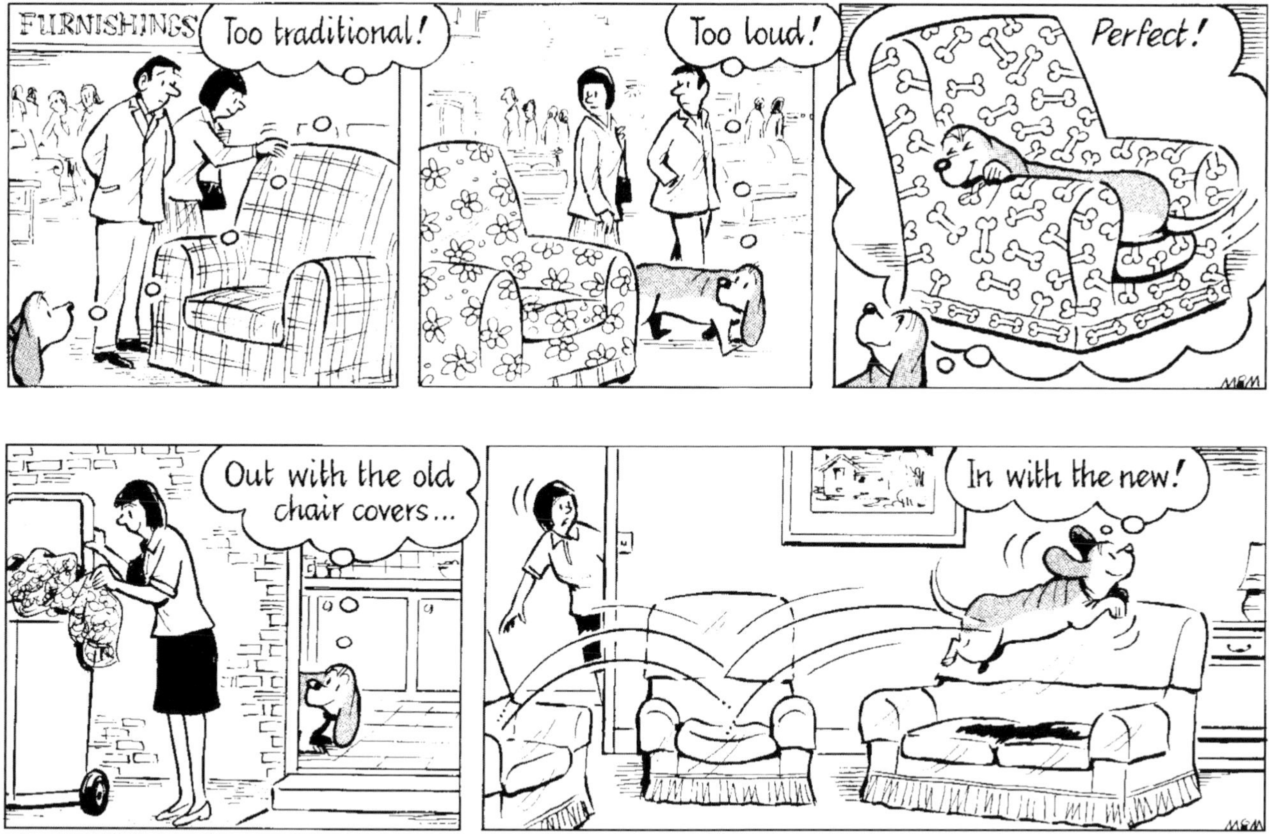
FURNISHINGS
Too traditional!
Too loud!
Perfect!
MGM
Out with the old chair covers...
In with the new!
MGM

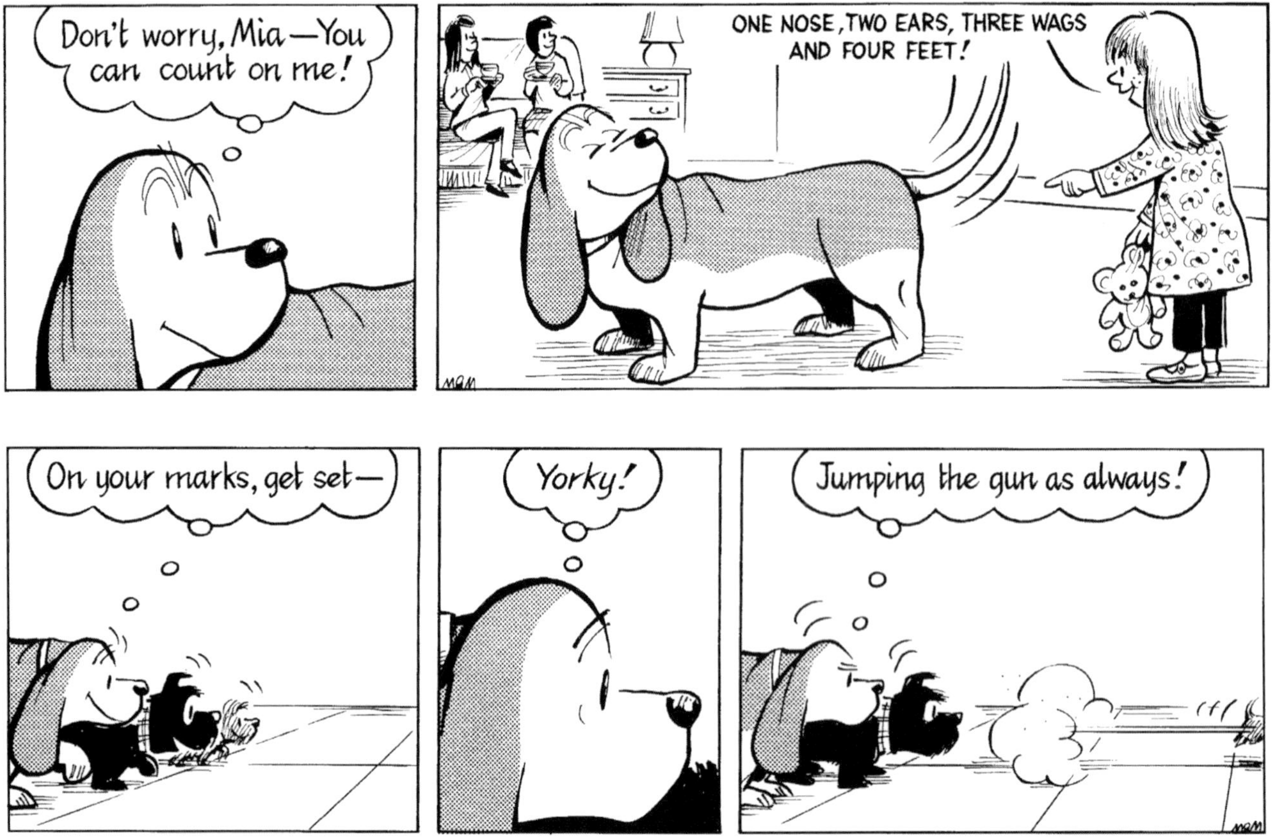
Don't worry, Mia—You can count on me!
ONE NOSE, TWO EARS, THREE WAGS AND FOUR FEET!
On your marks, get set—
Yorky!
Jumping the gun as always!

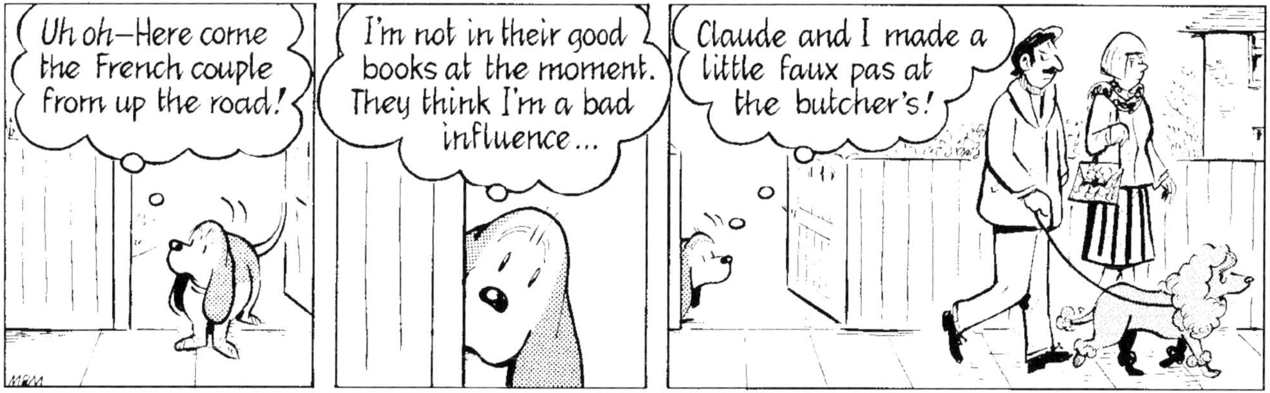
Uh oh–Here come the French couple from up the road!
I'm not in their good books at the moment. They think I'm a bad influence...
Claude and I made a little faux pas at the butcher's!

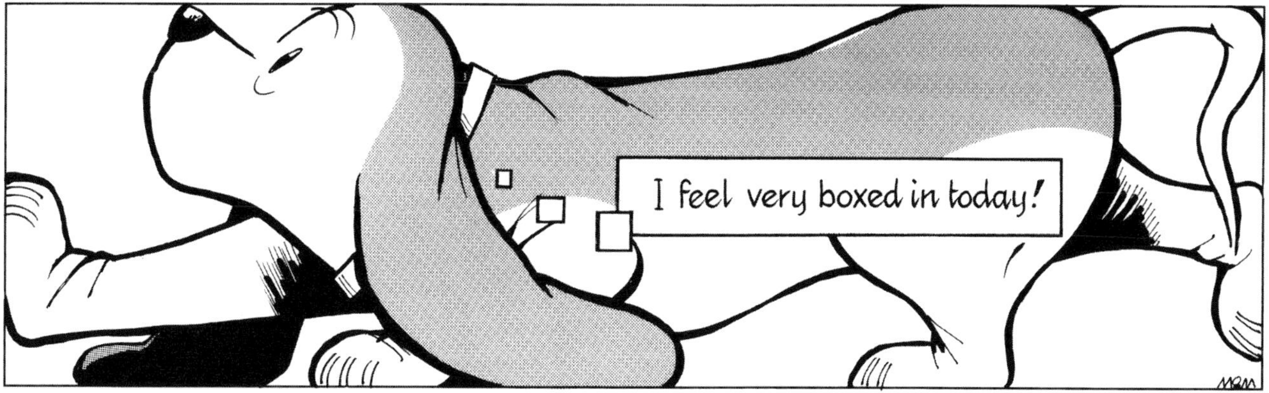
I feel very boxed in today!

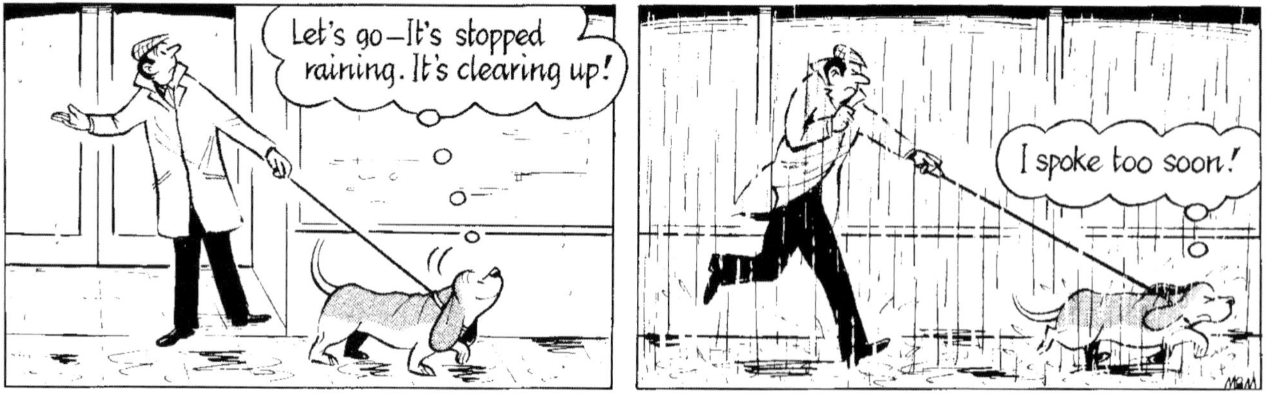
Let's go—It's stopped raining. It's clearing up!
I spoke too soon!

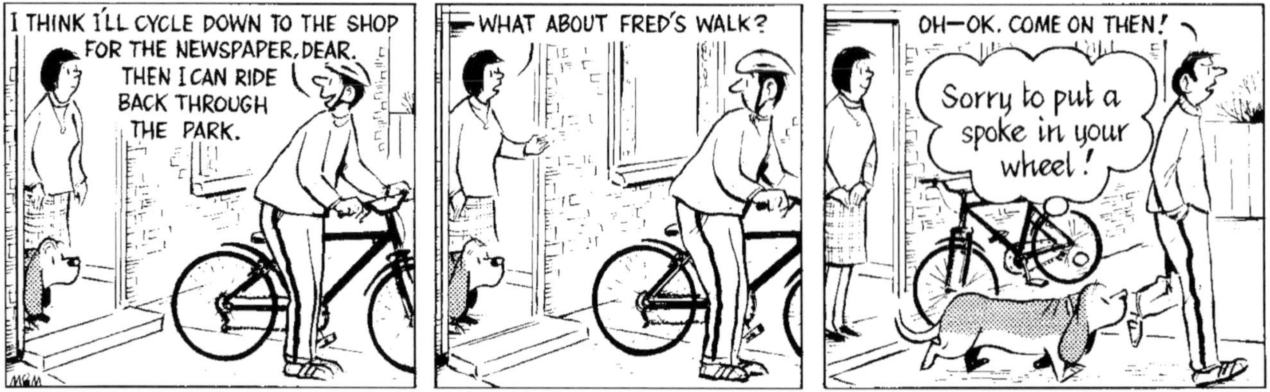
I THINK I'LL CYCLE DOWN TO THE SHOP FOR THE NEWSPAPER, DEAR. THEN I CAN RIDE BACK THROUGH THE PARK.
WHAT ABOUT FRED'S WALK?
OH—OK. COME ON THEN!
Sorry to put a spoke in your wheel!

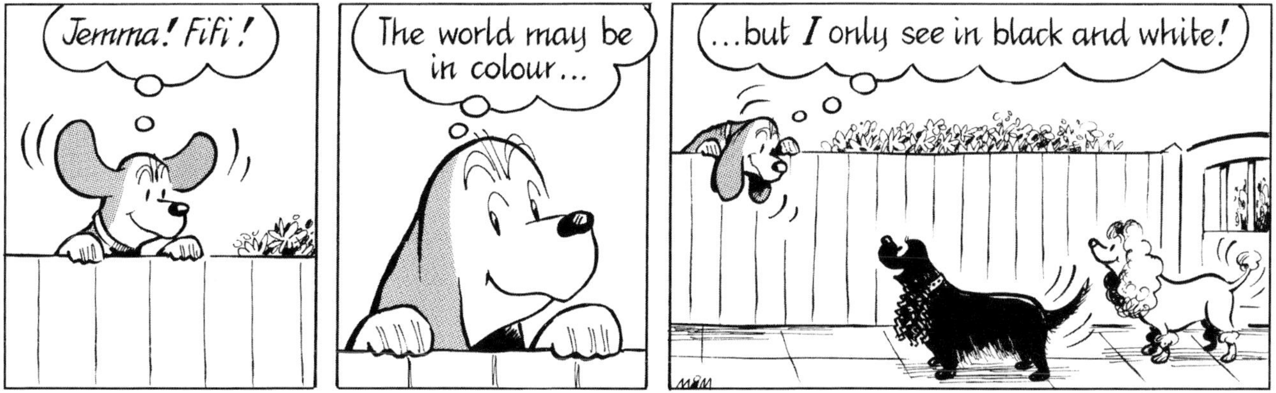
Jemma! Fifi!
The world may be in colour...
...but I only see in black and white!
M&M

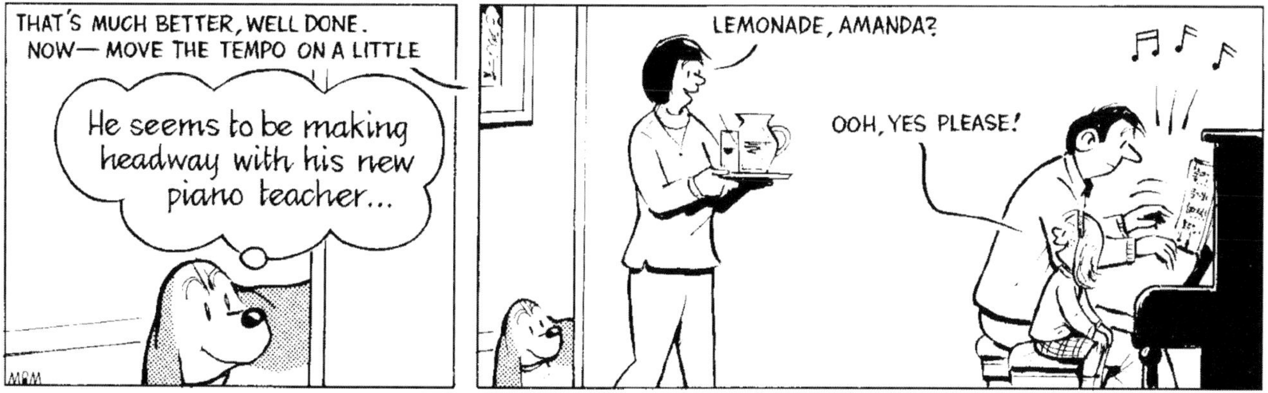
THAT'S MUCH BETTER, WELL DONE. NOW— MOVE THE TEMPO ON A LITTLE
He seems to be making headway with his new piano teacher...
M&M
LEMONADE, AMANDA?
OOH, YES PLEASE!

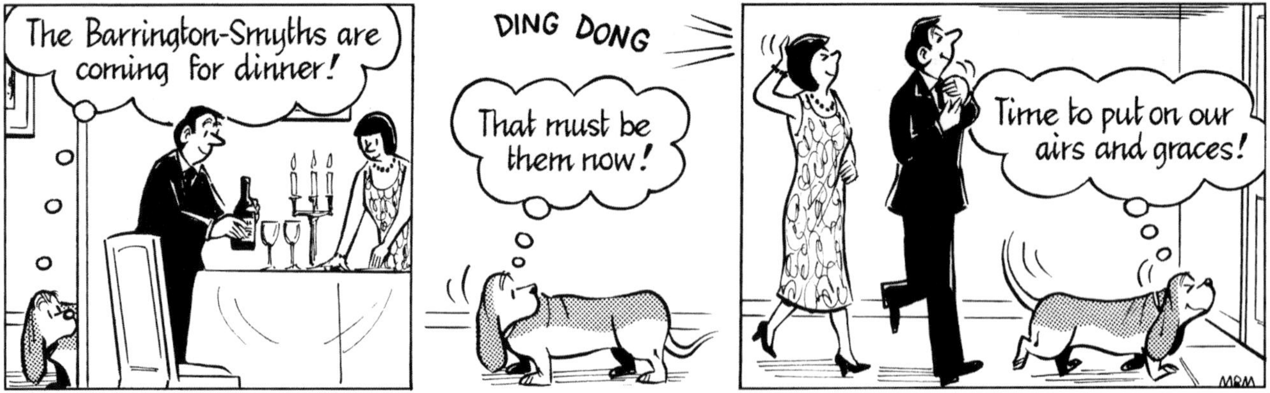
The Barrington-Smyths are coming for dinner!
DING DONG
That must be them now!
Time to put on our airs and graces!

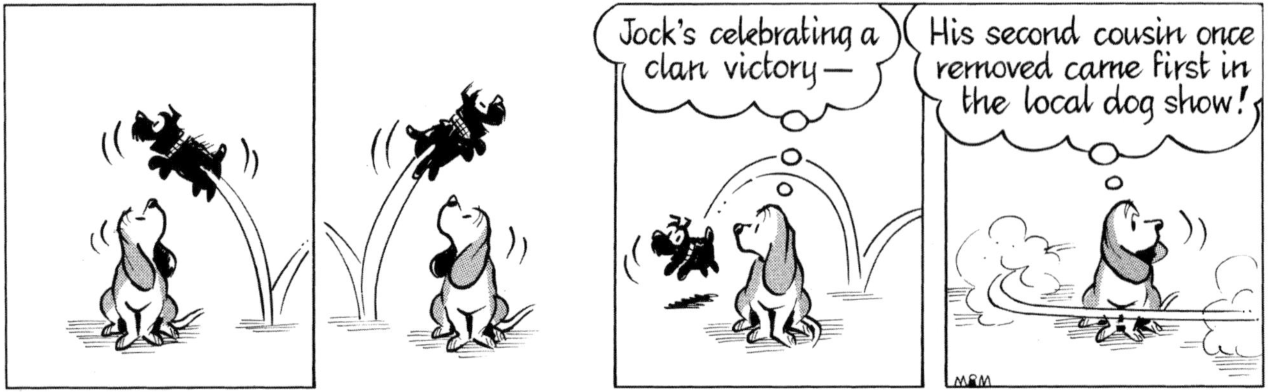
Jock's celebrating a clan victory —
His second cousin once removed came first in the local dog show!

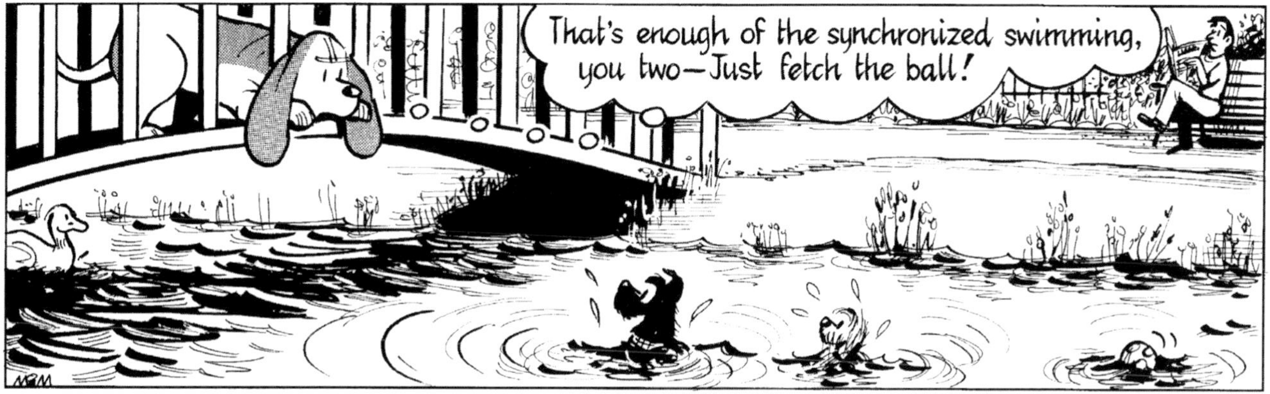
That's enough of the synchronized swimming, you two—Just fetch the ball!
MSM

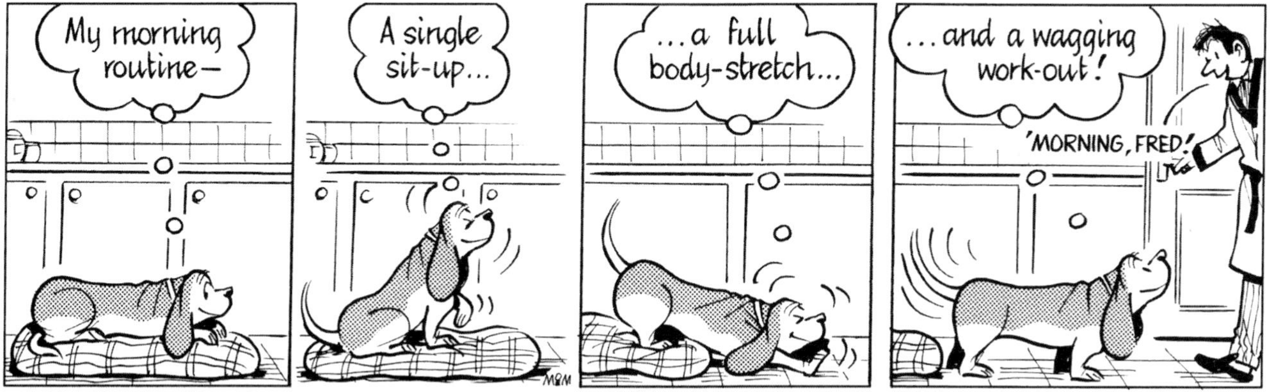
My morning routine—
A single sit-up...
...a full body-stretch...
MSM
...and a wagging work-out!
'MORNING, FRED!

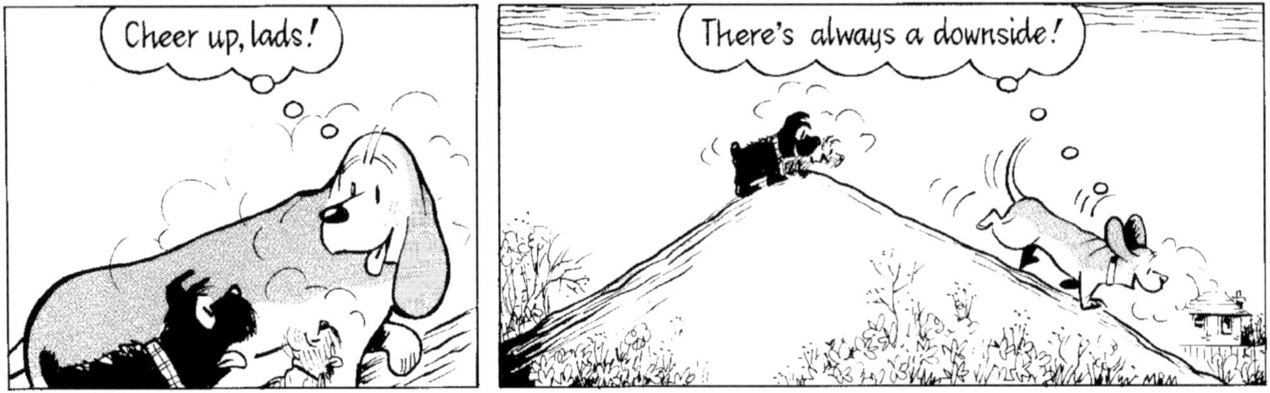
Cheer up, lads!
There's always a downside!
MGM

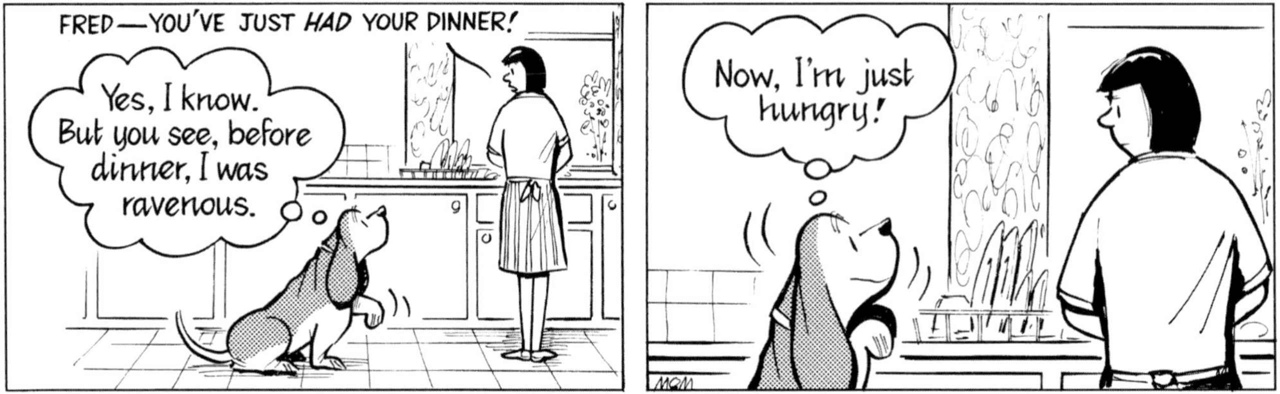
FRED—YOU'VE JUST HAD YOUR DINNER!
Yes, I know. But you see, before dinner, I was ravenous.
Now, I'm just hungry!
MGM

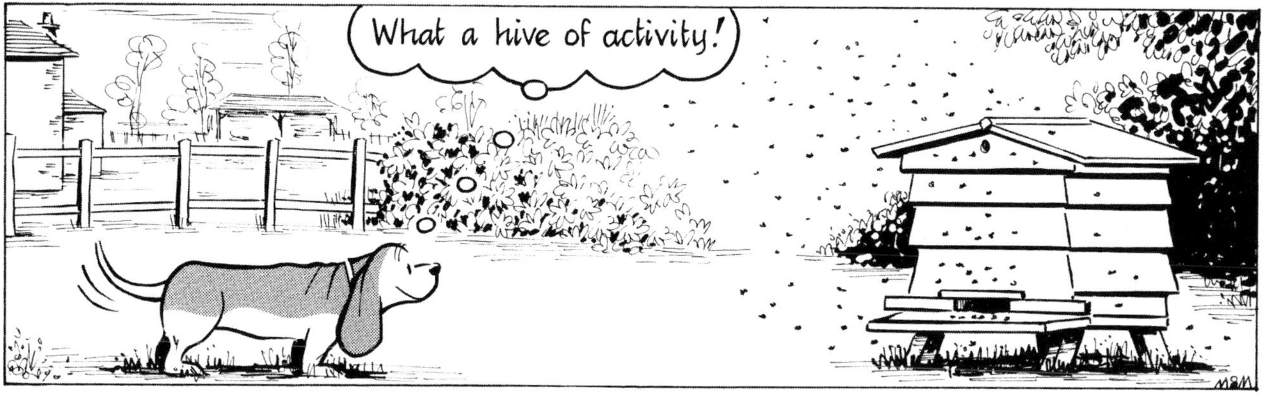
What a hive of activity!

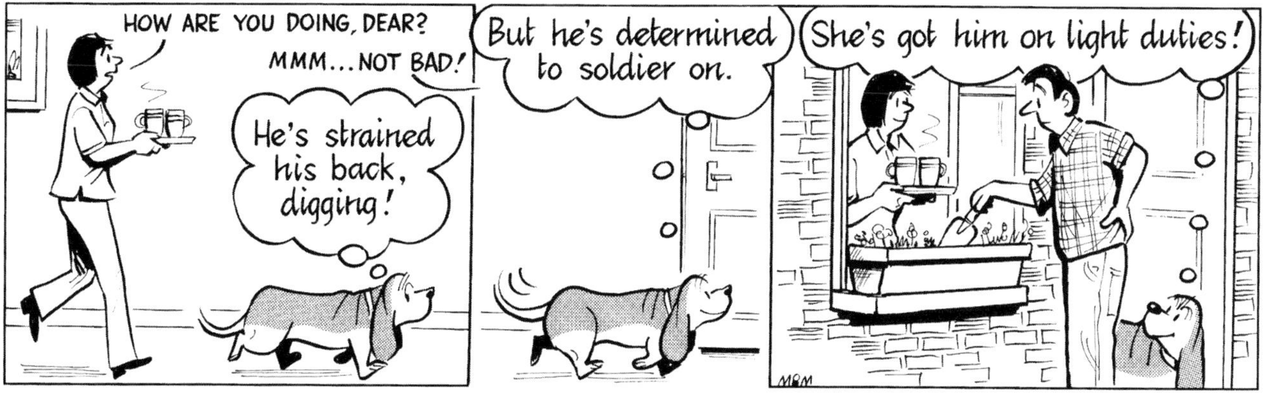
HOW ARE YOU DOING, DEAR?
MMM... NOT BAD!
He's strained his back, digging!
But he's determined to soldier on.
She's got him on light duties!

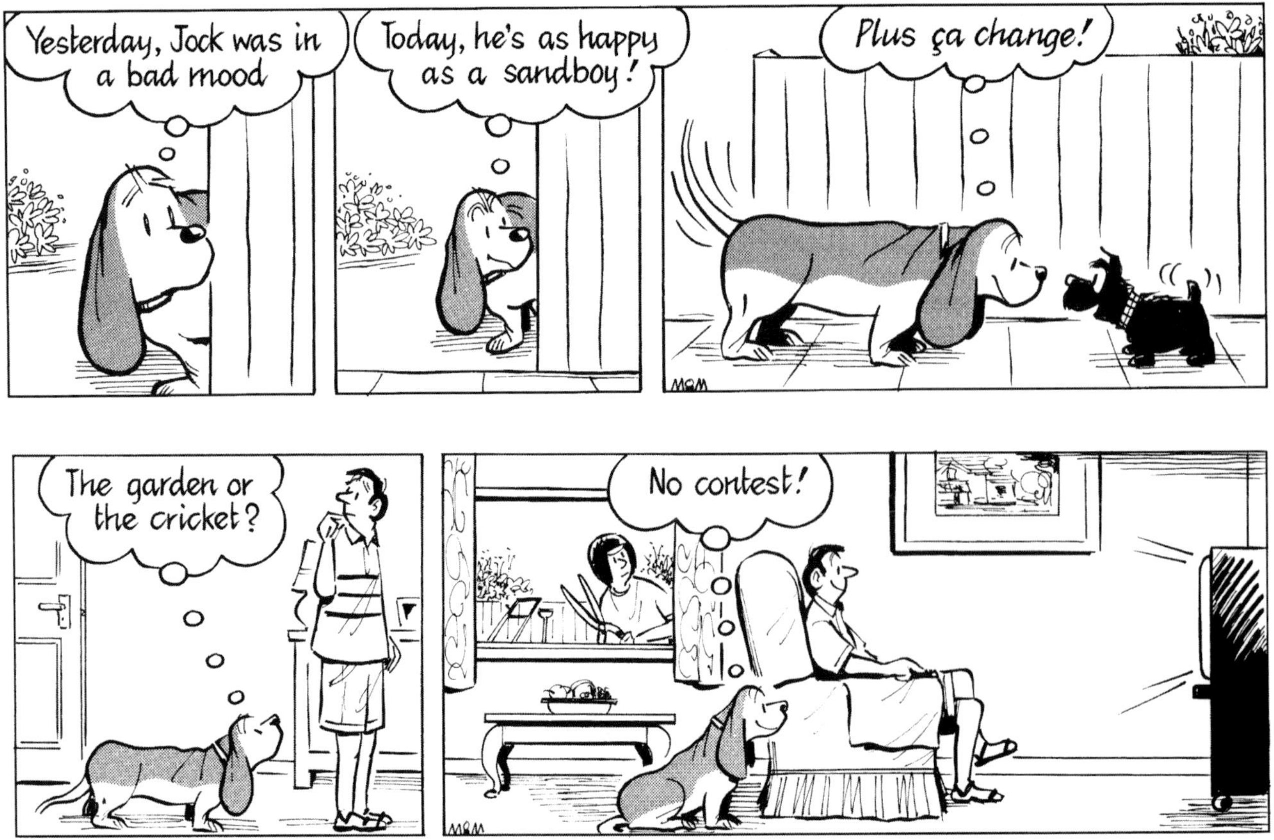
Yesterday, Jock was in a bad mood
Today, he's as happy as a sandboy!
Plus ça change!
The garden or the cricket?
No contest!

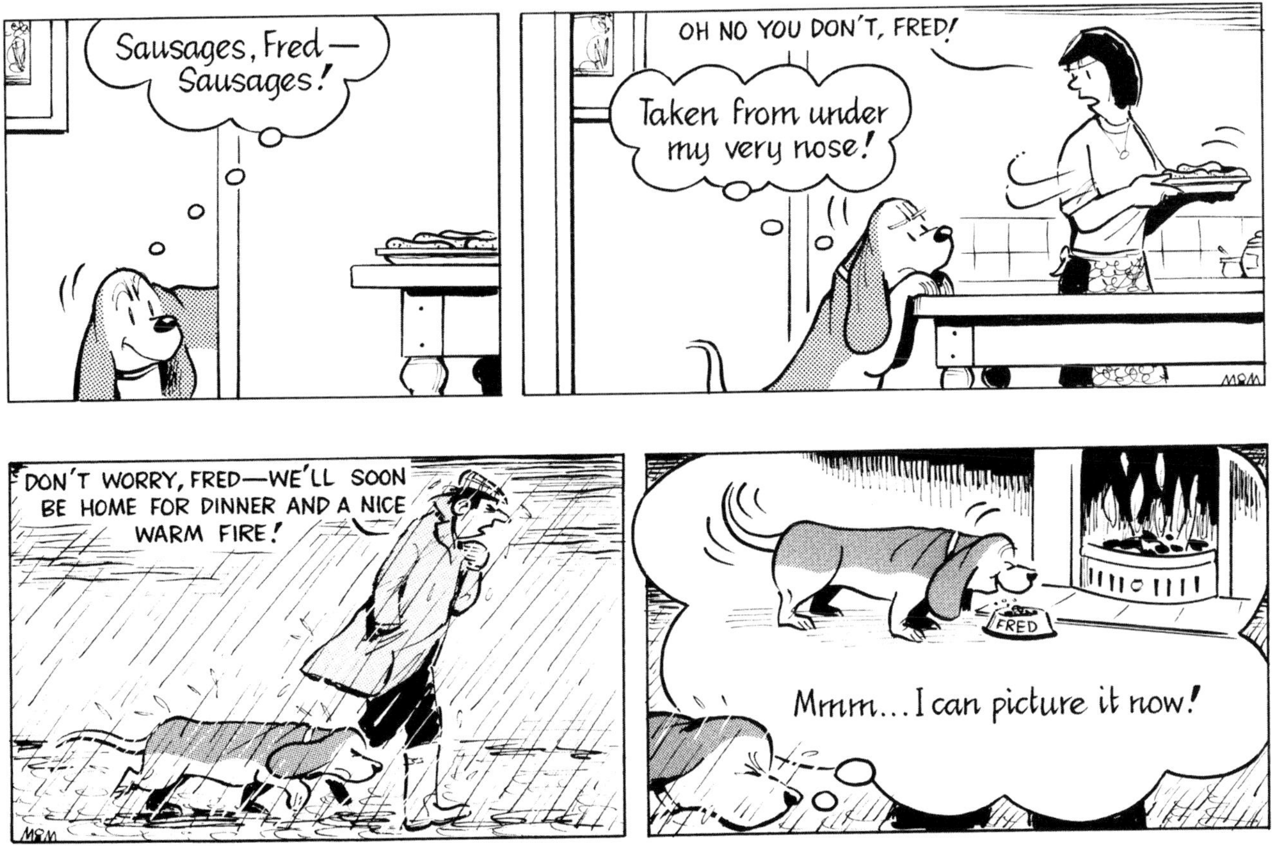

Sausages, Fred—
Sausages!
OH NO YOU DON'T, FRED!
Taken from under my very nose!
M&M
DON'T WORRY, FRED—WE'LL SOON BE HOME FOR DINNER AND A NICE WARM FIRE!
M&M
FRED
Mmm… I can picture it now!

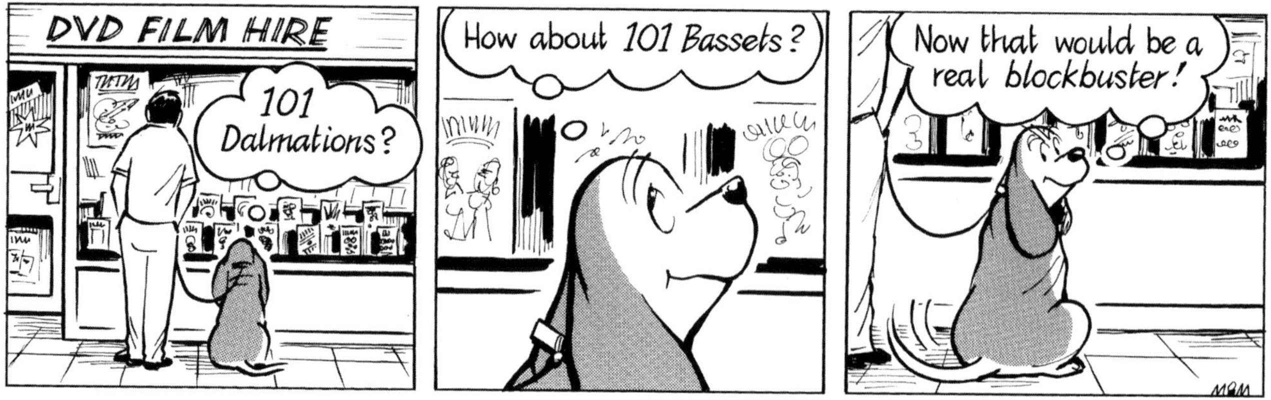
DVD FILM HIRE
101 Dalmations?
How about 101 Bassets?
Now that would be a real blockbuster!

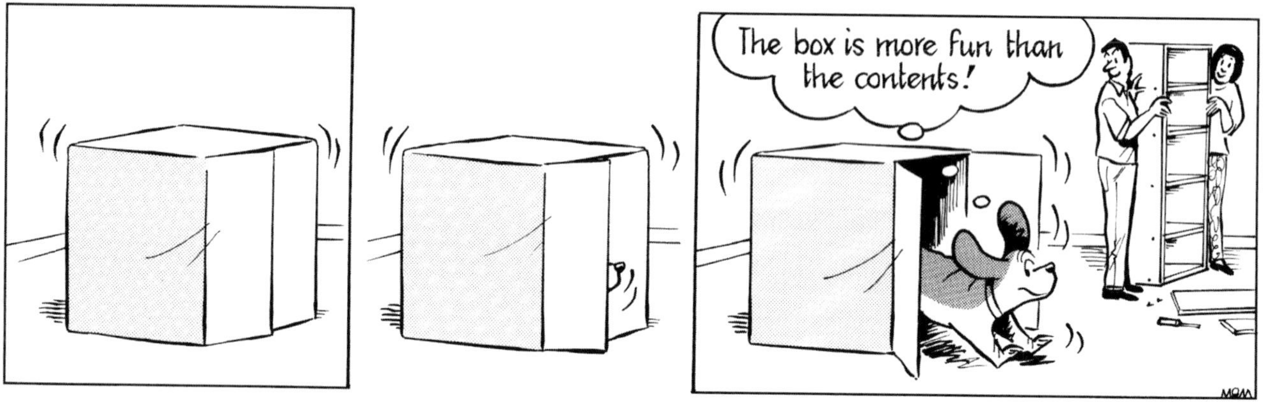
The box is more fun than the contents!

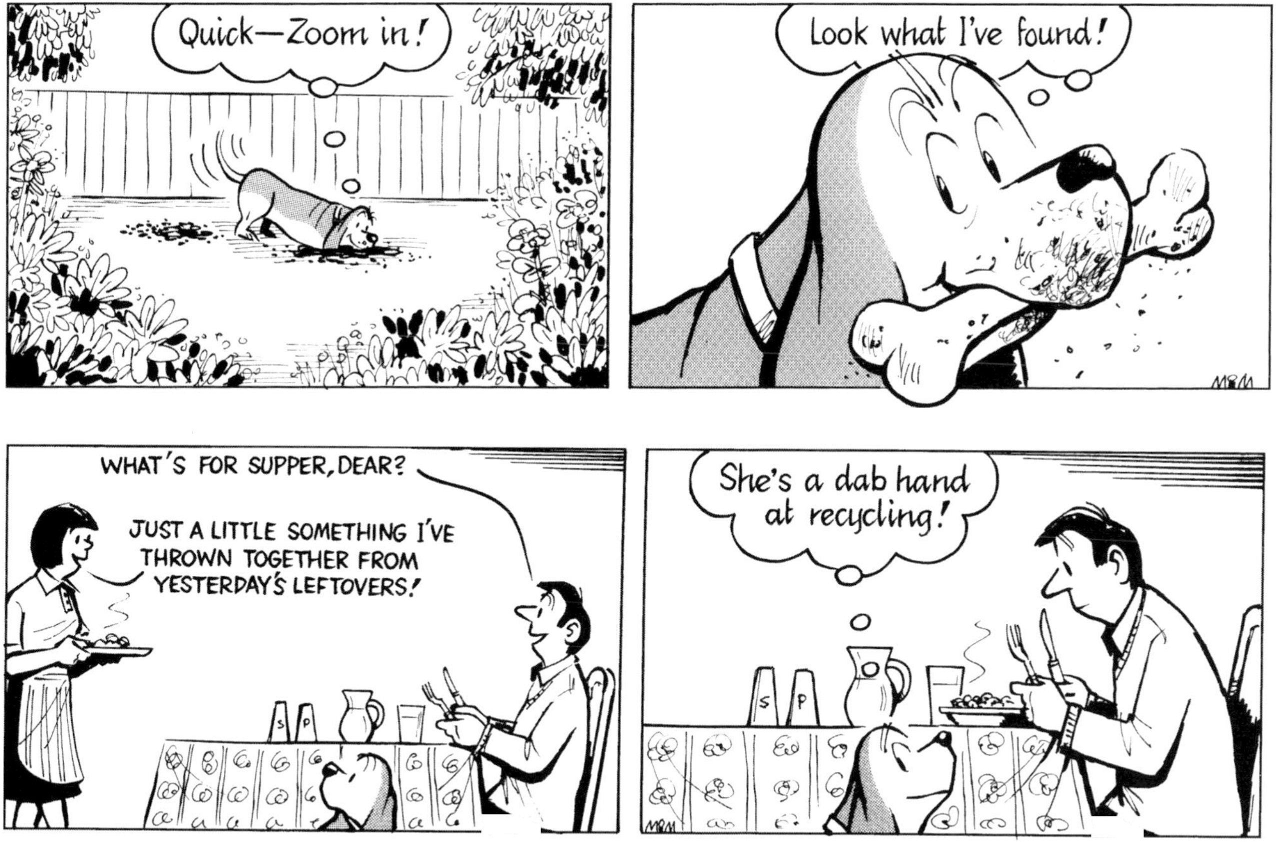
Quick—Zoom in!
Look what I've found!
MBM
WHAT'S FOR SUPPER, DEAR?
JUST A LITTLE SOMETHING I'VE THROWN TOGETHER FROM YESTERDAY'S LEFTOVERS!
She's a dab hand at recycling!
MBM

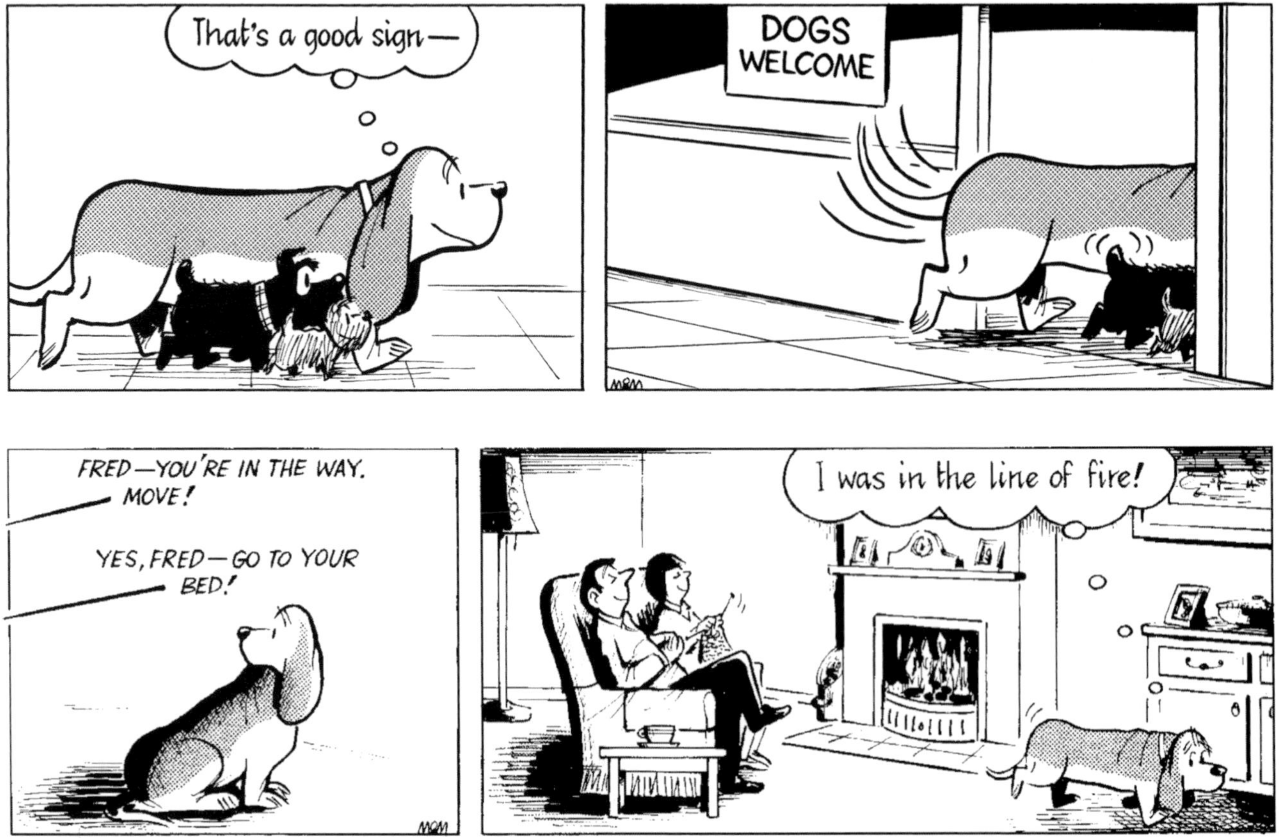
That's a good sign—
DOGS WELCOME
FRED—YOU'RE IN THE WAY. MOVE!
YES, FRED—GO TO YOUR BED!
I was in the line of fire!

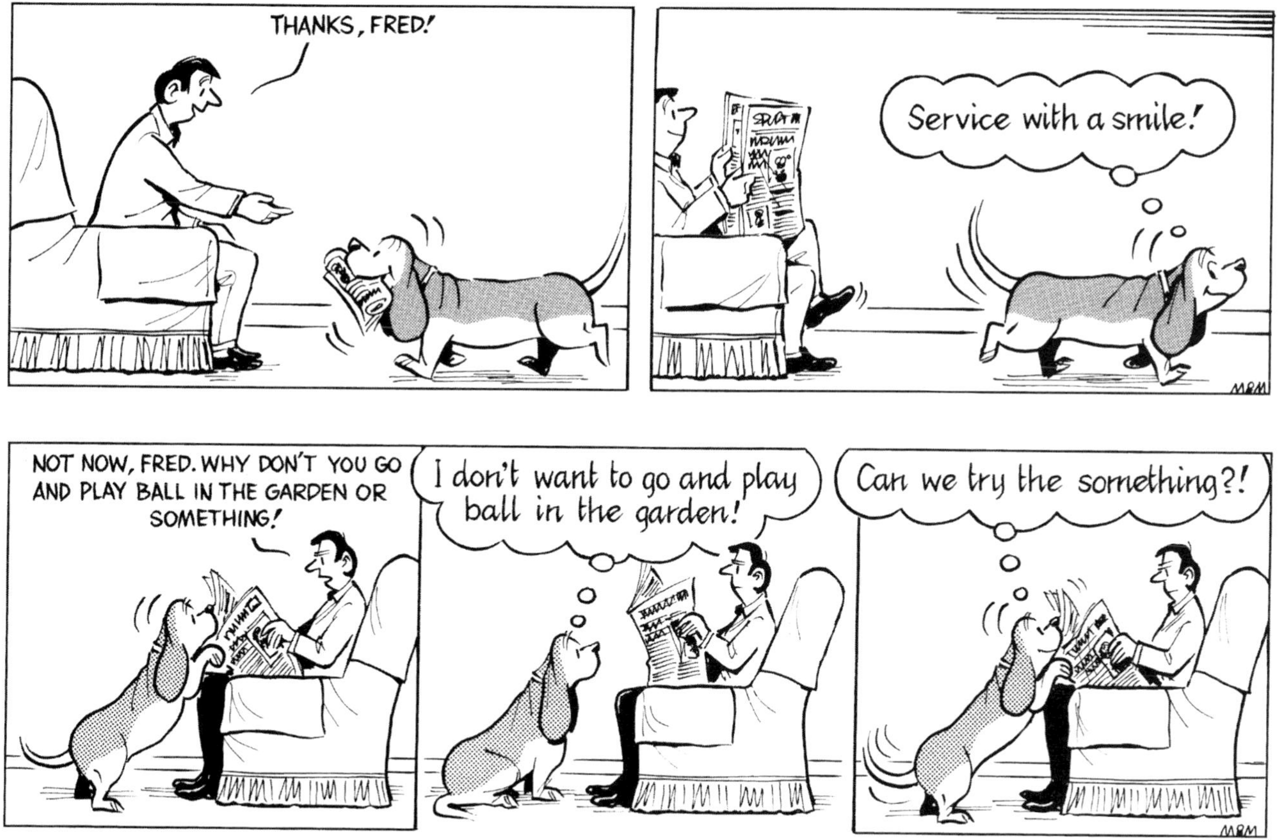
THANKS, FRED!
Service with a smile!
MBM
NOT NOW, FRED. WHY DON'T YOU GO AND PLAY BALL IN THE GARDEN OR SOMETHING!
I don't want to go and play ball in the garden!
Can we try the something?!
MBM

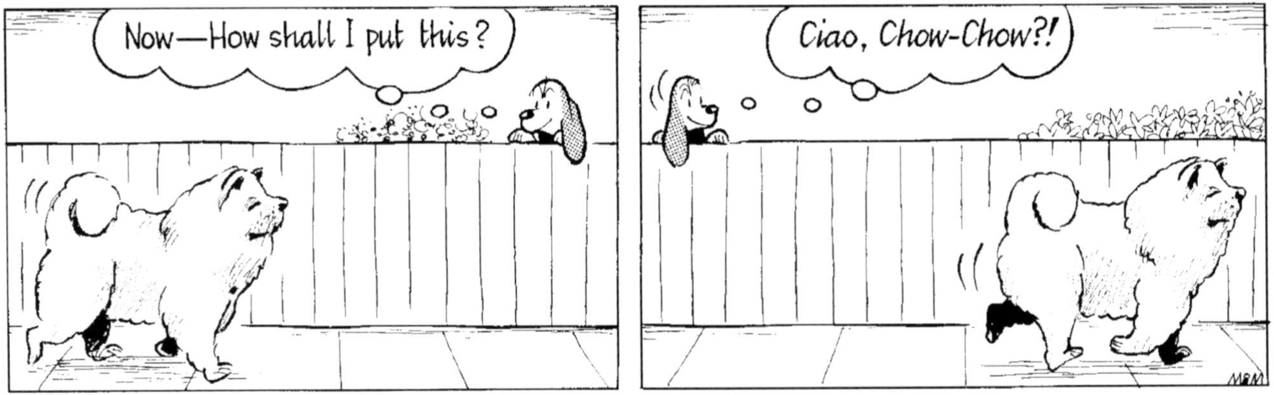
Now—How shall I put this?
Ciao, Chow-Chow?!
M&M

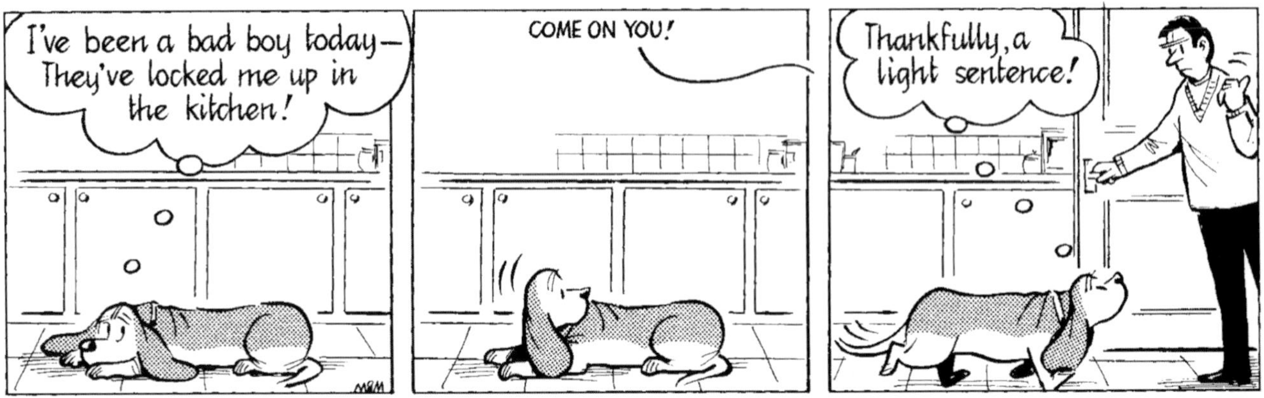
I've been a bad boy today—They've locked me up in the kitchen!
M&M
COME ON YOU!
Thankfully, a light sentence!

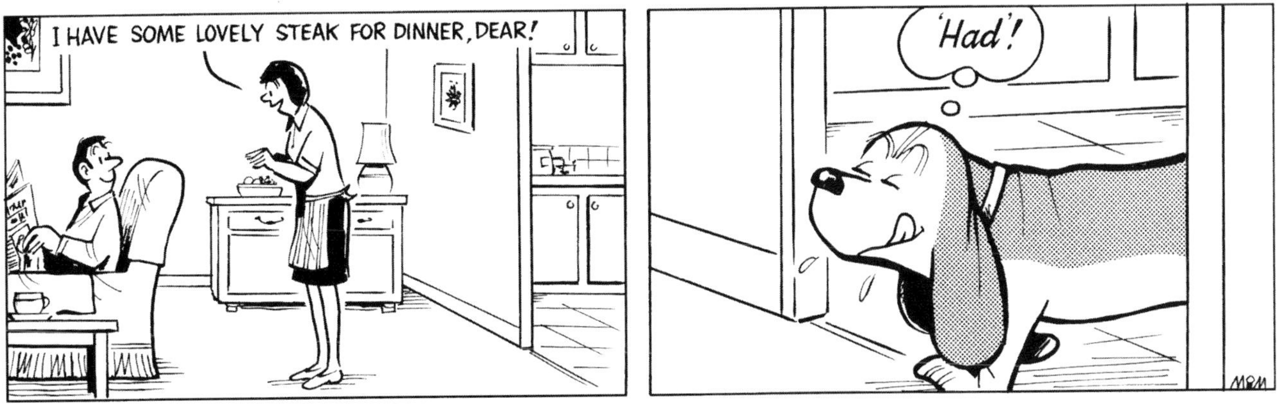
I HAVE SOME LOVELY STEAK FOR DINNER, DEAR!
'Had'!

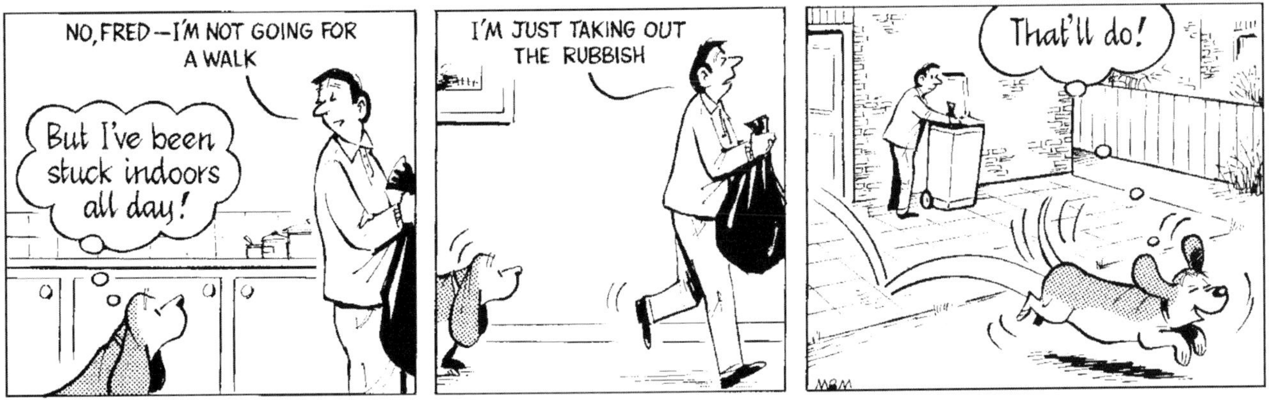
NO, FRED -- I'M NOT GOING FOR A WALK
But I've been stuck indoors all day!
I'M JUST TAKING OUT THE RUBBISH
That'll do!

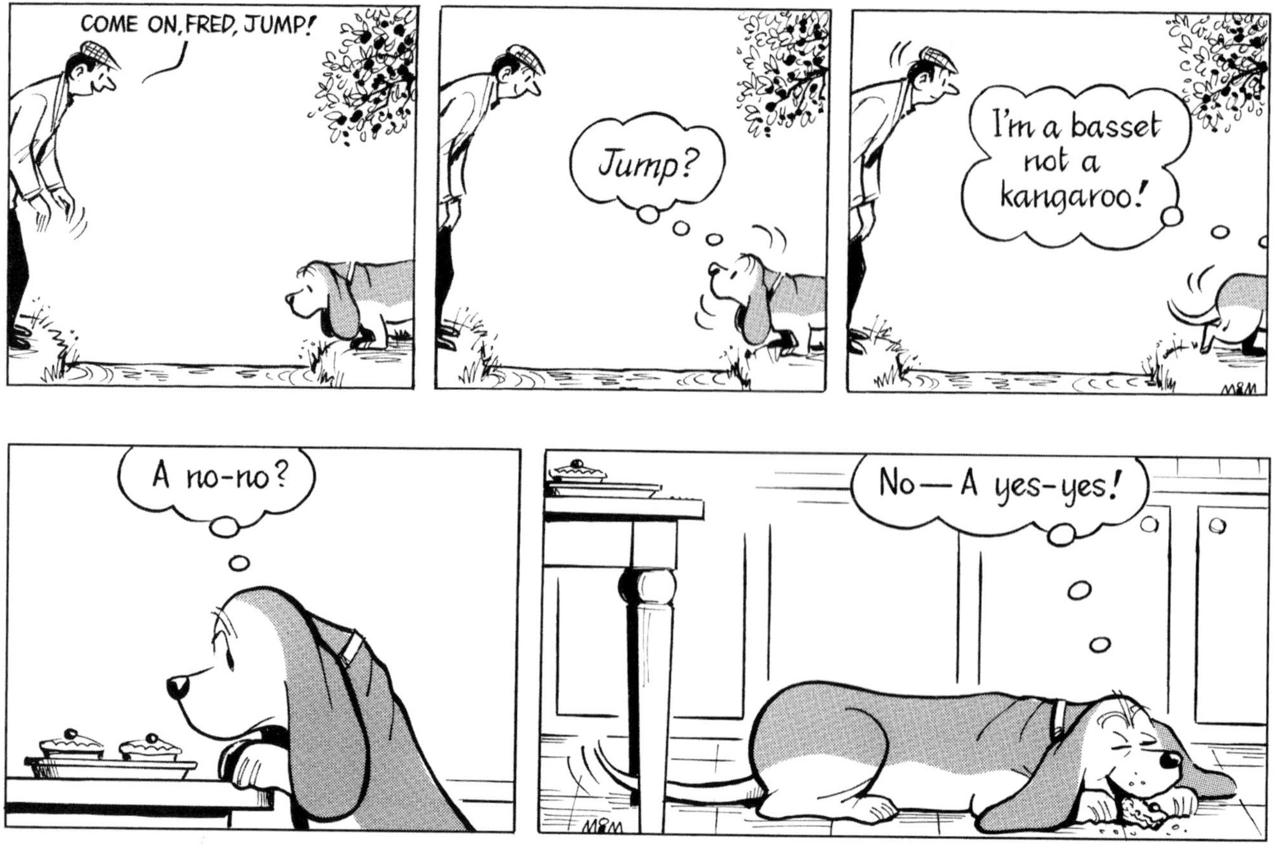
COME ON, FRED, JUMP!
Jump?
I'm a basset not a kangaroo!
A no-no?
No — A yes-yes!

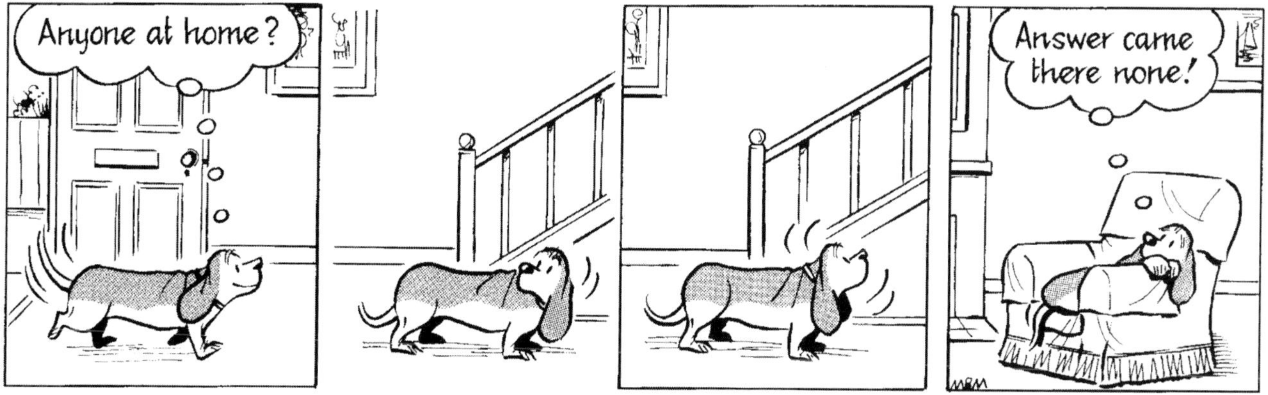
Anyone at home?
Answer came there none!
MGM

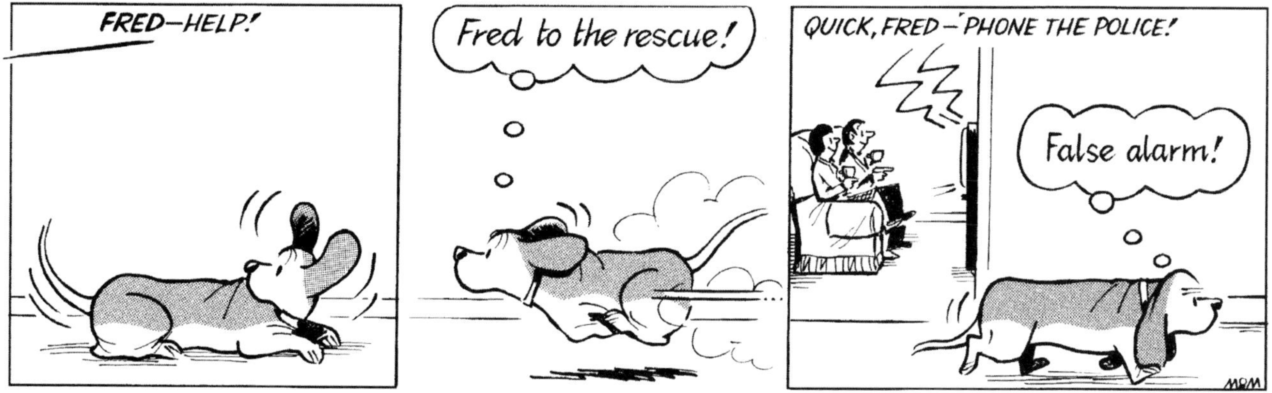
FRED—HELP!
Fred to the rescue!
QUICK, FRED—'PHONE THE POLICE!
False alarm!
MGM

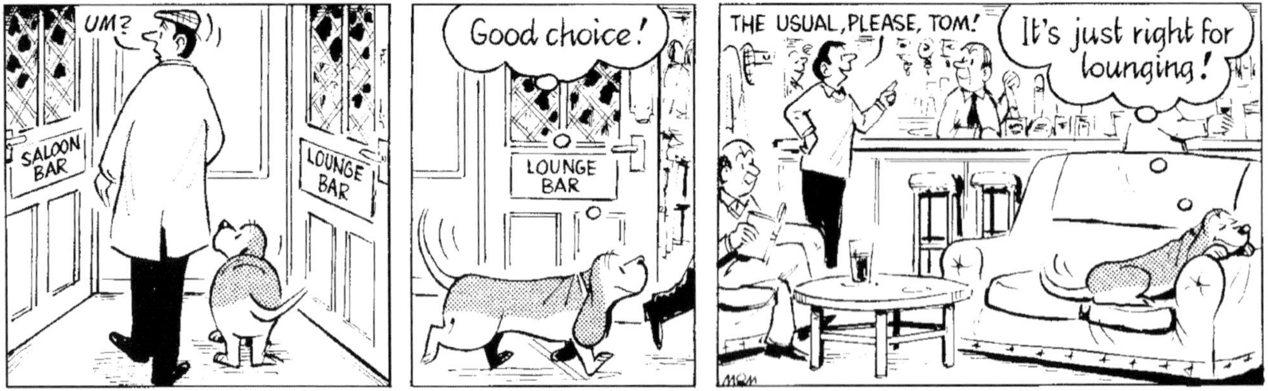
UM?
SALOON BAR
LOUNGE BAR
Good choice!
LOUNGE BAR
THE USUAL, PLEASE, TOM!
It's just right for lounging!
MRM

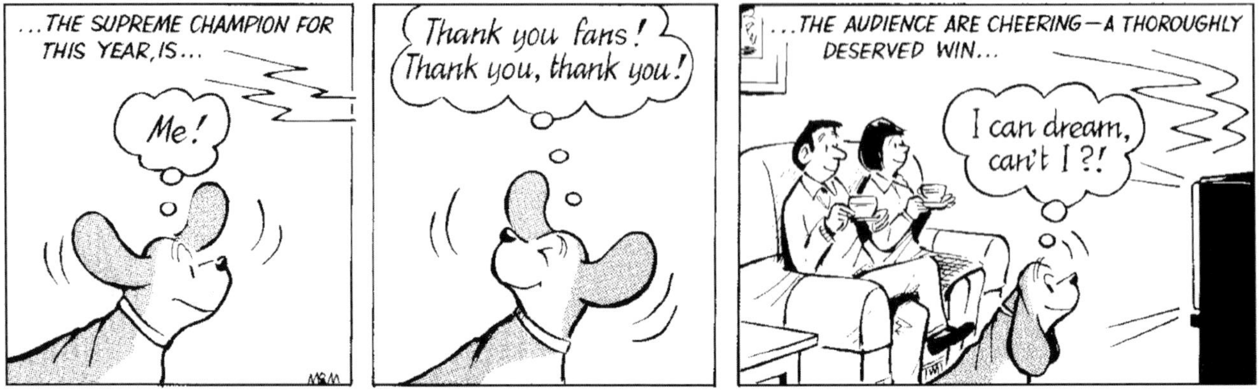
...THE SUPREME CHAMPION FOR THIS YEAR, IS...
Me!
MRM
Thank you fans! Thank you, thank you!
...THE AUDIENCE ARE CHEERING—A THOROUGHLY DESERVED WIN...
I can dream, can't I ?!

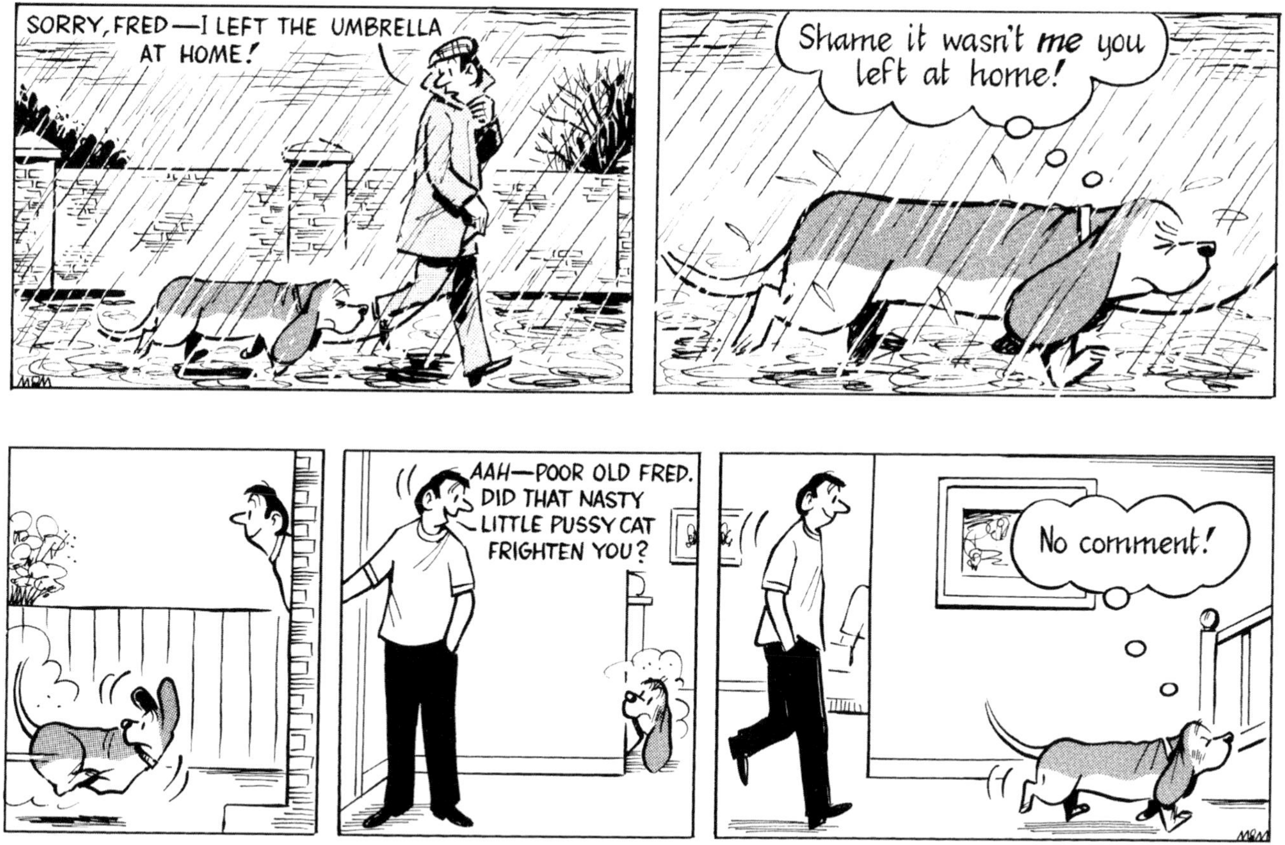
SORRY, FRED—I LEFT THE UMBRELLA AT HOME!
Shame it wasn't **me** you left at home!
AAH—POOR OLD FRED. DID THAT NASTY LITTLE PUSSY CAT FRIGHTEN YOU?
No comment!

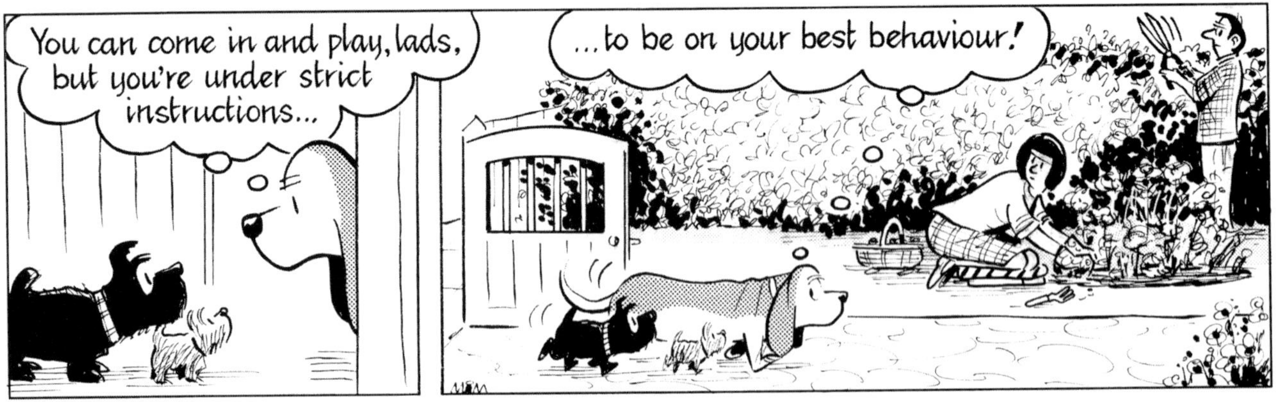
You can come in and play, lads, but you're under strict instructions...
...to be on your best behaviour!

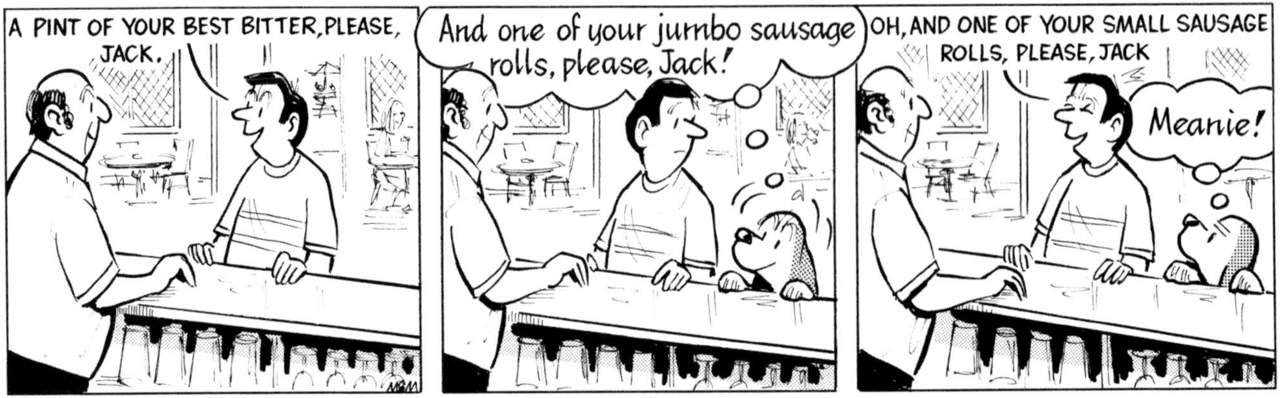
A PINT OF YOUR BEST BITTER, PLEASE, JACK.
And one of your jumbo sausage rolls, please, Jack!
OH, AND ONE OF YOUR SMALL SAUSAGE ROLLS, PLEASE, JACK
Meanie!

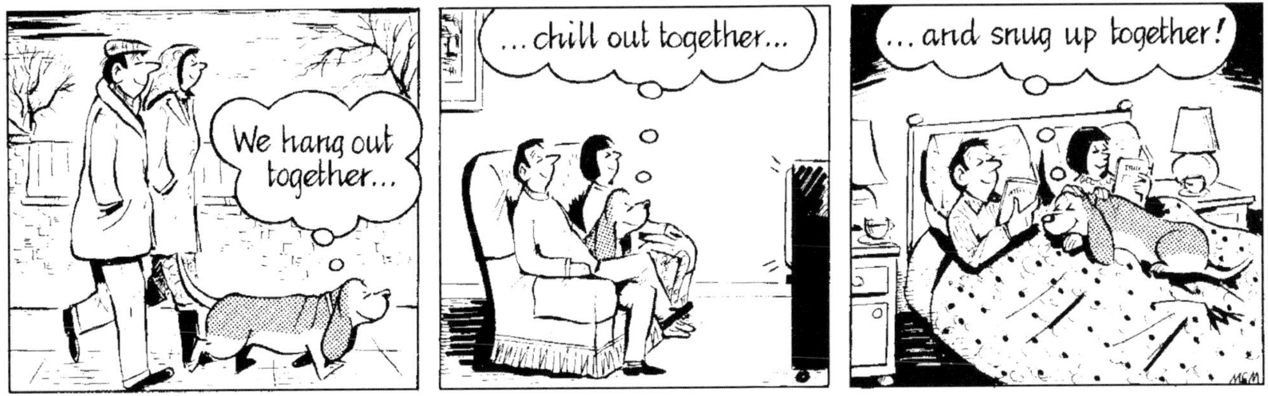
We hang out together...
...chill out together...
...and snug up together!

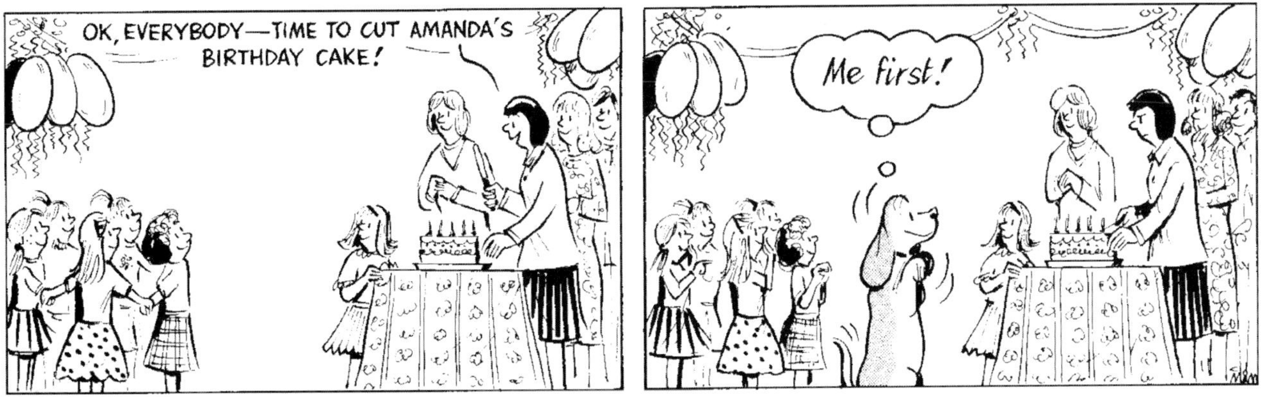
OK, EVERYBODY—TIME TO CUT AMANDA'S BIRTHDAY CAKE!
Me first!

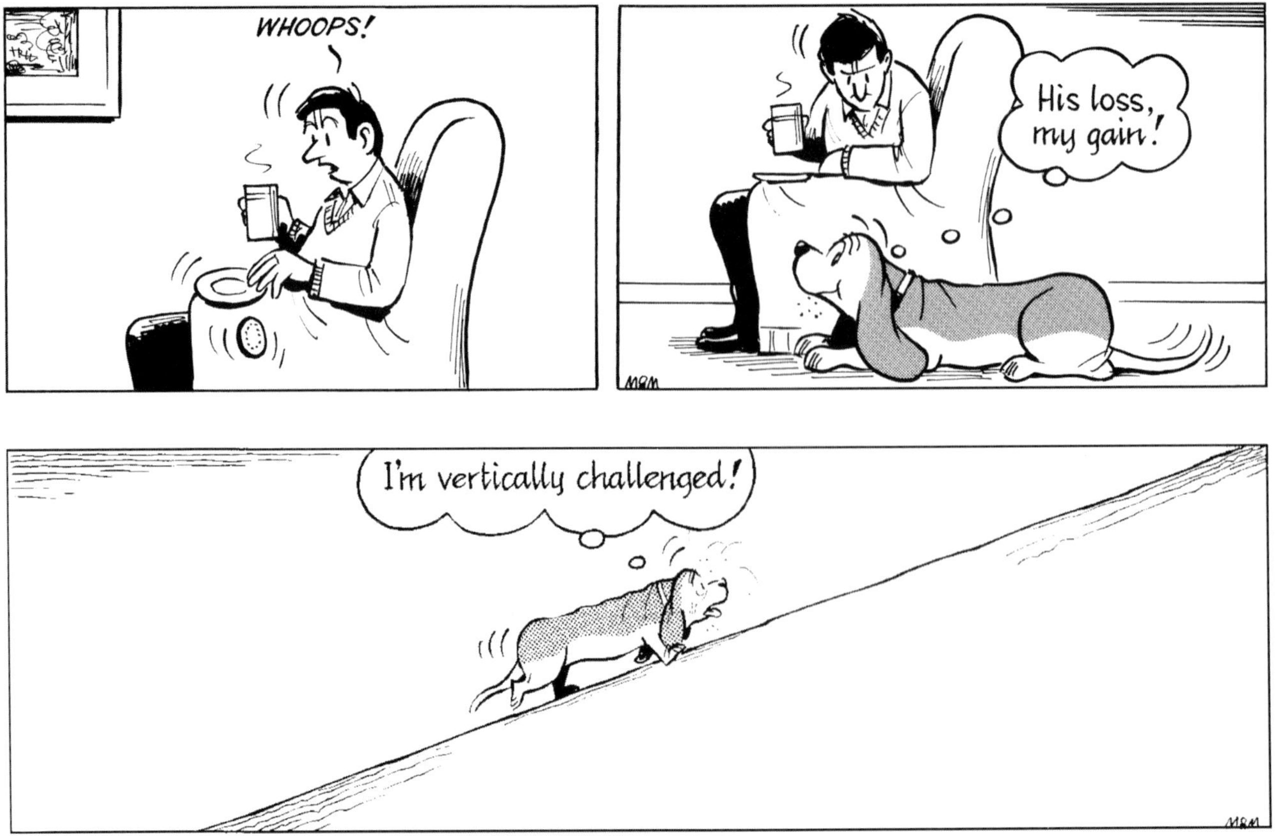
WHOOPS!
His loss, my gain!
M&M
I'm vertically challenged!
M&M

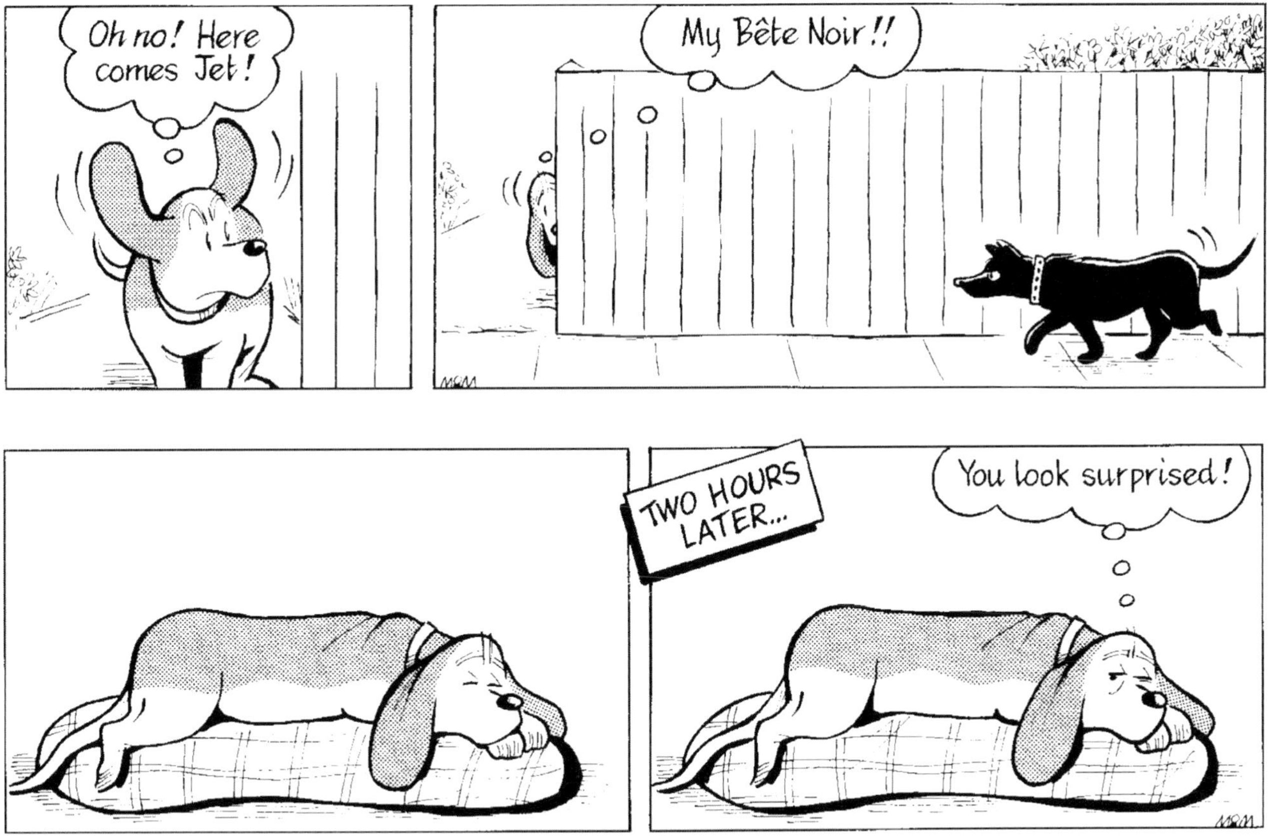

Oh no! Here comes Jet!
My Bête Noir!!
TWO HOURS LATER...
You look surprised!

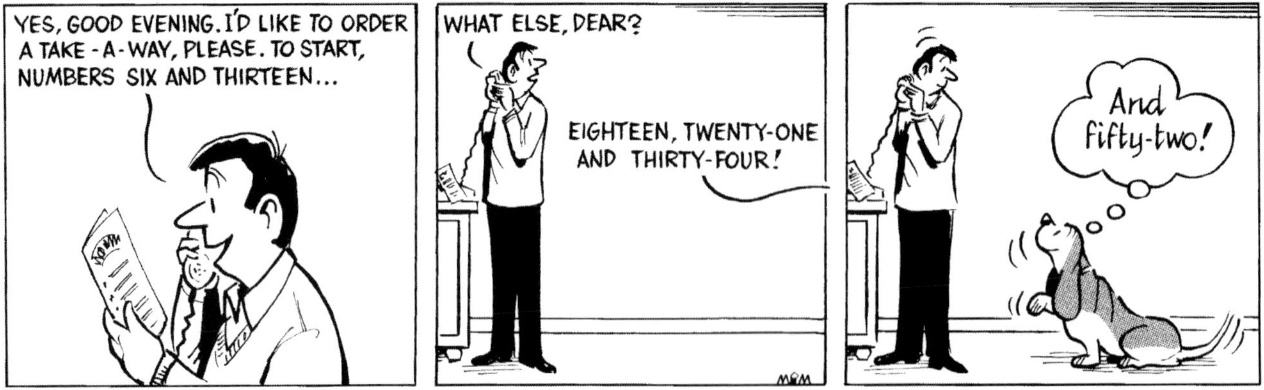
YES, GOOD EVENING. I'D LIKE TO ORDER A TAKE-A-WAY, PLEASE. TO START, NUMBERS SIX AND THIRTEEN...
WHAT ELSE, DEAR?
EIGHTEEN, TWENTY-ONE AND THIRTY-FOUR!
And fifty-two!

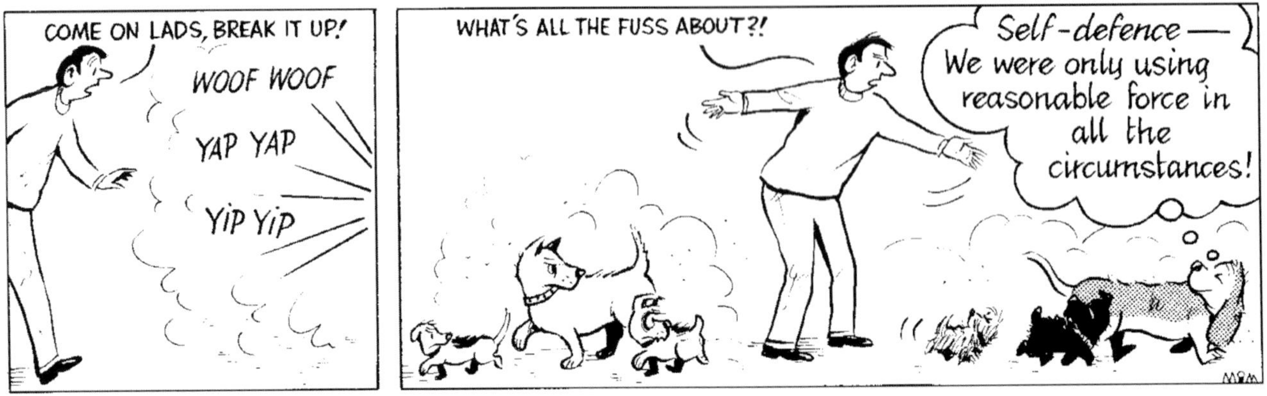
COME ON LADS, BREAK IT UP!
WOOF WOOF
YAP YAP
YIP YIP
WHAT'S ALL THE FUSS ABOUT?!
Self-defence — We were only using reasonable force in all the circumstances!

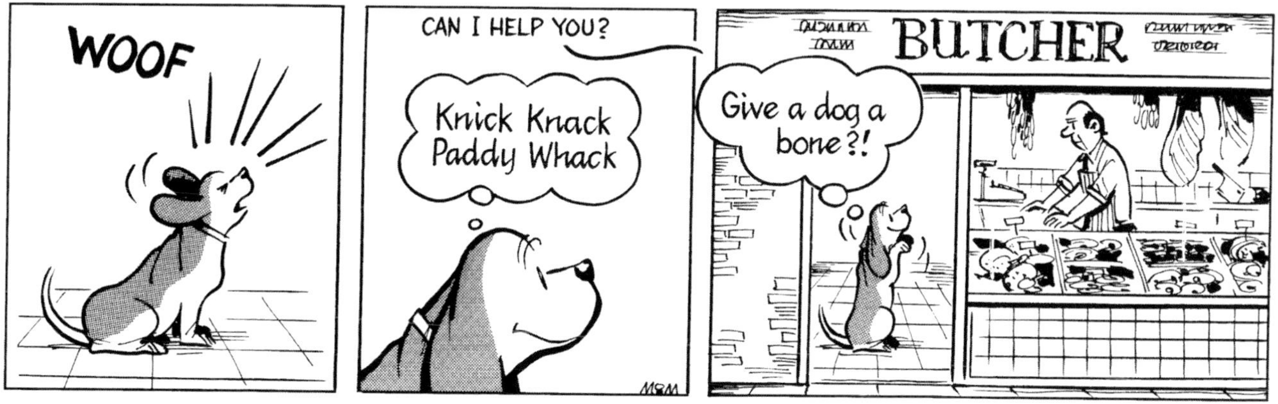
WOOF
CAN I HELP YOU?
Knick Knack Paddy Whack
BUTCHER
Give a dog a bone?!

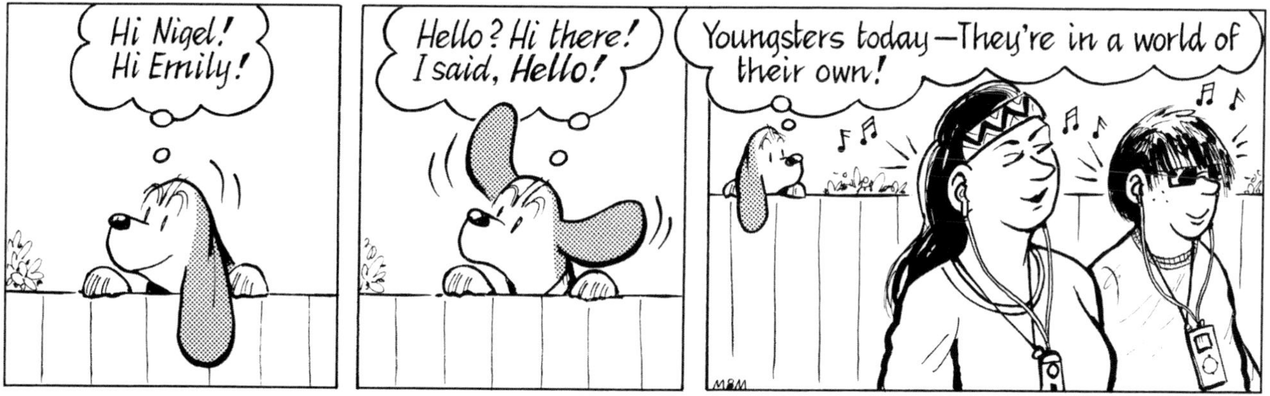
Hi Nigel! Hi Emily!
Hello? Hi there! I said, Hello!
Youngsters today—They're in a world of their own!

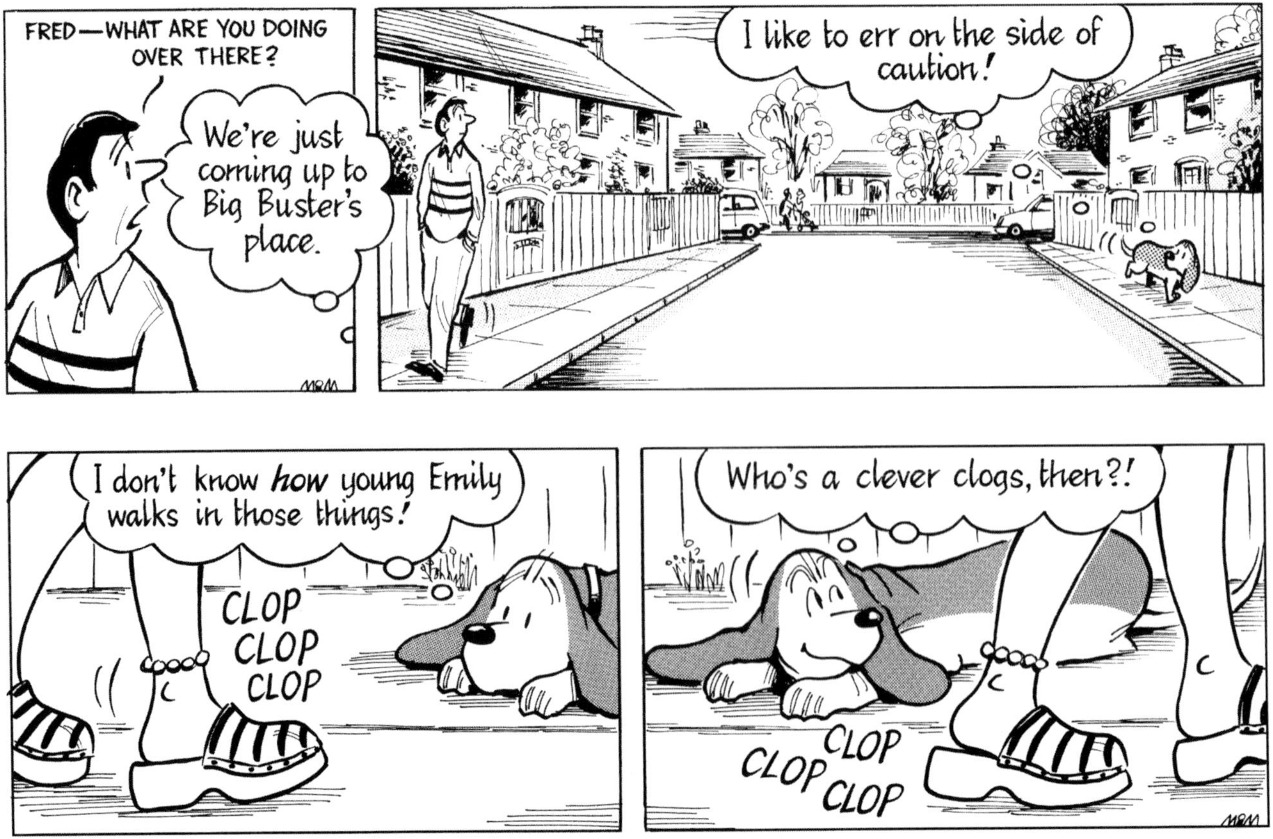
FRED—WHAT ARE YOU DOING OVER THERE?
We're just coming up to Big Buster's place.
I like to err on the side of caution!
I don't know **how** young Emily walks in those things!
CLOP CLOP CLOP
Who's a clever clogs, then?!
CLOP CLOP CLOP

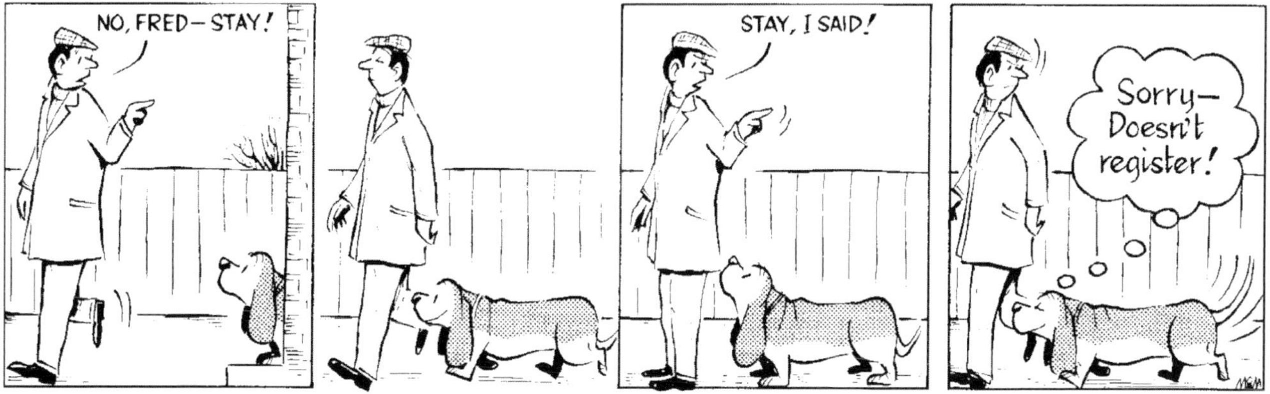
NO, FRED—STAY!
STAY, I SAID!
Sorry—Doesn't register!

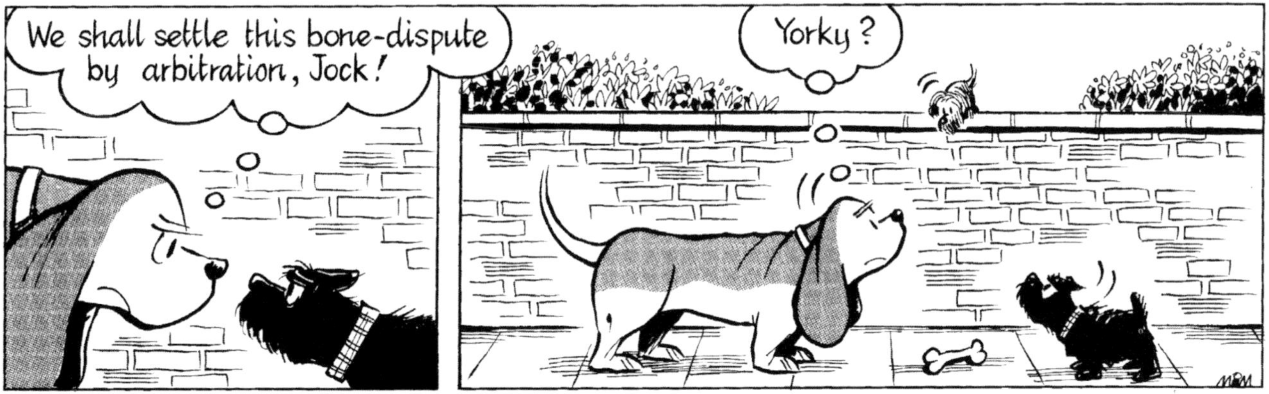
We shall settle this bone-dispute by arbitration, Jock!
Yorky?

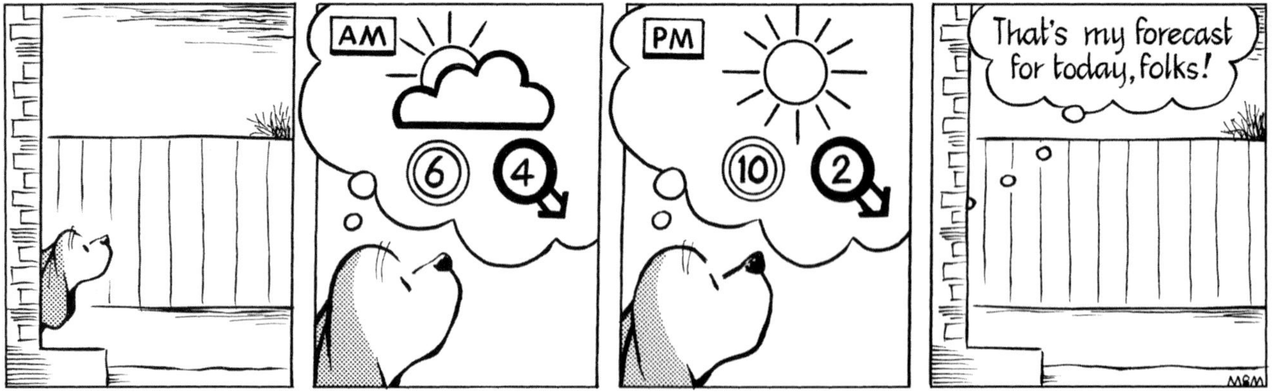
AM
6
4
PM
10
2
That's my forecast for today, folks!
M&M

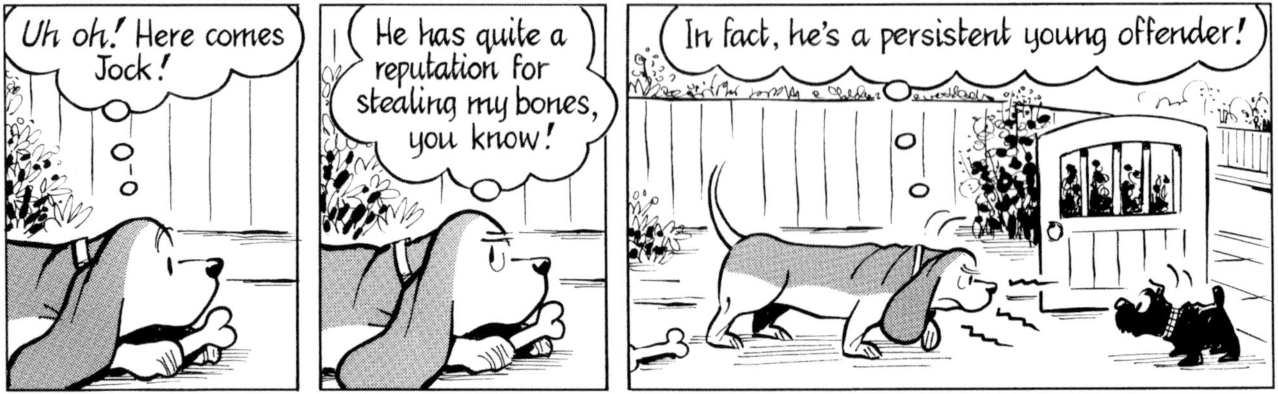
Uh oh! Here comes Jock!
He has quite a reputation for stealing my bones, you know!
In fact, he's a persistent young offender!

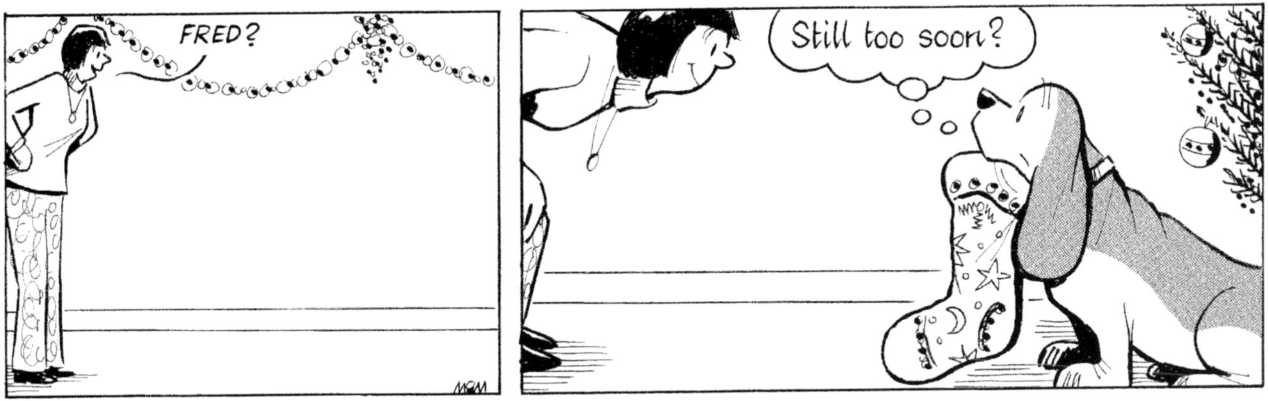
FRED?
Still too soon?
MSM

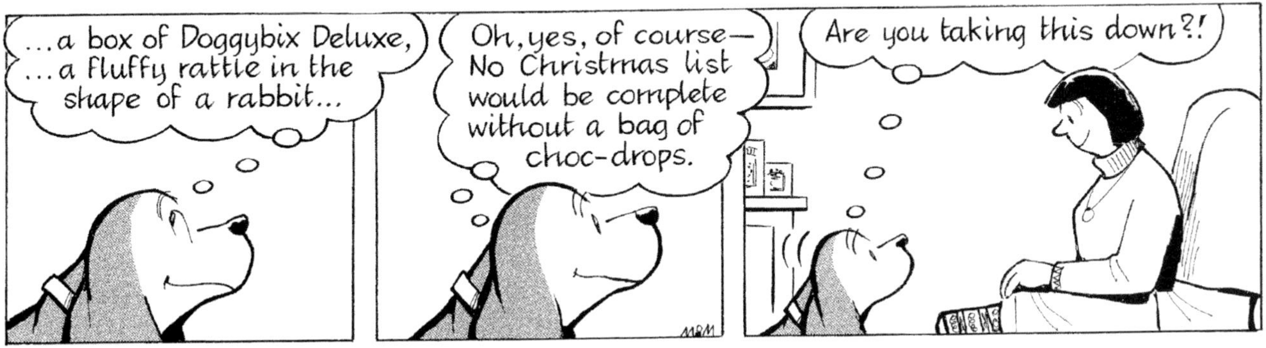
...a box of Doggybix Deluxe, ...a fluffy rattle in the shape of a rabbit...
Oh, yes, of course— No Christmas list would be complete without a bag of choc-drops.
MSM
Are you taking this down?!

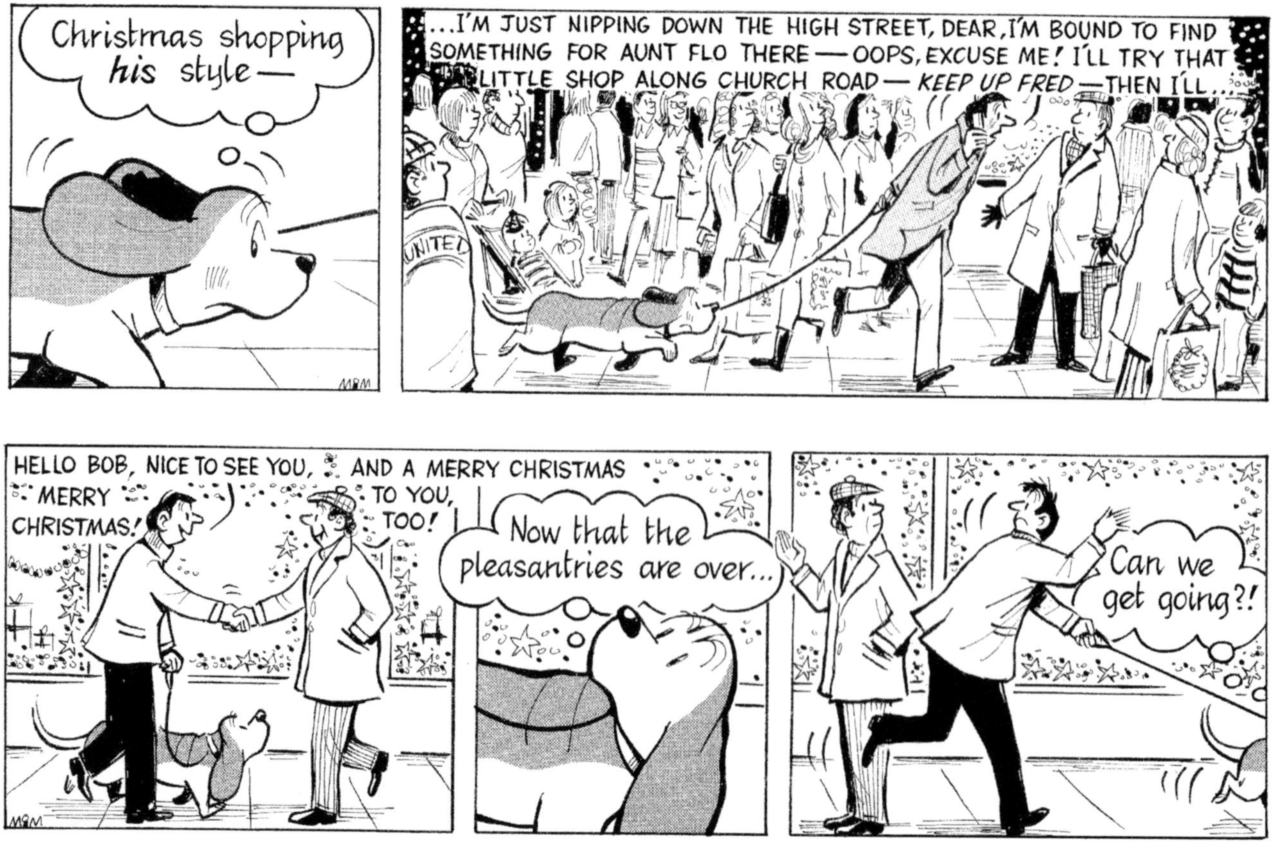

Christmas shopping *his* style—
...I'M JUST NIPPING DOWN THE HIGH STREET, DEAR, I'M BOUND TO FIND SOMETHING FOR AUNT FLO THERE—OOPS, EXCUSE ME! I'LL TRY THAT LITTLE SHOP ALONG CHURCH ROAD—*KEEP UP FRED*—THEN I'LL...
UNITED
HELLO BOB, NICE TO SEE YOU, AND A MERRY CHRISTMAS
MERRY CHRISTMAS!
TO YOU, TOO!
Now that the pleasantries are over...
Can we get going?!

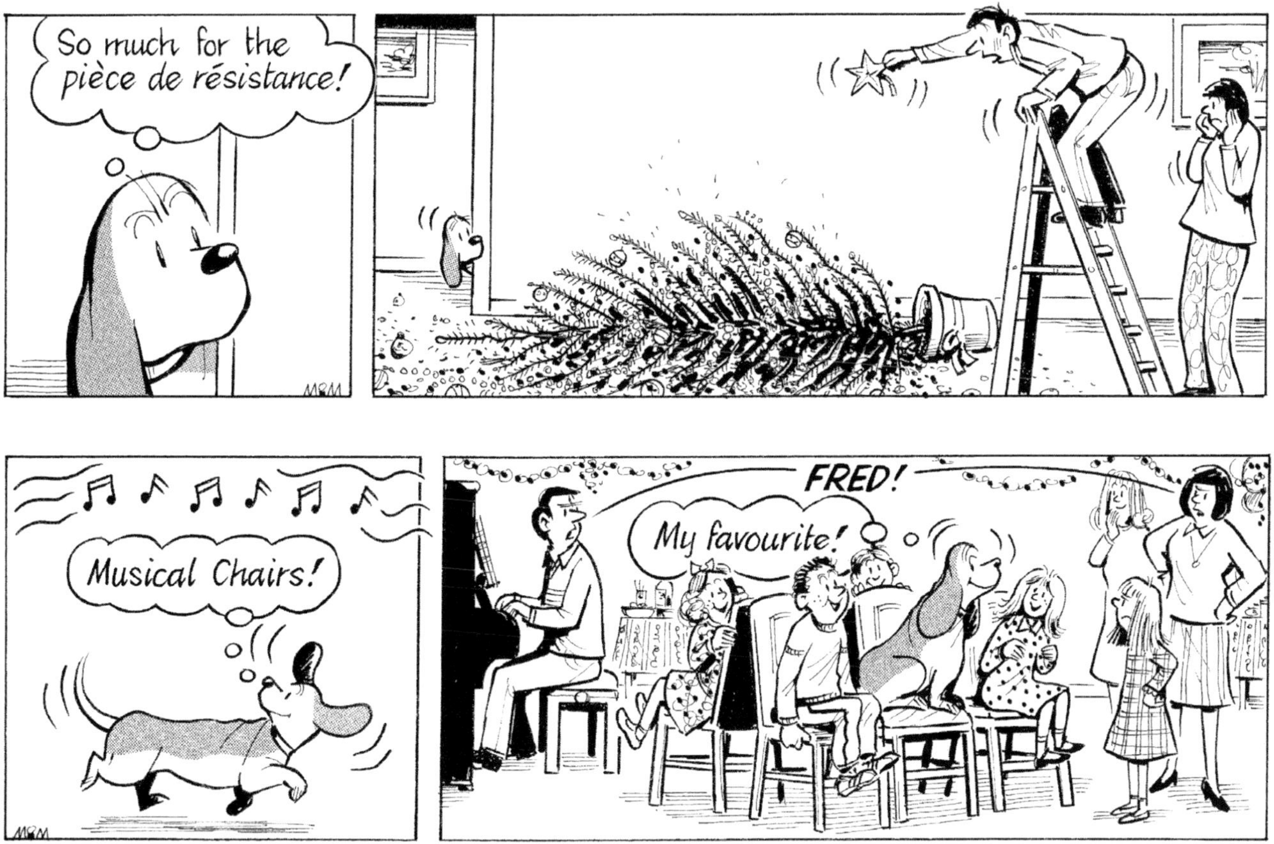
So much for the pièce de résistance!
Musical Chairs!
FRED!
My favourite!

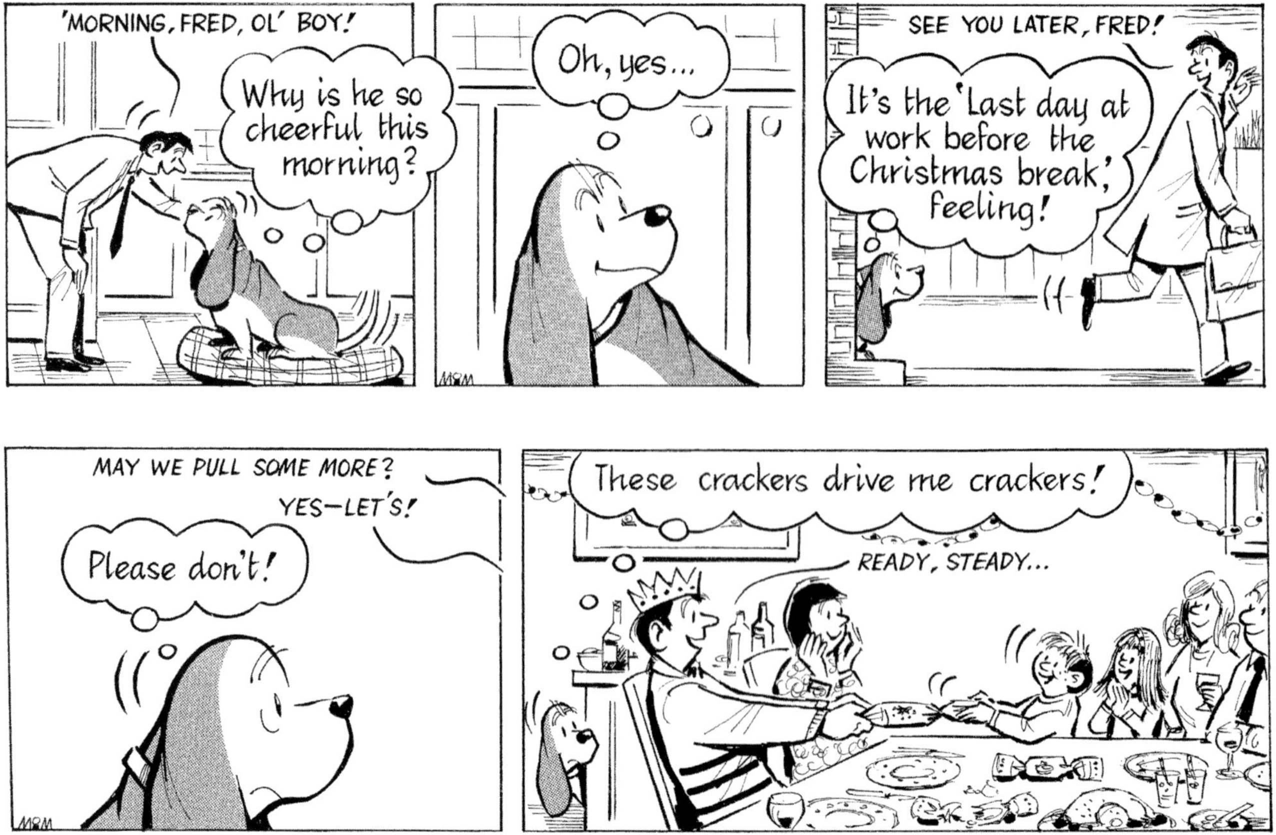
'MORNING, FRED, OL' BOY!
Why is he so cheerful this morning?
Oh, yes...
SEE YOU LATER, FRED!
It's the 'Last day at work before the Christmas break,' feeling!
MAY WE PULL SOME MORE?
YES—LET'S!
Please don't!
These crackers drive me crackers!
READY, STEADY...

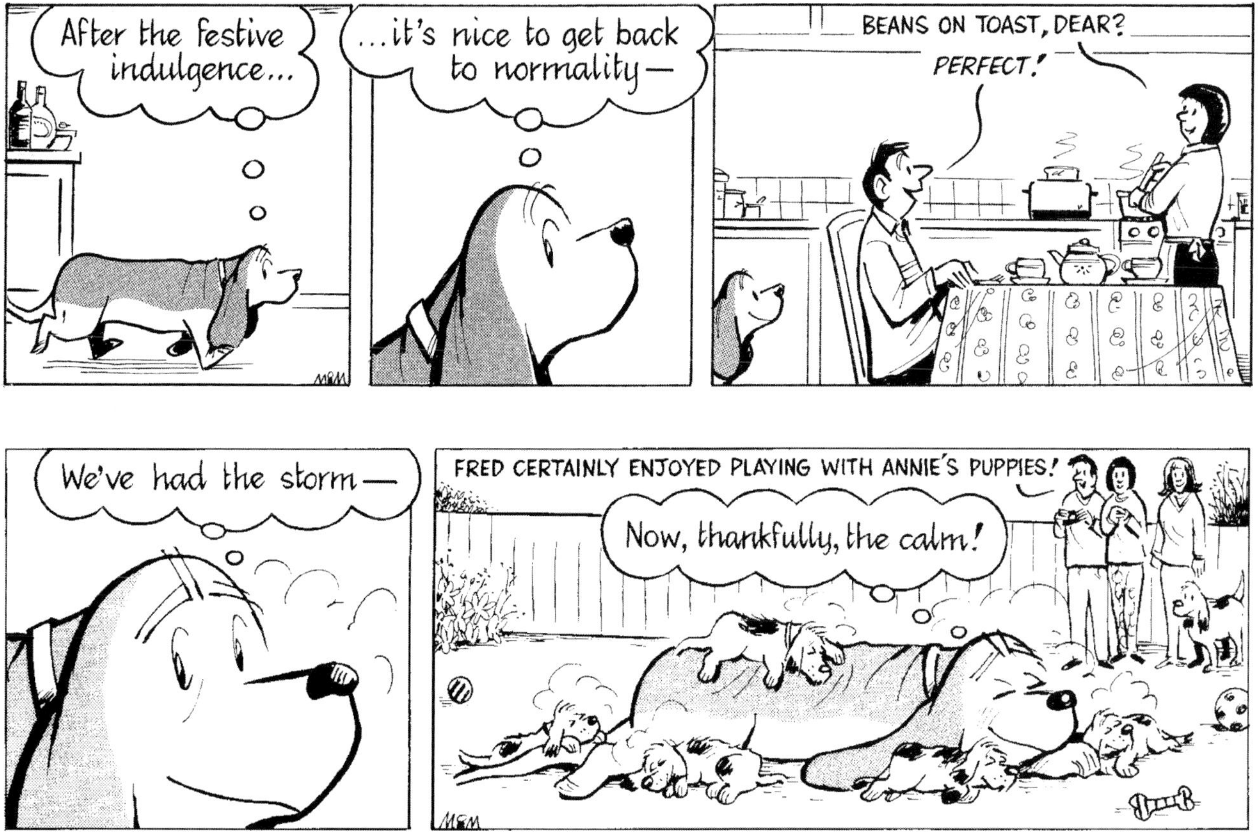
After the festive indulgence...
...it's nice to get back to normality—
BEANS ON TOAST, DEAR?
PERFECT!
We've had the storm—
FRED CERTAINLY ENJOYED PLAYING WITH ANNIE'S PUPPIES!
Now, thankfully, the calm!

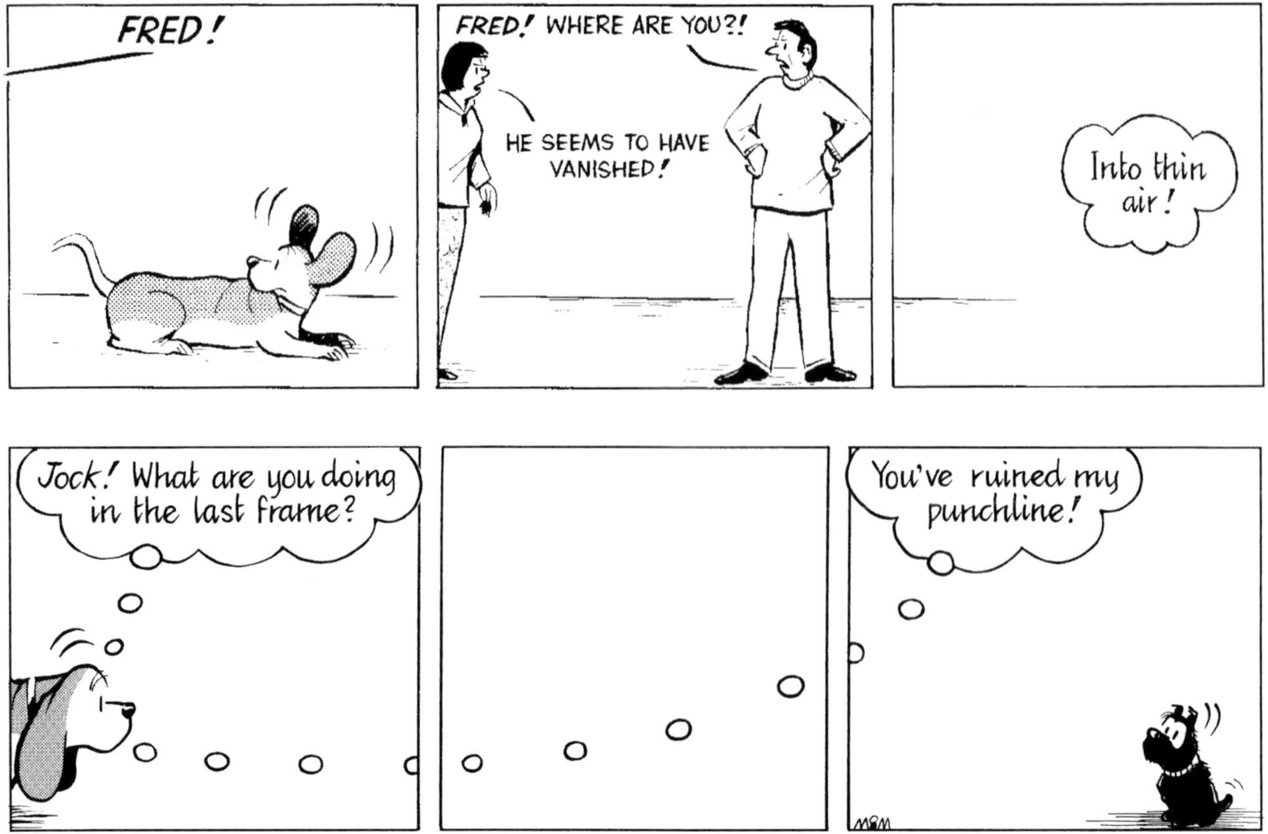
FRED!
FRED! WHERE ARE YOU?!
HE SEEMS TO HAVE VANISHED!
Into thin air!
Jock! What are you doing in the last frame?
You've ruined my punchline!
M&M